"Every college student studies literature. Some study it well, and profit from their assignments while enjoying them. Others study poorly or hardly at all. These may think they are studying hard—they do read all the assignments, and after all, what more is there to do?—but then their instructor gives them frustratingly poor grades. This book seeks to eliminate that kind of frustration. ⟪"In fiction, studying means more than reading to find out whether the head-hunters are eluded, more than knowing whether the boy like me gets the girl like my dream. In poetry, studying means more than summarizing in unadorned prose; more than daydreaming with book in lap. In drama, studying means more than reading to find out 'Who killed King Laius?' ⟪"What will you get from this book? Better grades, I hope; and perhaps fun. But more. Like your teachers, I hope you see beyond grades and beyond the mechanics, the techniques and methods of study, to the hard currency with which literature pays its students —the vision of life. Analysis is tearing apart, and synthesis is seeing whole. Most of us cannot see the whole until we have seen the parts. This book will show you how to find the parts and urge you to see the whole."

—from the *Introduction*

A
Student's
Guide to
Literature

C. Carter Colwell

WSP
Ⅲ WASHINGTON SQUARE PRESS   NEW YORK

To Christopher and Casey, who can read

A STUDENT'S GUIDE TO LITERATURE

A *Washington Square Press* edition

1st printing......................October, 1968
2nd printing...................September, 1969

L

Published by Washington Square Press,
a division of Simon & Schuster, Inc., 630 Fifth Avenue, New York, N.Y.

WASHINGTON SQUARE PRESS editions are distributed in the
U.S. by Simon & Schuster, Inc., 630 Fifth Avenue, New
York, N.Y. 10020 and in Canada by Simon & Schuster
of Canada, Ltd., Richmond Hill, Ontario, Canada.

Standard Book Number: 671-47790-0

Acknowledgments

My sincere appreciation to Educational Resources Corporation, and in
particular to Charles Sherover, for their editorial assistance; to James
H. O. Knox, Jr.; to the editorial staff of WSP, who are death on terminal
prepositions; to my most ruthless, relentless, and patient critic, who remains beautiful even while dismembering my prose; and to the students
of Stetson University.

Extracts from the following works are used by permission of the
publishers:

"Freedom Requires Responsibility: The Lack of Public Confidence in
Newspaper Editorials," Robert M. Hutchins. *Vital Speeches of the Day,*
City News Publishing Company, 1949.

The Heart of Darkness and *The Secret Sharer,* Joseph Conrad. J. M.
Dent & Sons, 1902, 1912.

Contents

v

Introduction:
The Study of Literature

Every college student studies literature. Some study it well, and profit from their assignments while enjoying them. Others study poorly or hardly at all. These may think they are studying hard—they do read all the assignments, and after all, what more is there to do?—but then their instructor gives them frustratingly poor grades. This book seeks to eliminate that kind of frustration.

Studying well means much more than simply reading through an assignment. Literature, in particular, usually means much more than it says, and does more than just make statements. Literature presents life. If I told you what life is, that would not be literature; but if I showed it to you, using words, that would be literature.

Homer does not tell us that "war is hell," which is what Goethe thought was the *Illiad*'s meaning. Instead, Homer shows us the experience of hell on earth, in merciless death after merciless death. The stated meaning "pride goeth before a fall" is quite different from the literary experience of feeling Oedipus' pride and sharing the agony of his self-abomination. Stating meaning is one thing; showing it is another. The photographer says, "One picture is worth a thousand words."

What he means is, "Presented experience communicates more than statement." Literature, like the great news photo, presents experience. Literature uses words, but it uses words to show you, not to tell.

Not only works of epic length, but even the single line of poetry shows its meaning: "Fools rush in where angels fear to tread," says the poet, his line starting with the "Fools" who crowd in at the first opportunity (the beginning of the line), the "angels" following more sedately, with more time for reflection, at the middle and end of the line. "Angels fear to tread where fools rush in" may state the same thing, but it does not enact the thought; even that simple change makes it less poetic. "If the assassination could trammel * up the consequence, and catch with his surcease success," Macbeth mutters to himself. "If by killing King Duncan I could take care of all the consequences, and at the very fact of his death achieve what I want. . . ." That is what the line states and it does what it says: it hurries pell-mell through a string of unaccented short vowels, rushing on toward the words of the wish. "Success" is to come at the same time as Duncan's "surcease." And in the line, success and surcease do come at the same time, not only side by side, but so much alike in sound that they seem practically the same. The poetry does not merely tell us Macbeth's anxiety, his hopes and fears; it asks us to experience them.

Studying literature well thus means getting beyond the surface statements to the heart of the experience itself. In fiction, studying means more than reading to find out whether the headhunters are eluded, more than knowing whether the boy like me gets the girl like my dream. In poetry, studying means more than summarizing in unadorned prose; more than daydreaming with book in lap. In drama, studying means more than reading to find out "Who killed King Laius?". One may read for excitement, for wish-fulfillment, for literal understanding, for escape, for the curiosity of the whodunit—all are legitimate reasons for reading. But all are less than enough.

Reading for fun, and that is what all of these reasons amount to, is less than enough twice over. Practically speaking, students do get grades; and the once-over-lightly is

* I.e., *net*.

unlikely to produce good ones. To speak even more practically —to speak, that is, about the lifetime of reading opportunities that awaits everyone when he has finished his formal education—reading for fun is less fun than reading critically, less fun than reading thoughtfully, less fun than studying, once you have learned how. Here's how.

In the first canto of Dante's *Inferno*, the ghost of the poet Virgil comes to lead the lost and wandering Dante safely through hell. But Virgil stands mute, saying nothing, until Dante begins the conversation and asks a question. This piece of medieval ghost lore—ghosts cannot speak until spoken to—is in itself a parable of study. To study is to ask questions. Even the scientist, who is sometimes thought of as far removed from the student of literature, studies nature in his experiments not by simply watching, but by posing questions, actively interrogating. The student of literature also must ask questions if he is to learn the inner nature of the books he reads.

Knowing what questions to ask is half the dance. Indeed, most of your literary instruction aims at teaching you what questions to ask. Fortunately, the questions are not entirely different for every new novel, poem, or play you read. The questions common to large numbers of works, perhaps all, constitute a technical critical vocabulary. If you know the technical vocabulary, then you know the questions to ask.

Your instructor will expect you to know such technical terms as sonnet, plot, crisis, developing character, tragedy, irony, and hyperbole. He will expect you to ask yourself questions about all your assignments, using these terms. One of the purposes of this book is to provide definitions of the most useful technical terms. Part I, "The Elements of Literature," contains these definitions in a series of short chapters, each of which deals with a related cluster of words. For example, Chapter 2, "Character," defines "developing character," "protagonist," "hero," and "blocking character," among other terms. Depending on your interests or needs, or on your instructor's analysis of them, certain chapters of major importance may simply be read as essay assignments in themselves. If, however, such thorough coverage is needed neither for introduction nor for review, "The Elements of Literature" may be used for reference as a dictionary of technical terms. The Index of Terms at the end of the book lists the pages on which each term is defined, as well as pages on which it is used in discussion. Thus, if you want to know what *hamartia* means, by checking the index you will find the appropriate page references, indicating where the term is defined and where it is used in illustrative discussion.

The major purpose of this book, however, goes beyond a knowledge of technical vocabulary. It aims at the process of applying that vocabulary in study itself.

Consider oceanography. The oceanographer, like the student of literature, needs many technical concepts. He must know something of biology, of geology, of chemistry, of meteorology, of ecology. Let's suppose he has been to all kinds of graduate schools and has studied all kinds of disciplines and knows all kinds of technical terms, biological, geological, etc. And let's suppose that he has been given a government grant for the study of the Antarctic Ocean. Where does he begin? At the northern edge? at the southern center? working down through the ice? rowing around the surface? diving beneath it? scraping the bottom? where?

The student of literature faces the same problem. He knows what *theme* means; he knows what *iambic* means; he knows what *cesura* means; but how does he begin to apply these terms to a poem? This book attempts to answer that question. The technical terms are explained in Part I. Part II, "Literary Genres," shows the methods by which the terms may be applied, in chapters on fiction, drama, poetry, and the essay.

The chapter divisions imply yet another distinction. How does one know which technical concepts to use? To some extent, knowing how to approach the work, to take hold of it, means knowing where to look for what. The oceanographer will not look for killer whales in the middle of an iceberg. If a student is looking for the rhyme scheme, he will not concentrate on the beginnings of the lines; although an occasional rhyme may wander to the beginning of the line, just as a killer whale might jump into the iceberg, rhymes don't live there. Where to look, and for what, depends on the subject being studied.

Which technical concept, which tool, to use depends on the nature of the thing being studied. Rhymes are rare in novels, plots rare in lyric poems. The nature of the different genres (novel, poetry, etc.) therefore serves as the organizing principle of Part II. The way technical vocabulary is relevant and the methods by which it is applied vary, partly according to whether the work studied is a play or an essay. Learning these differences is one way of learning what a play is, what an essay is.

What will you get from this book? Better grades, I hope; and perhaps fun. But more. Like your teachers, I hope you see beyond grades and beyond the mechanics, the techniques and methods of study, to the hard currency with which literature pays its students—the vision of life. Analysis is tearing apart, and synthesis is seeing whole. Most of us cannot see the whole until we have seen the parts. This book will show you how to find the parts and urge you to see the whole. May you see in the literature you study what the poet saw in man:

This Jack, Joke, poor potsherd, patch, matchwood, immortal diamonds,
    Is immortal diamond.*

* Gerard Manley Hopkins, "That Nature Is a Heraclitean Fire and of the Comfort of the Resurrection."

I. The Elements of Literature

1. Plot

Aristotle tells us that the plot of a tragedy should be a whole; that a whole is that which has a beginning, a middle, and an end; that a beginning is that which has nothing before it, and that an end is that which has nothing after it. Although his definitions of beginning and end are a little heavy-handed, Aristotle is getting at something very important. A *plot* is a causally related sequence of events. Each event results from the one that went before, according to the law of probability or necessity, and then produces the event that follows, according to that same law. In this causal chain, the first event is the only one not itself caused, and the last event is the only one not leading directly on to further action.

Surprisingly, what was apparently Aristotle's favorite play—Sophocles' *Oedipus the King,* on which he comments over half a dozen times—deals with the discovery of events that happened long ago concerning the birth and identity of Oedipus, and his unknowing murder of his father and marriage to his widowed mother. These crucial events are all in the past when the play opens. Therefore, in what sense can the beginning of the play have nothing before it?

There are two ways of eliminating the problem, both of

which introduce useful ideas. The first distinguishes between chronological plot and chronological unfolding. This solution to the problem includes events prior to the play as part of the plot. The events, that is, may have been causally related to each other as they originally occurred, but may now be presented or unfolded in a nonchronological progression (in this case, the succession of testimony produced by Oedipus' investigation). The flashback frequently appears when the unfolding and the plot do not follow the same order.

The second way of resolving the apparent conflict between Aristotle's insistence upon orderly progression and the retrospective nature of his favorite play distinguishes between story and plot by regarding story as overt event, physical action—giving birth, killing, marrying—and plot as a causal sequence that need not involve physical action at all. Although there are physical actions during *Oedipus* (Jocasta hangs herself and Oedipus blinds himself), the plot of *Oedipus* in the sense that Aristotle most probably meant it is a mental progression: the investigation and identification of the killer of the former king. The events that occur before the opening of the play are part of the story of *Oedipus,* but by this interpretation they are not part of the plot. The plot is the investigation that begins at the start of the play and runs to the end of the play. This investigation is what actually proceeds according to the law of necessity or probability.

Although there is some disagreement as to which of these Aristotle would have preferred, both distinctions are useful. The word "plot" has the same general meaning in both cases: a chain of causally related events (mental events must be included, no matter how one analyzes *Oedipus*). The disagreement concerns how it applies to *Oedipus.* The other two concepts also are useful: "unfolding," meaning the order in which events are presented in the play, whether chronological or not; and "story," meaning a group of overt events, not necessarily related as cause to effect. The difference between story and plot is stated by E. M. Forster in *Aspects of the Novel:* the audience hearing a story asks simply, "And then?" whereas the audience hearing a plot asks "Why?"

Aristotle prefers organic plots, which,

being an imitation of an action, must imitate one action and that a whole, the structural union of the parts being such that, if any one of them is displaced or removed, the whole will be disjointed and disturbed. For a thing whose presence or absence makes no visible difference, is not an organic part of the whole.*

An organic plot thus is one with no unnecessary events, and with all events in a necessary order. An episodic plot, by contrast, adds events and incidents (episodes) that are not necessary to the main line of development. This is the reason episodic plots are quite inferior to organic plots. Since most tragedies, says Aristotle, have organic plots, they are better than most epics, which have episodic plots. Note that an episodic plot still has a causal chain as its center; the wrath of Achilles and its consequences provide the necessary development that binds the parts of the *Iliad* together. An episodic plot is not a story with no connections at all, but around the central plot it clusters extraneous incidents and episodes. Aristotle's preference for organic plots should not be accepted unquestioningly; however, the distinction he makes is analytically sound, and applies to quite different literary works.

In a well-worked-out plot, then, the beginning is a cause of the middle; the middle is an effect of the beginning and a cause of the end; and the end is an effect of the middle. The introduction of a god at the end of the play, for reasons that do not arise out of the action itself but simply out of the author's inability to solve the problems he has created, a god who decrees how everything shall be resolved, is a grave flaw. This happened literally in some Greek plays, a *deus ex machina* (god from the machine) being lowered onstage in a mechanical contraption to dispense justice or at any rate terminate things. The phrase has come to mean any fortuitous ending, and is still critical. The child narrating a movie sometimes creates such an effect: "And so he fell off this cliff, see? and there was no way for him to survive, and—oh, yes, I forgot to mention this helicopter. . . ."

The crisis or climax divides the major parts of the plot.

---

* *Poetics*, tr. S. H. Butcher, in *Aristotle's Theory of Poetry and Fine Arts with a Critical Text and Translation of the Poetics* (4th ed.; London: Macmillan & Co., 1932), p. 35.

The crisis is the turning point in the protagonist's fortunes, the point of no return. (Calling it a "climax" emphasizes the moment's emotional intensity.) Usually it is marked by some significant decision, which will have irrevocable consequences. Everything leading up to the crisis is the complication, and everything from the crisis or turning point to the end is the unraveling or denouement. These are sometimes called "rising action" and "falling action." Sometimes, too, a new event that does not spring out of the given initial situation but converges on it from the side, so to speak, is called a "complication." Generally, however, such events are not treated as new influences but tend to appear in the exposition, which states the total initial situation, including any necessary background information. The exposition may be provided in a lump or incorporated piecemeal in the early part of the play.

Three other aspects of plot are reversal of intention, recognition, and tragic incident or catastrophe. Reversal of intention (*peripeteia*) is an attempt to do one thing that actually accomplishes its opposite. It is a form of irony. When a parent's shriek—"GET BACK!"—startles the previously calm child at the edge of the cliff into leaping straight forward and thence down, down, down, there has been a reversal of intention. Recognition (*anagnorisis*) is a "change from ignorance to knowledge, producing love or hate between the persons destined by the poet for good or bad fortune," as Aristotle defines it. It is a form of discovery. And catastrophe, as a technical term, simply means death, mutilation, and so forth. Aristotle says that in the best plots (such as that of *Oedipus*) the crisis or turning point is combined with reversal of intention and recognition.

These last terms imply the close connection between plot and character. Reversal of intention and recognition clearly deal with states of mind, and may well imply morality or personality, appropriate to a discussion of character. The basic connection between character and plot, of course, is purpose. Purpose or motive provides the connecting link that ties the events together in a causal chain. Any discussion of plot therefore tends quickly to involve characters, as it explores their motives and establishes the basic conflicts that generate the action. Even if the conflict is with nature, the protagonist's purposes are part of the plot. Without conflict of some sort, of course, there is no plot; for unresisted purpose is immediately fulfilled, like the magic wish. Since unresisted purpose is immediately fulfilled, there is no chain of events, the beginning and the ending being identical. With external conflict, however, fulfillment of purpose requires effort and overcoming counteraction. Of this stuff, plots are made.

One should recognize that internal conflicts are also possible. In the limiting case where there is only internal conflict and no external conflict, discussion of plot is virtually identical with discussion of character. For although Aristotle said that actions are what define character, it is as true to say that purposes are what define character. Aristotle's typically Greek inability to conceive of will as an independent faculty probably prompted him to minimize purpose and choice. The modern critic, his insight deepened by two thousand years of Christian thought and, most recently, psychoanalytic investigations, easily recognizes internal conflicts as the tension between incompatible motives within the same person.

Although he does not use the label, Aristotle hints at one more concept of importance: subplots. The name is self-explanatory, but a word of warning is needed: do not confuse everything that happens to a character, or everything he does, with a plot or subplot. Remember that an event must bear a causal relationship to those around it if together they are to constitute a plot.

Plot is discussed in somewhat different terms by Northrop Frye.* Like Aristotle, he approaches plot in terms of the relationship of beginning to end. Aristotle gives a definition of plot as the process by which one *gets from* the beginning to the end. Frye adds a classification of plot types based on a comparison of the state of affairs at the beginning to the state of affairs at the end. This classification identifies four basic plots: romantic, ironic or satiric, tragic, and comic.

The basis of Frye's classification of plots is a distinction between two realms, or states of affairs. One is desirable, the other undesirable; one is better than the way things are, the other worse than neutral. The better realm is idealized, the worse realm, sadly, is realistic. He then very simply identifies plots in which the initial and terminal situations are both idealized, or very good—romance; plots in which the initial

---

* *The Anatomy of Criticism* (Princeton, N.J.: Princeton University Press, 1957).

and terminal situations are both realistic, or disappointing and undesirable—satire; plots in which the initial situation is preferable to the terminal situation—tragedy; and plots in which the terminal situation is preferable to the initial situation—comedy. Or, to rephrase it, in romance things stay good, in satire they stay bad, in tragedy they deteriorate, and in comedy they improve.

Frye makes one additional distinction between romance and satire. Satirical plots tend to return to the initial situation, thus emphasizing the lack of improvement; romantic plots, however, involve a series of adventures and tend to be episodic, since variety and novelty are aspects of the desirable world that would be negated by a return to the initial situation and an emphasis on cyclical movement. Thus satires are cyclical, romances episodic.

The classification may be diagramed as follows, with the solid line dividing the desirable realm above from the undesirable realm below, and the arrows indicating the kind of progression for each plot:

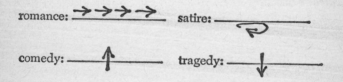

romance: ————→ satire: ————

comedy: ————↑———— tragedy: ————↓————

Applying these technical concepts is simply a matter of looking to see which ones apply. Questions therefore might be posed as follows:

1. *Do events lead by cause and effect from beginning to end?* (A detailed answer to this question should identify the plot. In summarizing the plot, be sure to state the causal links. E.g., "Because he wants to succeed, John asks the boss's daughter to marry him; being lonely, she accepts; because he doesn't love her, he gets bored; because he shows it, her feelings are hurt; because she is unhappy, her father fires John; because she prefers having a husband to being lonely, she joins him in his impoverished hovel; because she stays with him, John comes to love her; learning that John now loves his daughter, the boss reinstates John, promoting him to be

regional director for the south central area; everyone lives happily ever after.")

2. *Are there events or little chains of events that are not part of the main plot?* (The answer will indicate whether the plot is episodic or organic, and if there are actually subordinate chains of events, it will identify subplots.)

3. *Are events presented in their causal sequence, or not?* (If not, the unfolding differs from the plot, and some other organizing principle must be sought.)

4. *Does the ending develop logically out of preceding events and situations?* (If not, it is probably a *deus ex machina*.)

5. *At what point is the future development irrevocably determined?* (The answer identifies the crisis, and therefore also the complication and the unraveling or denouement. The "irrevocable determination" does not have to be a metaphysical necessity, but should be irreversible in terms of common sense.)

6. *How is necessary background information communicated?* (The answer will locate the exposition.)

7. *Does someone unintentionally do the opposite of what he intended?* (Reversal of intention.)

8. *What recognitions occur?*

9. *Are there any catastrophes?*

10. *Which characters oppose each other?* (The answer identifies external conflicts, and may have been included in the identification of the plot.)

11. *Are there any natural obstacles to be overcome?* (Most common in romances such as adventure stories, conflict with the environment is a type of external conflict.)

12. *Do any of the characters reveal ambivalence or uncertainty? Do they confront any dilemmas?* (The answer identifies internal conflicts. Note that a character in a poorly done work may simply be inconsistent.)

13. *Compare the state of affairs at the beginning to the state of affairs at the end, in terms of desirability.* (The answer should indicate whether the basic plot is romantic, satiric, tragic, or comic. The plot summarized in connection with question #1, for example, is comic.)

2. Character

Character involves two basic qualities, both of which affect current use of the word. The first quality is morality; the second quality is personality.

Character in the first sense, morality, has the older status as a technical concept in literary criticism. Aristotle's *Poetics* defined character exclusively as moral status, as goodness or badness.* Thus, he defines the most effective tragic hero as one who is pretty good. Not perfect, because then his misfortunes would just be outrageous; and not evil, because then his misfortunes would just be satisfying. That is, if the tragic hero is to arouse the sympathy of the audience without merely causing them to feel indignant that he suffers, he must be a lot better than average, but not perfect. Character is used in

---

* In a later section he talks of character as "appropriateness": e.g., a woman should not be portrayed as manly; but here also he seems to be thinking of moral qualities, since he illustrates with unintentional humor by saying, "This rule [appropriateness] is relative to each class. Even a woman may be good, and also a slave; although the woman may be said to be an inferior being, and the slave quite worthless."

this sense when one says, "He has a lot of character"—that is, he has a lot of moral goodness.

This sense of character is still important to the modern audience. If you cannot tell the good guys from the bad guys in the western, your reactions will be all wrong, like those of the apocryphal Indian boy who considered every western movie a tragedy except *Custer's Last Stand*. Character in its moral aspect is also important to an understanding of theme.

It is true that as sophistication increases it becomes increasingly difficult to distinguish good guys from bad guys. Thus, Indians may be treated sympathetically, confusing our stereotypes, that is, our preconceived classifications of people. And in really great art, the truth that no man is perfect and no man totally worthless will be expressed through characters who all blend, in some degree, moral goodness and moral badness. But this very point depends upon the audience's sensitivity to goodness and badness. Therefore, although the total evaluation may be complex, it is still an evaluation of character as moral worth.

What defines the individual character? In some cases, the author will, spelling out in so many words what he thinks this character is like. Choice, however, preeminently defines character, especially character in this first sense, moral excellence. For what a man chooses to do reveals his basic motives as good or bad—or, as in most cases, what he chooses to do reveals the particular blend of goodness and badness in his motivation.

Motivation is thus very important in determining character. Have you ever met someone who regarded with great suspicion your friendly inquiries as to where he came from and what his school or class was, someone who eyed you warily and said, "Why do you ask?" Treat the characters in literature with the same analytical suspicion, constantly asking, "Why?"

The question "why?" must be asked not just for the first decision, but for all decisions each character makes throughout the work. This necessity comes from two aspects of literary characters: first, any complex character must be revealed gradually; second, the character may in fact develop or change.

Gradual revelation of character may not be necessary for minor characters. They can be simpler and, if so, are usually called "stock" or "flat" characters because they are so routinely

typical (stock) or defined by so few characteristics (flat).
But even if the author describes the character for us, we still
need to see him in operation to be convinced that he is as
described. In art, seeing is believing, and no artist worthy of
the name will tell us a character is very good without letting
us see that goodness manifested in action at least once.
A fully developed character (usually called "round" or "three-
dimensional" to indicate his complexity and how much he
seems like a person you can know better and better) needs to
be shown in action much more than once—in different situations, making different decisions—so that all facets of his
character may be illuminated.

Because the simple, flat character has so few characteristics,
he cannot convincingly change without seeming to have been
transformed by a magic wand. The complex, round character,
however, by swinging from one aspect of his character to another that has been hinted at all along, can develop without
startling us. (This need for consistency is stated so emphatically by Aristotle that he says if a character is to be inconsistent, he must be consistently inconsistent.) Such a character is called, appropriately enough, a "developing character."
The opposite type, who does not change, is called a "static
character." Of course, not all round characters develop; but
very rarely does a flat character develop. Any development,
of course, will be shown in the decisions, usually involving
moral choices, the characters make.

Before leaving the topic of character as morality to take up
character as personality, a few further comments are needed.
According to Aristotle, characters in tragedy will generally be
somewhat better than average (especially the tragic hero),
whereas the characters in comedy will be somewhat worse
than average. In spite of his general nobility, however, the
main character of a tragedy ought to bring his misfortune
upon himself; not by vice, but by some *hamartia. Hamartia*
is a Greek word that is variously translated error or frailty,
tragic flaw, error of judgment, moral fault. The tragic hero
ought to bring his misfortune upon himself, but he ought not
really to deserve all the horrendous consequences. The trans-
lations of *hamartia* indicate uncertainty as to whether the
word means moral sin or intellectual mistake. That there is a
difference would probably not have occurred to Aristotle
as a possibility. For him, the good was what the intelligent man

would naturally choose; perversion or sin, in the sense of deliberate, fully rational choice of evil, was for Aristotle a contradiction in terms. A drunken, lustful, or enraged man might make an evil choice, but he could choose evil only because his reason was clouded. The word *"hamartia"* is derived from a term used in archery, which means literally a missing of the mark. The word obviously leaves open the question of the exact mechanics of the mark-missing; it does not tell us what the archer did that made him miss. But we automatically regard the archer as responsible for his score; the best archer hits the mark. By his *hamartia*, therefore, the tragic character is responsible for his own downfall.

Character in the second sense, personality, is a more modern concept. Perhaps Aristotle, a good Greek, just couldn't believe that what makes a man unique is either good or important, for this sense of the unique worth of the individual is a Judeo-Christian heritage, not a Greek one. In this second sense, character is the idiosyncratic qualities that make John John and Jim Jim. Character as personality includes speech habits, hair style, hobby, attitude toward work, and all of the complex attitudes and feelings that define the individual. The man who says of the campus oddball, "What a character he is!" uses the word in this sense—unique individual personality.

Character as personality is important in literature because, as most authors have discovered, people are interesting. Since the first requirement of any work of art is that it be interesting enough to prompt the audience to continue reading, looking, or listening, artists portray interesting people. Frequently, of course, morality and personality blend.

When a particular trait of personality is so emphasized that it becomes the defining characteristic, a type is created. This happens more often in comedy than in tragedy, partly because the rigidification of character is itself humorous.* By the Renaissance, a classification system based on a theory of four basic "humors" or character types developed, combining Aristotelian physics with Hippocratic psychochemistry. The bizarre psychochemistry of Hippocrates maintained that the predominance of one of four fluids or "humors" (blood, phlegm, black bile, and yellow bile) produced different per-

---

* See the discussion of mechanization of the living under "Comedy."

sonality types: the choleric, or angry, type (yellow bile); the melancholy type (black bile); the phlegmatic, or stolid, type (phlegm); and the sanguine, or lively and changeable, type (blood). In actual practice, the types found in comedy have always been more varied than this basic list of four might suggest. Those with special names come for the most part from Roman comedy. They include: the *miles gloriosus,* or braggart soldier, like Falstaff, or Barney Fife, Andy Griffith's television deputy; the *senex iratus,* or angry father, who characteristically forbids the young lovers to see each other again; the *dolosus servus,* or tricky slave, like Sancho Panza, Jeeves, Passepartout, the cartoon character Hazel; the gull, who is perpetually victimized; the churl; the buffoon (in English morality plays, called Vice or Iniquity); the fop; the country cousin. The list may, in fact, be extended indefinitely, naming any characteristic—for example, miserliness or religious zeal—that can become an obsessively dominant trait, that is, a humor. Most of the names of the types are self-explanatory.

Another classification is offered by Northrop Frye, who suggests two pairs of contrasting personality types that cover most dramatic characters: the self-deprecator (such as the tricky slave or the confidant who does not assert himself, like Horatio in *Hamlet*) in contrast with the impostor (anyone who claims to be more than he is, such as a proud tragic hero or a comic braggart soldier); and the increaser of festivity (usually a buffoon) in contrast with the refuser of festivity (frequently a churl or rustic such as the country cousin).* The latter pair, of course, apply particularly to comic characters; but the two pairs overlap. For example, a *senex* will probably be both a refuser of festivity and an impostor. He is the former because he does not want the hero to feast with the heroine, and he is an impostor because he seeks to make his will the law for others (which he doesn't have the right to do).

These, then, are the two basic meanings of character—morality and personality—and the various technical terms related to each concept. A few additional terms are based on neither meaning of character, referring not to the nature of

---

* The professional student of literature should know the original Greek words for these four: *eiron, alazon, bomolochos,* and *agroikos,* respectively.

the character itself but to the function of the character in the plot.

The most important character is known as the "protagonist" (*proto-* as in *prototype*, not as in *pro* and *con*), literally the proto-agonist, the first struggler, the leading actor. The character who struggles against the protagonist is called the "antagonist" in serious drama, more frequently a blocking character in comedy. A villain is usually a melodramatic antagonist; the *senex iratus,* or simply *senex,* usually functions as a blocking character in comedy, opposing the hero's wishes, in contrast to the tricky slave who usually works for the hero, helping him to win the heroine.

The very words "hero" and "heroine" are semitechnical terms. The former is perhaps the most ambiguous, even though it is the most common. Sometimes it is used to mean protagonist, most important character. Frequently, though, it includes a moral evaluation and implies courage, honor, great strength or achievement, or some other noble quality. In epics the hero is the doer of great deeds; in comedy he is the boy that gets the girl. It should be noted that the "hero" of a comedy, in this sense, may do practically nothing except want the heroine and finally get her, and thus not be the protagonist; frequently, too, he has very little personality, like Rock Hudson, although it is taken for granted that he is good in unspecified ways. The comic hero thus tends to be a self-deprecator, partly because he is rather neutral and unobtrusive (rather than self-assertive, as an impostor would be); partly, too, because he tends to adapt to circumstance* rather than to remain committed to some concept of his own worth.†

Among minor characters, the most common type defined by plot function is the foil, whose function it is to emphasize by contrast the protagonist's character. The straight man of most comic teams is a foil to the buffoonery of the clown or gagman.

All of these character types, traits, and functions are analytical concepts, and may be applied to any work of literature. Questions to ask when analyzing character include:

* See the definition of comedy.
† See the definition of tragedy.

1. *What does the author tell us directly of each character?*

2. *What do other characters, including a narrator if there is one, tell us of each character?*

3. *What decisions does each character make?* (All three of these questions are relevant both to character as morality and to character as personality.)

4. *Do any of the characters develop?* (Answering this involves comparing early decisions with late decisions, early reactions by other characters with late reactions by other characters.)

5. *Does describing each character require a few words or many?* (The answers will distinguish stock and flat characters from three-dimensional characters.)

6. *Who makes the most important decisions?* (The answer is the protagonist.)

7. *Does anyone oppose him?* (The one who does is an antagonist or one of the blocking characters.)

8. *To what extent is the tragic protagonist responsible for his fall?* (The answer will identify his *hamartia,* if there is one.)

9. *What stock characters do you find?* (Is there a *miles gloriosus?* a *senex?* a *dolosus servus?* a gull? a fop? etc.)

10. *Are there other characters who may be defined fairly well by a single trait?* (If so, and if they are at all important, they are humors of one sort or another. This question is closely related to question #5.) What is that trait?

Be sure that in answering all of the above questions you cite the evidence for your answers.

3. Theme

The *theme* of a piece is analogous to the moral of one of Aesop's fables. Most serious stories—including funny serious stories, that is, stories that make you laugh but are not mere pastimes—express a conviction about the world or some part of it. Many art forms other than stories and fables embody themes. In fact, all verbal forms tend to, including of course poetry and drama. Even comic strips may have themes; a young theologian, Robert Short, has shown in his book, *The Gospel According to Peanuts*, that many of the daily adventures of Charlie Brown and his friends intentionally and unmistakably express various parts of the Christian gospel as revealed in the New Testament. Such themes sound very much like the moral one finds at the end of a fable, stating a rule of conduct. But the theme does not have to tell you what to do; it must simply *express some conviction or belief about the way things are.* Frequently, this conviction may be stated in a proposition such as Goethe offered for Homer's great epic of war: "The lesson of the *Iliad* is that on this earth man must enact hell."

Theme, then, is what a story means; theme is a conviction about the real world you live in, and it may be stated in

17

several ways. Theme tends to be complex, and may include contradictory evaluations; rarely will theme be as simple as the moral following the fable.

Theme may be explicitly stated. Sometimes, however, theme is implicit, not explicit. A work may have a definite theme that nevertheless is nowhere directly stated. One of Aesop's fables with the moral omitted would be just such a work. Very frequently, theme is partly explicit and partly implicit.

Explicit theme is close to what Aristotle called "thought." *

It is all a character says when "enunciating some universal proposition." The modern critic insists that the theme of a work is not necessarily the same as the words of any one character, unless these words are in accord with the implications of the work as a whole. Thus, it would be rash to assume without careful investigation that what the *chorus* of a Greek play says is necessarily what the author meant as the theme of his work.

The analytical concept "theme" may be applied to a work by asking some or all of the following questions:

1. *If there is a narrator, does he enunciate any general truths?*

2. *Do any of the characters enunciate general truths?*

3. *Do they all agree?*

4. *Are the truths enunciated consistent with the events of the story, or are the characters wrong? or only partly right?*

---

* "Thought," for Aristotle, may be one of two things. First, it can be the reasoning process through which a character goes when arriving at a conclusion of some sort. For example, when Oedipus says, "Tiresias accuses me of regicide. I am not a regicide. Therefore Tiresias is a liar. A poor man like Tiresias would not lie to a king unless he had the backing of an important person. The only important person who would profit from my discomfiture is Creon. Therefore Creon must have prompted Tiresias to make this lying accusation," the argumentative process is an instance of this first meaning Aristotle gives to "thought." It falls under the heading of character. The second sense in which Aristotle uses the word is virtually the same as the modern concept of explicit theme.

If no theme is explicitly stated, the task is more difficult. How do you recognize implicit theme? This question is very hard to answer, for there are no set rules to be memorized and mechanically applied. The basic advice, then, is to read open-mindedly, alertly, aware that very frequently an author is trying to reveal something significant in the events, conversations, and thoughts that he describes and presents. Ask as you read:

5. *Is the author trying to tell me something, to express a truth or an attitude?*

6. *Does he think the lives of his characters typical of general human experience?*

7. *Does he adopt a moral attitude toward his characters?*

8. *Is there anything in this work that prompts me to say, "Yes, that is true," or "No, that is false," or "I had never realized that before"?*

4. Point of View

The question "What is the *point of view?*" is virtually the question "From where is the story seen?" Suppose you are watching a television show. As the story begins, you see a man and a woman sitting in a living room talking; it is as though you were in the doorway, or perhaps just outside the window, looking on as an observer. That is one kind of point of view, usually called "objective." * Suddenly the image shifts; now you see the back of a shoulder at the bottom of the screen and the back of an ear at the left side of the screen, and beyond these the face of the woman, looking slightly to your left. (She is looking, of course, at the man whose ear and shoulder you see.) This is another point of view; you are (literally, in this case) looking over the man's shoulder; you see what he sees, although not quite through his eyes. "I love you, John," the woman says. Again the viewpoint shifts, to a third vantage point: now the screen is filled with the face of the man, looking directly at the camera, at you, and at the woman. "I love you,

* Sometimes called "dramatic." In this, as in other areas of literary criticism, the terms used may differ from critic to critic. There is a consensus, however, on the ideas if not on the labels.

too, Mary," the man says. His face contorts in an expression presumably of love, and, still eyeball to eyeball with him, you hear the woman's voice as though over a telephone: "Aha! That stupid John believed my lie." Here your point of view is identical with the woman's. You see through her eyes (not just over her shoulder), and you share in her thoughts. Finally, as they kiss, the image shifts back to the original scene, as seen from the doorway or window, but this time a narrator's voice is heard, saying: "John, blinded by his mad, impetuous infatuation for Mary, does not realize that she is using him as a tool for her nefarious schemes."

Point of view on the screen is literally a viewpoint. In fiction, the scene is imagined from what is said. Fiction differs from screened art (TV and movies) because it is narrated rather than shown. (When screened art has a narrator, as in the last example above, the visual image still distinguishes it from written fiction.) The four viewpoints in our imagined TV show correspond to four different points of view that are frequently used in short stories. The first point of view was objective, looking at the characters from outside, without stating what they thought or felt, but leaving their thoughts and feelings to be inferred from their behavior and speech. The entire scene, if told from an objective point of view, might be as follows:

> John and Mary sat in the living room. "I love you, John," Mary said softly. John leaned forward, his expression softening. "I love you, too, Mary," he murmured deeply. They kissed.

Note that all is seen, but nothing is grasped telepathically. What the characters think is not told. Perhaps a clue to their thoughts may be given in an action presumably unnoticed by either, but recorded by the objective narrator: "Mary's hands tensed slightly as she spoke, but relaxed when John replied." Although the reader may not be positive at the time, subsequent events will indicate that Mary's hands tensed because she was afraid John would not believe her lie.

The second shot of our soap opera vignette corresponded to a less obvious point of view in fiction. In that shot, the camera looked over John's shoulder. The corresponding point of view in fiction might be called "limited objective." The distinctive feature of this point of view is that it stays with John, wherever he goes. Narration is still in the third person, as though a parakeet traveled with John and were now writing an impersonal account of "What Was Seen from John's Shoulder." From this point of view, the episode might be rendered thus:

> Mary sat facing John. The dark wood of the doorway framed her golden hair. "I love you, John," Mary said softly, parting her ruby lips. John leaned forward. "I love you, too, Mary," he murmured deeply. They kissed.

Note that Mary is described as seen by John, although John himself is not the narrator. If Mary leaves the room, her actions cannot be described from this point of view, because she cannot be seen by the narrator looking over John's shoulder. In a more common form of this point of view, we are told by the narrator (who is looking over John's shoulder all the time) what John himself thinks. In such a case, we might be told: "John did not notice Mary's hands relaxing slightly as he answered her." This point of view is called "limited omniscient," "selective omniscient," or "third person limited to one character."

The third shot represents a simpler point of view. In that case, the camera stood where Mary's eyes would have been, and John spoke directly to her, the camera, and the audience; simultaneously, we knew what Mary was thinking. The short-story writer or novelist would achieve much the same effect by using first-person narration:*

> As we sat in the living room, I knew I had to convince John I loved him. "I love you, John," I said as earnestly as I could. John looked at me sickeningly and said, "I love you, too, Mary." I knew he believed the lie I had told. We kissed.

The fourth and last point of view resembled the objective in one sense, but differed in another: the camera was looking on, as in the first shot, but the thoughts of the characters were

---

* For definition of interior monologue, which might be considered a variation on the subjective point of view, see "Fiction," p. 97.

known to the observer—that is, to author and to audience. The point of view in such a case is usually called "omniscient," obviously because the narrator knows everything, even what characters think and feel. For a last time, then, our scene might be rendered thus from an omniscient point of view:

John and Mary sat in the living room. Mary knew she had to convince John she really loved him, or he would expose her to the FBI. "I love you, John," Mary said softly, and tried to conceal her nervousness as she waited for his reply. But John, blinded by his mad, impetuous infatuation, suspected nothing of her evil intent. "I love you, too, Mary," he murmured deeply. Mary relaxed inwardly. They kissed.

"What is the point of view?" then is equivalent to "Who sees how much?" The types discussed may be outlined as follows:

I. Looking on.
  A. *Objective*. Third-person narration; no thoughts are read.
  B. *Omniscient*. Third-person narration; all thoughts may be read.

II. Looking through a character's eyes.*
  Subjective. First-person narration; the narrator may tell his thoughts and feelings.

III. Looking over the character's shoulder.*
  A. *Limited objective*. Third-person narration; the thoughts of the character with the shoulder may be told.
  B. *Limited omniscient*. Third-person narration; the thoughts of the character with the shoulder may be told.

* It is worth distinguishing whether the character in types II and III is a major participant in the main action or merely an observer.

5. Scene

Scene is what surrounds characters when they act, or think, or simply look about them. Scene is place or location, or locale, or context, or environment.

It can be simply what the author tells us or shows us of the place inhabited by his characters. In its simplest sense in drama, scene is what we see when we look at the stage (what Aristotle called "spectacle"): the visual impact of the presentation or staging. In its simplest sense in fiction, scene is local color: those details that make a place be itself and not some other place. Scene in poetry may range from the complete specificity of a detailed landscape description to any indeterminate location in which mental activity, at least, is possible.

In a broader and more sophisticated sense, scene begins to take on nonphysical qualities. Thus, when date is added to place in identifying scene, not only are changing styles in human architecture and dress referred to, but also social structures, such as feudalism or the Greek city-state, are identified. In this sense, scene is not mere place or location; it is social context.

In its broadest and most profound sense, scene is the

whole world presented by the author. The satirist describes a different world from the writer of romances, for the satirist fills his scene with a chaotic hodgepodge of discreditable people and events, whereas the world of romance presents idealized actions in a world of plenty. The satirist presents a world in which clear rational perception and high ideals cannot survive, except as deliberate self-deception. The world of romance, on the contrary, is one in which cynicism exists only as foolish irritability. For example, although the *Iliad* is ultimately tragic, it is still largely an idealized world, filled with golden cups and divinely wrought armor, with men as strong as ten alive today and wiser than any you or Homer knew. The difference is not simply physical, but includes a whole attitude toward human possibility. In such a world Thersites' cynicism is crabby stupidity, and he deserves no answer but the beating Odysseus gives him. But in Shakespeare's largely satirical *Troilus and Cressida*, the situation is reversed. Thersites' cynicism defines the impossibility of true nobility and characterizes a world in which the nobility of Hector cannot survive.

In this broadest sense, including the ultimate spiritual environment the work presents, scene is closely related to theme. Theme is what the work implies about the world; and scene in this sense is the world presented. For most purposes, scene can be understood and applied to works of literature in its simpler initial sense, the literal and physically describable location of the action. But at times broadening the description of scene may make it easier to reach an understanding of theme.

Scene frequently strengthens other aspects of a work, perhaps by specific symbolism, perhaps by general tone. Distortion of the natural world in order to express the mood of some one of the characters is termed, by its critics, the "pathetic fallacy," because it fallaciously attributes emotion (pathos) to nature. Rain at funerals is an example. Ingmar Bergman's movie *The Magician* achieves a comic tone by switching, completely improbably, from pouring rain to bright sunshine when the hero is given a last-minute reprieve. If the device is not intended to have a comic effect, such a change in the weather must be made inconspicuously and without violating the audience's standards of realistic probability.

Questions to ask in literary analysis when considering scene include these:

1. *What am I told, or do I see, about the appearance of the place where the action occurs?* (This is scene in the simplest sense.)

2. *Does the date or country affect my expectations for the action, for the characters' behavior and attitudes?* (Scene in this second sense includes historical and social factors.)

3. *What limitations does the context of the work seem to place upon human action? Or, conversely, what possibilities for human action does it seem to open up?* (Scene in this broadest sense begins to approximate theme. It is also very close to what Northrup Frye means by "mode," a term which the advanced student should explore in *Anatomy of Criticism.**

4. *How is the scene related to mood?* (The answer will identify instances of the so-called "pathetic fallacy.")

* See p. 7.

6. Versification

The study of *versification,* that is, the formal devices of poetry, encompasses a large number of literary terms. Also called "prosody," versification comprises the structured or technical features of verse. It includes the repetition of sounds and rhythm (the musical quality produced by arrangements of accented and unaccented sounds and pauses) and the grouping of these sounds and rhythms into varied patterns in words. Repetition of sound and rhythm is necessary to establish a pattern, and the pattern must be established before it can be varied. Each of the three components of versification (repetition of sounds, repetition of rhythm, and patterns of repetition and variation involving sound and rhythm) is further subdivided as follows:

Repetition of sound
1. Rhyme
2. Alliteration
3. Assonance
4. Consonance

Repetition of rhythm
   5. Foot (iamb, anapest, etc.)
   6. Meter (tetrameter, pentameter, etc.)
   7. Syllabic count (rare in English)
   8. Stress count (typical of Old English and some modern verse)

Patterns of repetition and variation
   9. Stanza (rhyme royal, heroic couplet, etc.)
   10. Specific verse forms (sonnet, limerick, etc.)
   11. Free verse
   12. Refrain

1. Rhyme is the repetition of the final accented vowel and following consonants. Usually the rhyming words are at line ends; when one or more rhyming words are within the line, the rhyme is called "internal." Rhymes may be masculine or single (i.e., occurring in the last syllable, as in re*d*—be*d*, rem*ain*—abst*ain*), feminine or double (i.e., occurring in two syllables, as in h*andy*—c*andy*, g*iver*—r*iver*), or polysyllabic (i.e., occurring in more than two syllables, as in tr*aveling*—r*aveling*, cap*ability*—inst*ability*). Note that *sound*, not spelling, determines rhyme: *cough* rhymes with *off*, but not with *through*.*

Certain sound repetitions that do not strictly follow the rules of rhyme (lovel*y*—bab*y*, si*tt*ing—fi*t*ly, dang*le*—hand*le*) are known as imperfect rhyme, half-rhyme, slant-rhyme, approximate rhyme, or near-rhyme.

2. Alliteration, strictly speaking, is the repetition of the initial consonants of words (as in *l*anky *l*egs, *f*avorite *ph*one); in a broader sense, it is the repetition of any consonant (*l*ead ba*ll*, *th*ick pi*th*). In this latter sense alliteration can be synonymous with consonance, defined below.

3. Assonance is the repetition of any accented vowel (r*e*d p*e*ncil, b*a*by m*a*y, s*o* alth*ou*gh).

4. Consonance is the repetition of both initial and final consonants of a syllable (*r*e*d* *r*o*d*, *p*in*g* *p*on*g*); or the repeti-

---

* Although a visual resemblance like that between *cough* and *through* is called "eye rhyme" and appears in some English verse, it is not true rhyme.

tion of the final consonants (ha*rd* boa*rd*); or, more broadly, the repetition of any consonant.

Repetition of sounds may be used to produce a pleasing effect, called "euphony." "O my love is like a red, red rose / That's newly sprung in June" repeats the easy-to-say and soft sounds of *l* in "love," "like," "newly"; *r* in "red, red rose"; *u* in "newly" and "June."

The same device can also be used to produce an unpleasing effect with harsh sounds, called "cacophony." "I am a bastard begot, bastard instructed, bastard in mind" repeats the heavy *b* of "bastard"; the explosive *t* sounds of "bastard," "begot," and "instructed"; and the guttural stops *g* in "begot" and *k* in "instructed"; and it has a heavy ratio of consonant sounds to vowel sounds.

5. The foot is the basic unit of meter, a rhythmic pattern determined by the relationship between the stressed, accented, or strong syllables and the unstressed, unaccented, or weak syllables of the words in a line of verse. The four kinds of feet most commonly used in English verse are:

the iamb: light–heavy (aLACK, atTACK, in HASTE)

the trochee: heavy–light (BATtle, STOP it)

the anapest: light–light–heavy (pirouETTE, to the WOODS)

the dactyl: heavy–light–light (SWIMmingly, CHARiot, HURrying)

There are names for more complicated combinations, but they are rarely used. With the addition of two unusual feet, the pyrrhic foot (light–light) and the spondee (heavy–heavy), most English prosody can be scanned (analyzed rhythmically), into repetitions of the four basic feet. (Occasionally, a line will include an extra accented syllable, a monosyllable foot.)

The poem most often quoted to illustrate different feet is one by Coleridge entitled "Metrical Feet":

Trochee trips from long to short;

From long to long in solemn sort
Slow Spondee stalks: strong foot! yet ill able
Ever to come up with Dactyl trisyllable;
Iambics march from short to long;
With a leap and a bound the swift Anapests throng. . . .

Here is a device that I find helps me to keep the basic four straight, as long as I can remember what iambs are (da-DUM), the names of the other three, alphabetical order, and symmetrical contrast. In alphabetical order:

anapests dactyls iambs trochees (ADIT)

When you identify iambs—they are far and away the most common foot, found in blank verse, heroic couplets, rhyme royal, sonnets, ottava rima, etc.—you have:

da-DUM
anapests dactyls iambs trochees

That much you have to remember. The rest fills itself in. Trochees contrast with iambs:

da-DUM/DUM-da
anapests dactyls iambs trochees

and anapests and dactyls contrast in the same pattern:

da-da-DUM/ DUM-da-da   da-DUM/ DUM-da
anapests   dactyls   iambs trochees

Thus, if you can remember "ADIT" and what an iamb is, you are on your way to reminding yourself what trochees, anapests, and dactyls are.

6. Meter is traditionally defined in terms of the number of feet in the line. From one to eight feet per line, the meters are: monometer (one foot), dimeter (two feet), trimeter, tetrameter, pentameter, hexameter, heptameter, and octameter. Lines of greater length, and even the longer of these, tend to break into shorter units. A clear break in the line, which may or may not be marked by punctuation, is called a

"cesura." A clear break at the end of the line makes it end-stopped; if it runs on to the next without pause, it is enjambed.

Note that in scansion, the division into feet need not correspond with the division into words: "I never saw a purple cow" is iambic tetrameter even though each foot involves a divided word: "I NEV/er SAW/ a PUR/ple COW." Note, too, that not all feet in a line of verse need be the same: "When in the chronicle of wasted time . . ." begins with a trochee (WHEN in) but is basically iambic. Normal pronunciation would probably accent: "WHEN in/ the CHRON/ i cle/ of WAST/ed TIME." The *cle* of "chronicle" is followed by a light cesura, which helps compensate for the difference between normal pronunciation and the accentuation called for by the line as a whole. Strict metrical pronunciation would accent: "When IN/ the CHRON/ i CLE/ of WAST/ed TIME." This tension between the underlying metrical pattern, which must be established by a good bit of repetition, and the natural accentuation of speech, provides a contrast that should be heard and felt just as syncopation and rhythmic variety in music are heard and felt.

7. Syllabic count as the basis for the rhythmic patterning of verse lines is infrequently used in English poetry, although it is regularly used in French. The French language tends to give each syllable in a phrase except the last one (which is stressed) equal emphasis. In English the variation of stress makes the pattern of syllabic verse difficult to perceive. Lines with the same syllabic count tend not to seem equivalent if they do not have the same number of stresses distributed in the same order.

However, the *haiku*, a Japanese verse form based on syllabic count (usually alluding to a season of the year), is increasingly popular in this country. It consists of seventeen syllables in three lines (five in the first and third, seven in the second).

8. Stress count measures the number of stresses in a line of verse, rather than the number of syllables. A line based on stress count is divided into feet containing varying numbers of syllables (as opposed to the relatively fixed number of syllables in the foot of a conventional verse line), with the accent or stress on the first.

Verse based on stress count is called "accentual verse." Typical of Old English poetry, it has been repopularized in modern poetry by such poets as Gerard Manley Hopkins (who developed an obscure theory about "sprung rhythm") and, more recently, W. H. Auden.

9. The stanza is the grouping of lines into which a poem is divided. A pair of rhyming lines is a couplet. A three-line unit with a rhyming pattern is a tercet. A four-line unit with a rhyming pattern is a quatrain, five—cinquain (rarely used), six—sestet, eight—octave.

The rhyme scheme (pattern of rhyming lines) of a stanza or verse form is usually indicated in studies of versification by using letters of the alphabet to stand for each rhymed line ending. The rhyme scheme of the first stanza of "Daffodils" is *ababcc*, as follows:

I wandered lonely as a cloud	*a*
That floats on high o'er vales and hills,	*b*
When all at once I saw a crowd,	*a*
A host, of golden daffodils;	*b*
Beside the lake, beneath the trees,	*c*
Fluttering and dancing in the breeze	*c*

Following are some common stanza forms:

Blank verse consists of ungrouped lines in unrhymed iambic pentameter.

Heroic couplets are couplets (rhymed) in iambic pentameter, usually "closed"—that is, the thought stops at the couplet's end.

Terza rima (Italian for, literally, "third rhyme") is the rhyme scheme of a poem (or section of a poem) consisting of tercets rhyming *aba bcb cdc* . . . ending with a couplet *nn*.

Ballad stanzas are quatrains of which the first and third lines are in tetrameter and the second and fourth in trimeter, rhyming *abab* or *xaxa* (*x* indicates an unrhymed line).

The rhyme royal stanza consists of seven lines of iambic pentameter rhyming *ababbcc*.

The *ottava rima* ("eighth rhyme") stanza consists of eight lines of iambic pentameter rhyming *abababcc*.

The Spenserian stanza has nine lines, eight in iambic pentameter and one (the last) in iambic hexameter, rhyming *ababbcbcc*.

Of course, many poems have a stanzaic form which falls into none of these categories; nevertheless, these terms are among the most useful in literary study, and the forms they represent are among the most common in English verse.

10. Some specific verse forms have been established for complete short poems. Perhaps the most popular is the limerick, consisting of five anapestic lines, rhyming *aabba*, the *a* lines in trimeter, the *b* lines in dimeter.

The sonnet consists of fourteen lines of iambic pentameter, rhyming *ababcdcdefefgg* (Shakespearean or English sonnet) or *abbaabbacdecde* (Petrarchan or Italian sonnet). In the latter type, the first eight lines form the octave, and the last six form the sestet, which may vary in rhyming pattern.

The sestina, an unusually rigid form popular in the Middle Ages, has six six-line stanzas and a seventh three-line stanza. Although it is usually unrhymed, the last word in each line of the first stanza reappears, in different order, as the last word of one of the lines of the second stanza; they are rearranged again in the third, and so on. In the short seventh stanza, three of the six words appear in the middle and three at the end of the lines. Such very different poets as Sir Philip Sidney, Rudyard Kipling, and Ezra Pound have tried this rigorous form.

The villanelle is another rigid form. Consisting of five tercets and one final quatrain, it has only two rhymes. The entire first line of the first stanza reappears as the last line of the second and fourth stanzas and as the third line of the quatrain. The third line of the first stanza reappears as the last line of the third, fifth, and final stanzas. Dylan Thomas' poem "Do Not Go Gentle into That Good Night" is a villanelle.

11. Free verse follows no set patterns of foot or meter and has no rhyme scheme, but bases its rhythmic flow on the thought or emotion being expressed.

12. A refrain is a phrase, line, or group of lines recurring at regular intervals in a poem.

7. Figurative Language

Figures of speech include almost any unusual way of conveying meaning through words. As a means of communicating through careful control of diction, figurative language is most typical of poetry, and is discussed at length in the chapter on that genre. Here are some of the more common classifications of figurative language:

Apostrophe is direct address of something personified or of someone not literally present. For example: "Milton! thou shouldst be living at this hour. . . ." An ode frequently apostrophizes its subject ("O wild West Wind, *thou* breath of Autumn's being"). A dramatic monologue does not, but instead assumes the literal presence of the person addressed, even though only one person speaks throughout the poem. Apostrophe requires the absence of the person addressed.

Hyperbole is probably more easily remembered as overstatement; the two are synonyms. "You could have knocked me over with a feather" is a hyberbolic description of surprise. Vituperation or invective (verbal abuse; a heartfelt chewing out) is often hyperbolic and is used for comic or satiric purposes. Shakespeare's *Henry IV, Part 1*, Act II, Scene 4, provides some delightful nonsatiric examples of vituperation in the exchanges between the fat Falstaff and the slender Prince Hal:

PRINCE: Why, thou clay-brained guts, thou knotty-pated fool, thou whoreson, obscene, greasy tallow-ketch, . . . this sanguine coward, this bed-presser, this horse-back breaker, this huge hill of flesh;—

FALSTAFF: 'Sblood, you starveling, you eel-skin, you dried neat's-tongue, you bull's pizzle, you stock-fish! O! for breath to utter what is like thee; you tailor's yard, you sheath, you bow-case, you vile standing tuck.

But hyperbole can also praise, as the language of love shows. Since my wife happens to be the most beautiful woman in the world, everyone else who has told his beloved that *she* is the most beautiful woman in the world is of necessity engaging in hyperbole.

Imagery in its broader sense can simply mean figurative language. As a distinct concept, however, it refers specifically to verbally communicated sense experience. The most common, of course, is the visual image, or word picture; any vivid description creates such an image. Also included, however, are the other senses, such as taste:

> . . . he from forth the closet brought a heap
> Of candied apple, quince, and plum, and gourd;
> With jellies soother than the creamy curd,
> And lucent syrups, tinct with cinnamon;
> Manna and dates, in argosy transferr'd
> From Fez; and spiced dainties, every one
> From silken Samarcand to cedar'd Lebanon.*

Say that when dieting, and your mouth waters.

Metaphor equates what is literally meant with something else, whether explicitly or implicitly. "You are a dog, sir!" is an explicit metaphor (although by now a dead one; that is, it has been used so often that "worthless person" has become one of the literal denotations of "dog," a meaning that can be found in the dictionary). "You forgot your collar and leash" is also metaphorical, the equation being implied rather than stated. (Note that a simile is an explicit comparison, rather than an explicit equation; see below.) An important general concept is the difference between the literal meaning of a

---

* John Keats, "The Eve of St. Agnes."

figure of speech and what is metaphorically equated with it. I. A. Richards introduced the terms "tenor" and "vehicle" to distinguish these two. The tenor is what is literally meant; the vehicle is equated with it. The tenor of "you forgot your collar and leash" is your worthlessness, perhaps subservience; the vehicle is the implied dog. The purpose of metaphor is usually to attach the connotations (associations) of the vehicle to the tenor, and thereby to enrich the tone and say more than a literal statement would.

A metonymy is the use of a closely related thing to represent what is literally meant. The word "brass" meaning a high-ranking officer is a metonymy, the insignia representing those who hold the rank with which it is associated.

Onomatopoeia is a kind of imagery, and also a technique related to sound control in versification. Onomatopoetic words imitate the sounds they name: hiss, buzz, slither, bang, meow, blat, zap, pow, zowie. The word "ring" is extended and reverberates like the sound of a bell:

> . . . Your name is like a golden bell
> Hung in my heart; and when I think of you,
> I tremble, and the bell swings and rings—*Roxane!* . . .
> *Roxane!* . . . along my veins, *Roxane!* . . .*

Words that suggest their meaning by their sound are called onomatopoetic even if they do not themselves name sounds, such as slither, flutter, spit.

A paradox is a seemingly impossible statement that on closer consideration is realized to be true. "He who would win his life must lose it" is a paradox, apparently self-contradictory, but expressing a truth when properly understood. One of John Donne's "Holy Sonnets"—a prayer—ends paradoxically:

> Take me to you, imprison me, for I
> Except you enthrall me, never shall be free,
> Nor ever chaste, except you ravish me.

Personification speaks of nonhumans as though they were

---

* Edmund Rostand, *Cyrano de Bergerac,* tr. Brian Hooker (New York: Henry Holt, 1923), reprinted in *The Book of the Play,* ed. Harold R. Walley (New York: Charles Scribner's Sons, 1950), p. 619.

human; logically, it is a special case of metaphor. Apostrophes which are not addressed to humans are also personifications, since they imply the possibility of conversation.

Puns enrich poetic meaning by introducing more than one denotation or literal meaning. Because they are witty, their tone is sharp, perhaps light; but they are not used just for humorous purposes, as Donne's puns on his own name in serious religious verse show. "A Hymn to God the Father" states "And having done that, thou hast done—" that is, God has finished and so also has John Donne. Sir John Suckling, after exclaiming in the first stanza of "The Constant Lover" that he has actually loved for three whole days together, puns on "discover" and "constant" in the next stanza:

> Time shall moult away his wings
>   Ere he shall *discover* [find; make bare, like the wings]
> In the whole wide world again
>   Such a *constant* lover. [faithful; frequent]

A simile is an explicit comparison (cf. the implicit or explicit equation of metaphor) between unlike things. A literal comparison is not a simile; "Jane is more beautiful than Janet" is not a simile, but "Jane is more beautiful than the first A on my record sheet" is a simile.

Synecdoche is one of several substitutions, similar to metonymy, such as the particular for the general (America's fighting men will protect her), the general for the particular (tell the world of high finance to finish his paper and come help me with the dishes), the thing contained for the container (pass the juice, please), the part for the whole (lend a hand, here), and so forth.

Understatement (the opposite of hyperbole) is just what the name implies, saying less than is the case; a special form of understatement, called "litotes," consists of asserting something by denying its opposite: "He's no fool; she's no beauty; that test was no snap." Translated, these literally mean: "He's very smart; she's very ugly; the test was very hard."

All of these technical concepts can be checked out one by one for any poem or apparently figurative passage, by asking whether the definition fits. The most general question is:

"What is really meant? How do the words actually written relate to what is really meant?"

8. Irony

Irony involves a tension or conflict between what is said and what is meant; this tension is not a slight difference but a real contrast. When a man's best friend, whom he has not seen for a month, slaps him on the back and says "Hey, you old s.o.b., how've you been?" no offense is taken. The man knows his friend is not really imputing to him canine ancestry on the distaff side. Usually, the tone of voice in irony is more biting. The grumpy child who says "Oh, goody. Spinach again," is bitterly ironic: he means not "Oh, goody" but "Oh, baddy."

Some critics and some textbook authors distinguish between kinds of irony, depending on whether the conflict is between what one speaker says and what the author means, or between what the same speaker says and what he means, or between what one speaker says and what you know to be true, or between what you expect and what is actually the case. Since there is some variation in how these terms are defined, check your individual text or your instructor for the types of irony. But remember the general case—*a conflict, a contrast, between what is said or thought from one point of view or attitude and what is said or thought from another.*

Irony is intimately associated with satire; and, although it may be bland or biting, contributes to the total tone of a work.

The analytical concept irony may be applied to a work by asking:

1. *Does the author mean what the speaker says?*

2. *Does the speaker mean what the speaker says, and not the opposite?*

3. *Does the speaker say what you or any other reasonable person would believe?*

4. *Does the speaker know what he is talking about?*

5. *Do events reverse your expectations? not simply not fulfill them, but reverse them?*

Answering "no" to any of the first four questions, "yes" to the fifth, implies irony. In justifying the answers you will describe the specific ironic contrast.

9. Comedy

Comedy is a pretty broad term. A horde of words associated with comedy pop immediately into mind: wit, humor, folly, affectation, the ridiculous, merriness, joy, jokes, puns, caricatures, laughter, and more. Defining it therefore requires some limiting. The discussion that follows will concentrate on comedy as a literary form associated with laughter.

What makes people laugh? Something funny. Not always, of course; one can laugh from embarrassment or for other reasons. As the little girl remarked proudly, "My friend and I have a wonderful sense of humor. Sometimes we laugh and laugh for no reason at all." Even apes do something very like laughing when tickled, and baboons grin broadly, showing their fighting teeth, not as a threat but as a gesture of submission, a friendly or nervous apology. These types of laughter do not concern us. Instead, our question is, What kinds of things are funny? Having attempted an answer, we can then turn to literary form.

Most answers to the question "What is funny?" involve either disparity or surprise. Surprise, of course, is simply a reaction to disparity or incongruity. Not all disparity, however, is funny. A gross violation of our sense of justice tends to enrage us, not amuse us.

The first specification, then, might be that the funny disparity must be painless. This limitation is not sufficient, but it does express a truth. People cannot laugh at what gives them a real sense of hurt. If a man tries to stop a rolling volleyball with his foot, twists his ankle, and in the process of falling down stands for a few seconds straight upside down on the back of his neck (if you detect an autobiographical sincerity here you are right), he may in fact laugh in spite of the agony caused by his sprain; but the laughter is prompted by his ability to disassociate himself from the sprain pain and regard his stepping on a rolling ball and his ridiculous headstand as they would look to someone who felt nothing.

Suppose you see a little old lady carrying a bag of groceries slip on the ice, her feet shooting straight out in front of her, leaving her for a brief instant in a sitting position above the sidewalk, blankly startled, then suddenly galvanized into gyrating action as she attempts to avoid the fall, with arms, legs, cabbages, and ketchup bottles flying in all directions and to no avail; for finally she comes down with a thump accompanied by tinkling shards of glass and splattering fruit. When you see such a sight you may well laugh. But you laugh only as long as you see the fall objectively, not empathically. When you realize that she may have broken a hipbone and that age may prevent it from ever healing fully, the fall is not so funny. The difference depends upon the onlooker: if he sympathizes, if he feels the suffering, to that extent he tends not to laugh. If, however, he sees the misfortune from outside, and does not sense the pain involved, to that extent he may well laugh uproariously.

The artist who wishes to make you laugh attempts to control your response by controlling your tendency to empathize. A basic technique is to make the pain obviously unreal. Clowns are clearly not really suffering. Animated cartoons show incredible mayhem, but people laugh with no sadism, for the suffering is obviously unreal. The cat who breaks into little cracks and then shatters is clearly going to be reassembled and once more chasing the mouse in the very next frame.

Besides making the suffering unreal, the comic writer may simply minimize the suffering, placing it below the point at which our amusement is overcome by sympathy. That is, the suffering may be merely discomfort. Instead of falling on ice, the stumblebum may fall into a swimming pool.

Making the suffering unreal and making it trivial are two aspects of the same technique for allowing otherwise painful events to seem funny. A somewhat different technique involves making the suffering acceptable to the audience because it is deserved. Comic villains frequently get it in the end, and their misfortunes are much more acceptable because we do not sympathize with someone who is simply getting what he deserves. The cat who chases the mouse does most of the suffering, as does the coyote who chases the roadrunner. Of course, the suffering is clearly unreal anyway; but the success of the roadrunner cartoons is partly due to the exaggerated villainy of the coyote, whose three-thousand-foot fall or two-ton smash is preceded by a malevolent smirk.

According to Aristotle, comedy deals with that species of the ugly which is not painful: to wit, the ridiculous. The examples of disparity thus far have all involved some degree of pain, controlled by the author in one of the preceding ways. Limiting pain, however, or preventing empathy, is essentially negative. What positive characteristics make disparity funny? One convincing answer is offered by Henri Bergson in his essay, *Laughter*.* The essential characteristic of something funny, says Bergson, is the mechanization of life. Life, or any living being, has two relevant characteristics: life is purposive; and life is adaptable. Since a living creature has purposes, he goes out and encounters the world, trying to achieve his purposes; and since he is adaptable, he adjusts to the world's attempts to frustrate him and to the obstacles he encounters. A machine, however, although it may have an apparent purpose—doing what it was designed to do—is not adaptable. Therefore, it does not encounter obstacles the way a living creature does; rather than adapting, it persists futilely in its predetermined direction, and crashes. When something that ought to be alive, such as a fictional character, encounters an obstacle the way a machine does, the observer's sense of the disparity wells up in a bubble of laughter. The living, which ought to be adaptable, has been shown mechanized, that is, unadaptable and rigid.

Consider, for example, the little old lady carrying groceries. Her purpose is to reach the subway. Suddenly, the world

* In *Laughter and an Essay on Comedy*, ed. Sophie Wyler (Garden City, N.Y.: Doubleday, 1956).

thrusts an obstacle in her way: a slippery patch. Now a human being, as a purposive living creature, should say, "Aha! A slippery patch, as I live and breathe! I shall adapt by stepping carefully around this patch, and thus achieve my purpose by reaching the subway upright." A machine, however, perceives nothing, operates entirely on the basis of its built-in patterns, and does not adapt;* the robot goes clump, clump, clumping right over the patch. When the clump becomes a swish, down it goes. Insofar as the little old lady goes clump, clump, swish, thump, she is a robot. And that, says Bergson, is funny.

Bergson's essay applies this basic concept with great ingenuity to a wide variety of circumstances usually conceded to be funny, such as puns, caricatures, and the humors (or types) of comic character. Although some of the applications are more convincing than others, the basic concept of humor as mechanization of the living seems valid over a very wide range of human and literary experience. The question remains, How does literature express this idea of what is funny?

First, and less significantly, individual episodes, events, or lines may be humorous within practically any literary form. It is true that if the whole work is not funny, a few scattered jokes may pose a problem concerned with mood. Sometimes it is hard to laugh and cry at the same time. However, it is not as hard as Aristotle thought it was, and even the Greeks wrote "tragedies" with humorous elements (for example, Euripides' play *Alcestis* in which Hercules comes on drunk). The terms "tragicomedy" and "comic relief" express the possibility of combining humor with seriousness. The first piece of practical criticism in English literature, John Dryden's *Essay of Dramatic Poesie*, defends Shakespeare's mixture of tragic and comic elements against attacks by neoclassical French critics. The single laugh line or episode, its humor depending on Bergson's "mechanization," is compatible with predominantly serious works.

The more significant answer to the question of how literature is funny concerns form. This second answer is more complex than the first. There seems to be a critical consensus that comedy differs in form from tragedy. Although there is

---

* Even a machine with detectors and feedbacks operates within built-in limits on its flexibility.

not yet unanimity on how that comic form may best be described, two modern statements deserve serious attention. Northrop Frye and Suzanne K. Langer have both offered descriptions of comic form that may be related to Bergson's definition of the basis of humor.

Like Henri Bergson, Suzanne Langer sees in comedy an expression of life itself.* Moreover, life for her also depends essentially upon adaptability, upon adjustment to accidental circumstance. She and Bergson agree that anything that draws our attention to the adaptability of a living creature is cheering, bracing, invigorating, revitalizing, what-have-you. Instead of focusing upon the single laughable accident, however, she looks at the larger issue of the plot structure of a whole comedy. In a comedy as an entire work, the audience's sense of vitality will be most enhanced by the sight of a hero who is flexible and adaptive enough to adjust to the accidental misfortunes that assail him. The typical comic plot, therefore, involves a hero who keeps running into accidental difficulties and successfully overcoming them, not by ruthlessly or fatalistically imposing his will, but by adapting to them. The comic plot therefore tends to be episodic: constructed, that is, of separate incidents which do not lead logically and inevitably into each other. The hero skips down the road of life, is knocked off balance, staggers a bit perhaps, but then recovers by a dexterous skip and a slight change in direction, to continue on his way and be bumped again.

The difficulties must be accidental rather than foreordained; Miss Langer explains that destiny in the guise of fortune is comic, whereas destiny in the guise of fate would be tragic. After all, if the whole universe is against you in any purposeful way, the possibilities of life keeping ahead of the game— in literary comedy, the possibilities of the happy ending— would be very slim indeed. The joyous sense of life, therefore, is created by a plot showing successful adaptations to one misfortune after another.

Now, Bergson and Langer seem to disagree on a striking point. For Bergson, laughter is produced by the mechanization of life, that is, failure to adapt; whereas for Langer, a plot is comic (invokes a happy sense of life) if it shows not failure to adapt but repeated adaptation. This difference is,

---

* *Feeling and Form* (New York: Charles Scribner's Sons, 1953).

I believe, more apparent than real. Our first point about comic misfortune was that it must not involve real suffering. Any misfortune which cannot be ultimately adapted to will kill laughter, not provoke it. The old lady on the ice and the stumblebum in the swimming pool must both get up and continue to live their lives if the audience is to be amused. Their continued lives may be different because of the accidents—ketchup-less in the one case, sopping wet in the other—but the characters must make the minimal adaptation of going on their way with adjusted purposes—the old lady may settle for mustard, the stumblebum borrow ill-fitting dry clothes. Bergson's theory, that is, requires the additional concept of adaptation.

Similarly, Miss Langer's emphasis on adaptation minimizes the other half of the situation—the blind unpreparedness for what may arise. In her typical comic plot, the accident occurs, and the hero is caught off guard. (If he were totally prepared, there would be no sense of conflict at all; the effect would suggest not life but an unreal mastermind manipulating the world like a toy.) Now, at the moment when he is caught off guard, at the moment when destiny in the guise of fortune jolts him, he is manifesting precisely the mechanized lack of adaptation which Bergson emphasizes. For an example, go back to the little old lady on the ice. Bergson would emphasize the failure to maintain balance, the wild gyrations, the plumping fall; the Bergsonian joke-teller would probably assume that she would get up, and tell the story in a light enough way that his audience would assume it too, without even perhaps bothering to refer to it. But the adaptation of getting up is still assumed. Miss Langer's comic hero, in a similar situation, would probably have the same experience up to the plumping fall. That is, her hero would whistle jauntily, slip on the ice, gyrate violently, and recover his balance in the last instant by throwing away the bag of groceries, thus managing to land on all fours; then, with a rueful grimace, he would pick up the largest fragment of bottle that held a little ketchup, and continue toward the subway. If he *did* wind up prostrate like the little old lady, he would certainly get up and keep going. Thus, just as Bergson on the one hand minimizes adaptation, so Langer on the other hand minimizes the initial maladjustment; but both the initial maladjustment (which is increasingly mechanical the longer it is continued) and the final adaptation are necessary to comedy.

Bergson's emphasis is more apt to produce laughter; Langer's to produce well-being, even joy. Clearly, though, one could not base a unified work on a series of Bergsonian jokes. The comic victim who does not get up and go on cannot appear in the next episode. Continued emphasis on the failure to adapt therefore wears out a whole cast of characters in no time at all, and is most appropriate to the stand-up comic who tells a series of unrelated jokes. If the comedy is to have a story of some sort, then the hero must get up and adapt at least well enough to be ready for another misfortune or obstacle to appear. If you are going to keep knocking a man down, he has to keep getting up. Miss Langer's description is therefore more satisfactory for the analysis of comedy as literary structure, Bergson's description more satisfactory for the understanding of comedy as momentary experience.

Northrop Frye offers a somewhat different approach to the nature of comic form. Like Miss Langer, he emphasizes the sense of freedom, of possibility, the absence of restriction. But whereas she tends to see this free possibility primarily in terms of the adaptability of the individual comic hero, Frye sees it primarily in social terms. The comic plot thus presents a society (perhaps as small as a single family) initially dominated by the blocking characters, a society restricted by too precise laws and tyrannous rules which keep boys from girls and feasters from the tables. But by the end of the typical comedy (there are many variants) a new society has been established, free of the life-inhibiting restrictions of the older society, usually focused on the hero's getting the heroine, and winding up with a wedding feast in Greek old comedy or a fade-out on the kiss in the modern Doris Day movie.

If the example of the pratfall on the ice is used in a comic structure such as Frye defines, it gets much more complicated. First, it is necessary to introduce all kinds of other characters; secondly, the before and after situations become more crucial. Instead of our initial Bergsonian little old lady, we will stick with our Langerly young man. We will provide him with a home and father, and also a heroine, with whom he is going to elope, and perhaps add a valet. The initial situation is that the father refuses to let the boy see the girl, and is keeping him at home by hiding his galoshes. The boy has tried once to meet his beloved, and has taken a bad tumble because his patent leather pumps won't grip the ice. The valet (a *dolosus servus;* see "Character") takes the young man's side, partly because he likes to see young men marry and partly because the father has threatened to fire him if he doesn't stop drinking the after-dinner port and pinching the maids. Therefore the valet hatches a scheme: he leads the young man on his way, scattering rock salt before him to melt the ice and afford him firm footing en route to that fair flower, the fiancée. The final situation will most typically be resolved if the father is clearly no longer able (or no longer inclined) to impose his restrictions. A further development would therefore be necessary, in which say the father pursues, but himself falls on the refrozen ice, and either reforms rather improbably or else becomes permanently bed-ridden, hence to be lovingly tended by his new daughter-in-law with his money controlled by his son's power-of-attorney. Everybody celebrates and lives happily ever after.

Frye's stress on the single social development from one kind of society to another can be reconciled with Miss Langer's stress on the successive adaptations of an individual.

Bergson focused on the moments leading into the fall; Miss Langer focuses on the moments leading out of the fall, to an adjusted but restored equilibrium; and Frye focuses on the *context* of both—the society that creates obstacles that may trip one up, and the society one must establish if such obstacles are not to be created again.

For all their differing emphases (which, although they are real, I have stressed more strongly than the critics themselves might), all three are in accord on one central principle: comedy is a celebration of the freedom and vitality of life.

In deciding how comic a work is, these analytical questions should be asked:

1. *Who fails, errs, or suffers?* (If no one does any of these, the work is not a comedy—for that matter, it has no plot.)

2. *Is suffering minimized? how? because temporary? slight? unreal?* (The less the suffering is minimized, the more you empathize, the less comic the work.)

3. *What obstacles have to be overcome?* (The answers may identify moments of Bergsonian mechanization, or the blows of Langer's comic fortune. If the obstacles are human objections, the answer may identify the blocking characters who are opposing a free and happy society. Note that there are also obstacles and conflict in tragedy and other forms.)

4. *Whom do you want to get his way?* (The answer should identify the comic hero.)

5. *Who tries to impose his way on others?* (If the tone of the whole is not tragic, the answer will identify blocking characters. When such a character is the protagonist, the work will have tragic aspects.)

6. *In what ways do any characters fail to adapt?* (If suffering is minimized, as suggested in question #2, the answer should identify funny situations.)

7. *Are there any rigid repetitions, implying mechanization?* (This is really question #6 in a more specific form. An affirmative answer to this question must involve comedy or satire. An affirmative answer to question #6 could involve tragic commitment or integrity, if the characters knowingly refuse to adapt.)

8. *Is the hero well off at the end?* (In comedy, he should be.)

9. *What hindrances to a free and easy life have been eliminated or corrected?*

10. *Is there a new set of rules governing conduct at the end?*

11. *Has the center of power within the society of characters shifted?* (Questions #9, #10, and #11 all concern the applicability of the comic shift from a restrictive to a flexible, life-oriented society, as described by Frye.)

12. *Are you amused? by what?*

13. *Does the work as a whole make you feel good? joyful? vigorous?* (The last two questions concern the general impact of comedy. Tragedy can make one feel good, but in a different way: able to bear the world; comedy makes one feel on top of the world.)

10. Satire

The entry under *satire* in the Thrall, Hibbard, and Holman *Handbook to Literature* opens with this definition:

Satire: a literary manner which blends a critical attitude with humor and wit to the end that human institutions or humanity may be improved.*

Here is a definition from Webster's *Seventh New Collegiate Dictionary:*

1. A literary work holding up human vices and follies to ridicule or scorn. 2. Trenchant wit, irony, or sarcasm used to expose and discredit vice or folly.

The basic distinction between the first and second meanings in this definition depends on whether or not the satire is literary. I have included Webster's second meaning because

* William Flint Thrall and Addison Hibbard, *A Handbook to Literature,* revised and enlarged by C. Hugh Holman (New York: Odyssey Press, 1960), p. 436.

it reveals that irony and sarcasm are not satire in themselves, but only when they are used for the satirical purpose of exposing and discrediting vice or folly. Sarcasm is simply nastiness, without any necessary intent to improve, and irony is saying one thing and meaning the opposite. If your instructor says to a student, "Well, Jones, don't you want to ask another stupid question?" he is being sarcastic, but neither ironical nor satirical; if he says, "You will all be disappointed to hear that we are not having a quiz this morning," he is being ironical, but neither sarcastic nor satirical. If however your instructor says, "It's wonderful! You sit there with your notebooks and faces open and your minds closed!" he is being ironical (for he does not think it wonderful) and satirical (he wants you to unfold your mental shutters).

The etymology of the word "satire" is illuminating:

F[rench], fr. L[atin] *satira, satura,* a poetic medley, . . . fr. *satura* . . . a dish filled with various kinds of fruits, a mixture, a medley, fr. *satur* full of food, sated.[*]

A satirist, you see, is someone who is fed up.

So much for the general definition of satire. What follows is a classification of satiric devices, or kinds of satire, into nine categories.

You will note that all the definitions of satire refer to an element of morality. Therefore, the classification takes as its base a moral evaluation with three gradations: badness, mediocrity, and goodness. This division, however, does not give us the three categories bad, mediocre, and good satire. Rather, we must distinguish between the subject of the satire or what is satirically evaluated, and what the satire does with its subject, the way the subject is treated. (The subject of satire is in the work of art, and may be evaluated in various ways; the object of satire is the real vice or folly, outside the work, that the author is ultimately attacking. Satire is like voodoo in this respect: the wax doll is the subject of the attack, but the object of the attack is the real person whose toenail clippings are inside the doll.) We

---

[*] Webster, *New International Dictionary of the English Language, Second Edition* (Springfield, Mass.: G. & C. Merriam, 1934).

classify satire according to the real value of the subject and the value attributed to that subject. Satire may present bad things, good things, or mediocre things; and it may evaluate those things as bad, as good, or as mediocre. This gives nine possible types of satire (by which I mean satirical devices or methods): for satire may treat the bad as bad; it may treat the bad as mediocre; or it may treat the bad as good. Similarly, it may treat the mediocre as bad, mediocre, or good; and it may treat the good as bad, mediocre, or good. (As will be explained, three of the nine possibilities are not really satirical.) Let us examine these types in some detail, with examples.

The first group includes the three ways in which satire may treat bad things. The first type in this group is that satire (or that part of a larger satire) which treats the bad as bad. There are two ways of identifying the bad as bad: explicitly and implicitly. The first is vituperation or invective, in which the bad is called bad in so many words. In one example of vituperative satire, from *Gulliver's Travels*,* the following words are addressed to Gulliver by the giant King of the Brobdingnagians after listening to Gulliver's description of humankind:

> I cannot but conclude the Bulk of your Natives, to be the most pernicious Race of little odious Vermin that Nature ever suffered to crawl upon the Surface of the Earth.

Here is another example of vituperative satire, written in defense of Jonathan Swift by his cousin Deane Swift ("Deane" is a proper name, not the title):

> . . . shall we condemn a preacher of righteousness, for exposing under the character of a nasty unteachable Yahoo the deformity, the blackness, the filthiness and corruption of those hellish, abominable vices, which inflame the wrath of God against the children of disobedience; and subject them without repentance, that is, without a thorough change of life and practice, to

* Jonathan Swift, *Gulliver's Travels and Other Writings,* ed. Ricardo Quintana (New York: Random House, 1958), p. 101.

everlasting perdition? Ought a preacher of righteousness; ought a watchman of the Christian faith, (who is accountable for his talents, and obliged to warn the innocent, as well as terrify the wicked and the prophane) to hold his peace, like a dumb dog that cannot bark when avarice, fraud, cheating, violence, rapine, extortion, cruelty, oppression, tyranny, rancour, envy, malice, detraction, hatred, revenge, murder, whoredom, adultery, lasciviousness, bribery, corruption, pimping, lying, perjury, subornation, treachery, ingratitude, gaming, flattery, drunkenness, gluttony, luxury, vanity, effeminacy, cowardice, pride, impudence, hypocrisy, infidelity, blasphemy, idolatry, sodomy, and innumerable other vices are as epidemical as the pox, and many of them the notorious characteristicks of the bulk of humankind? *

I will not repeat for you the pejorative or critical words in this passage of invective. You may notice that vituperation is generally hyperbolic. The reason vituperation usually overstates the evils of the case is simply that things usually just aren't that bad. Furthermore, to believe that something is all bad is to despair of it; and despair is incompatible with satire's purpose of improving. If, however, the satirist simply described things as exactly as bad as everyone knows them to be, he probably would not produce a strong reaction. After all, if everyone really loathed the evils the satirist attacks, the evils should already have been eliminated. For the sake, therefore, of prodding sluggards into a positive reaction, satire will engage in hyperbolic vituperation.

Vituperation, then, is explicit denunciation of badness as bad. Another way to treat a bad thing as bad is to equate it allegorically with something inferior or bad. Take, for example, the two Englishmen, Alf and Herman, who were engaged in conversation one sunny English afternoon. Alf made reference to the doctrine of reincarnation, probably showing off; and Herman asked him what that was. "Whoi, 'Erman!" said Alf, "ahin'tchoo ever 'eard of reincarnytion?"

---

* From Deane Swift, *An Essay upon the Life, Writings, and Character of Dr. Jonathan Swift* (London, 1755), pp. 218–221, reprinted in *A Casebook on Gulliver Among the Houyhnhnms*, ed. Milton P. Foster (New York: Thomas Y. Crowell, 1961), pp. 74–75.

"Naoh, aw ahin't," said Herman. "Whoi, 'Erman," said Alf, "h'it's loike this: yew doies, see, an thay plantcha h'under-ground; an pretty soon, h'oop coomes a dahysy; an h'along coomes a caow an crops the dahysy; an pretty soon, caows bein' as haow thay is, ther caow drawps somethin' h'on ther path; an then Oi coomes h'along, an Oi says, 'Whoi, 'Erman! yew ahin't chainged a bit!' An that's reincarnytion."

This is a pretty simple allegory; but there are more complicated examples of allegorical satire. The fourth book of *Gulliver's Travels* presents two clearly allegorical creatures, the beastly Yahoo, referred to by Jonathan Swift's cousin in the passage quoted above, and the Houyhnhnm, a rational horse. They represent beastliness and reason, as extremes between which man stands. The Yahoo, however, is super-ficially human, and is apparently equated with mankind. Insofar as sinful and vicious man is allegorically represented by the Yahoo, Swift is allegorically equating the bad objects of his satire (evil men) with clearly bad things (repulsive Yahoos).

Vituperation and (sometimes) allegorical satire treat bad things as bad. A different technique, and a different effect, result when the bad is treated as mediocre. This, of course, is understatement: it consists of treating something as less bad than it really is. This kind of understatement, under-statement dealing with bad things, usually rates them just on the negative side of mediocrity. (If it rates them on the positive side, it belongs in the next group, among the types that treat the bad as good.) Treating the bad as mediocre, or not so bad, is therefore the opposite of hyperbolic vituper-ation, which overemphasizes bad qualities.

A marvelous sentence from Swift's *Tale of a Tub* is often quoted: "Last week I saw a woman flayed, and you will hardly believe how much it altered her person for the worse." This is a masterpiece of understatement. Part of the impact of this particular sentence comes from its semblance of hyper-bole: the words "you will hardly believe how much" suggest that a really emphatic statement is to come; but the conclu-sion of the sentence displaces the speaker's attention from its proper concern, human agony, to a comparatively trivial and therefore improper concern, feminine pulchritude. The understatement is therefore compounded: first, the hideous-ness of rent meat is inadequately described as an alteration for the worse; second, the speaker concentrates on the least important drawback in the situation (disfigurement) rather than the most important (agony and death). The effect of the disparity between what is referred to and the evaluation of it, between the badness of the subject and the mediocrity attributed to it, shows the power of understatement.

Allegory also may be used to treat the bad as mediocre, or slightly bad; the effect is usually ridicule. The first book of *Gulliver's Travels* makes extended use of this kind of satiric allegory. For example, the kind of heels one wears stands for political affiliation; the way one eats eggs, for religious affiliation. Trying to straddle the political fence is equated with wearing one high and one low heel, which causes a decided hobble; and religious persecution becomes ridiculous, for clearly everyone ought to be allowed to eat eggs the way he wants to. In both of these cases, Swift is allegorically equating the bad things, which he is attacking, with not so bad, but slightly ludicrous, things.

The next satiric type or device is that which treats the bad as good. This, of course, is a form of irony, or saying one thing and meaning the opposite. The tone of this irony may vary greatly from one work or passage to another. Chaucer's *envoi* to the *Clerk's Tale* wields this satiric device with heavy bitterness:

> Arch-wives, stand up, defend your board and bed!
> Stronger than camels as you are, prevail!
> Don't swallow insults, offer them instead.
> And all you slender little wives and frail,
> Be fierce as Indian tigers, since destined
> To rattle like a windmill in a gale.*

When the Clerk says, "Be nasty," he doesn't really mean it. He may fear it will happen, but he is not honestly recommending shrewishness as proper wifely conduct. The tone of this example is heavy and bitter, because the speaker of the lines that call badness good (the Clerk) doesn't believe what he is saying. (When the speaker *does* believe what he is saying, although the author doesn't, the irony and the tone

* Geoffrey Chaucer, *The Canterbury Tales*, tr. Nevill Coghill (Baltimore, Md.: Penguin Books, 1958), p. 371.

are both different. This problem is discussed later in this chapter.) Satire with a bitter tone, such as the Clerk's lines, and most vituperation, is sometimes called "Juvenalian," after the Roman satirist Juvenal; when the tone is mild, as is frequently the case when treating the bad as mediocre, the satire may be called "Horatian," after the Roman satirist Horace.

The next major group of satiric devices all deal with the mediocre. Like the really bad, the mediocre too may be treated by a satirical work as bad, as mediocre, or as good. It is possible for the characters within a work to treat the mediocre as bad, for the author's satiric purposes. In Joseph Heller's novel *Catch-22* there are numerous incidents in which military machinery of an awesome nature devotes itself to eradicating evils that in fact are quite mediocre. A striking example of this treatment of the mediocre as bad is the incident involving the chaplain. A flyer, forced to censor enlisted men's letters while recuperating in the hospital, had amused himself by forging the chaplain's name, and writing at the bottom of a number of letters, "I yearn for you tragically. A. T. Tappman, Chaplain, U.S. Army." * A counterespionage agent has been sent to the hospital to investigate this subversion, and a counterespionage agent-investigator has also been sent, to keep an eye on the counterespionage agent. Since Chaplain Tappman is not in fact in the hospital at all, he is not found for a long time. Finally, however, he is kidnapped by three extremely vicious officers, who take him to an isolated basement and threaten him with torture unless he confesses that he has written, "I yearn for you tragically. A. T. Tappman, Chaplain, U.S. Army," at the bottom of the letters he was censoring. The investigation is cruel and terrifying, especially for Chaplain Tappman, but even a little for the reader. What is really being satirized in this case, the real object of satire, is military and cloak-and-dagger investigations; but dramatically it presents the treatment of the mediocre subject (A. T. Tappman, Chaplain, and his alleged crime) as bad (i.e., deserving of the third degree and the time of five highly paid investigators). The chaplain, by the way, confesses, and is released unharmed.

So much for treating the trivial as bad. For logical sym-

* Joseph Heller, *Catch-22* (New York: Dell Books, 1962), p. 8.

metry, I next take up treating the mediocre as mediocre, and immediately put it down again. This approach cannot incite to moral improvement, it is simple literalism, and it is probably extremely dull. Some forms of very delicate satire may approximate this successfully, as Jane Austen's work perhaps does; but *only* as an approximation. The impact derives precisely from the extent to which she does *not* present mediocrity mediocrely. To do that would not be satire.

The next category, however, treating the mediocre as good, is one of the time-honored forms of satire. This form is ironically hyperbolic mock-heroic satire. The common name is mock-heroic. When the mediocre or trivial or inconsequential is treated as terribly important, the form of satire is mock-heroic. "The Rape of the Lock," by Alexander Pope, is a mock-heroic poem which ironically elevates stealing a lock of hair to the stature of Paris' abduction of Helen or the descent of Zeus to Danae as a shower of gold. As in the case of A. T. Tappman, Chaplain, the real object of satire here is not the mediocre triviality (in this case, the theft of a lock of hair). The real object of satire for Pope is the angry furor that the historical theft of the lock produced. Not the mediocre itself, but regarding the mediocre as important, is what is satirized. Within the satire, however, the device employed is to treat the subject, a trivial theft, as even more important than the historical personages thought it, making it semidivine in the manner of mythic epic—to wit, mock-heroic. (Heller's bringing of the innocuous A. T. Tappman to the secret inquisition torture chamber might, by analogy to "mock-heroic," be called "mock-demonic.")

Another mock-heroic poem, "Mac Flecknoe," by John Dryden, also elevates the trivial and mediocre to semidivine status. Dryden is attacking poor poetry, most particularly the poetry of one Thomas Shadwell. The poem is allegedly spoken by a recently dead poet, also no good, named Flecknoe; Dryden represents him as seeking a worthy successor, and in the person of Flecknoe says the following:

> Shadwell alone my perfect image bears,
> Mature in dullness from his tender years.
> Shadwell alone of all my sons is he
> Who stands confirm'd in full stupidity.

The rest to some faint meaning make pretense,
But Shadwell never deviates into sense.
Some Beams of Wit on other souls may fall,
Strike through and make a lucid interval;
But Shadwell's genuine right admits no ray,
His rising fogs prevail upon the Day;
Besides, his goodly Fabrick fills the eye
And seems design'd for thoughtless Majesty:
Thoughtless as Monarch Oakes that shade the plain,
And, spread in solemn state, supinely reign.

Notice here that Shadwell is not positively bad, he simply
has no virtues; he is mediocre. Notice that he is spoken of in
words of praise: "Perfect, mature, confirm'd, never deviates,
genuine, goodly, majesty," etc. Note particularly that Flecknoe,
the speaker, really means what he says as praise. Yet note also
how you are persistently reminded of the actual quality of the
item being praised: perfect, but perfect in the image of
Flecknoe; mature, but mature in dullness; confirm'd, a word of
praise, but confirm'd in full what? full stupidity. Shadwell
never deviates, but what he never deviates into is sense; he
has the quality of genuineness, but genuine night. He prevails,
but it is his Fogs that prevail upon the Day; and, in the
apotheosis of mediocrity, he "seems design'd for thoughtless
Majesty/Thoughtless as Monarch Oakes that shade the plain/
And, spread in solemn state, supinely reign."

This poem is mock-heroic, because of the discrepancy between trivial subject matter and a laudatory, heroic style; it
is, like all mock-heroic satire, hyperbolic, because it treats
trivia (particularly, Shadwell) as more important than they
really are; and, like all mock-heroic satire, it is ironical, because it is a mockery: Dryden doesn't mean his praise, even
though the fictional speaker Flecknoe does.

We come now to the last three categories of satiric methods,
all of which present good things. Only one of them, treating
the good as bad, is really satirical. I will therefore comment
on the other two first. Treating the good as mediocre is
cynical, blasé, or merely reserved; it is not satiric. To treat
good things as good, the other possibility that I wish to dispose
of, is not satiric either, because it is not a critical procedure nor
is it ironical. Let us consider, then, that form of satire which
treats good things as bad ones.

Treating good things as bad is the final satiric device. It is, of course, ironical. Swift once wrote, in a satirical essay:

> I hope no Reader imagines me so weak to stand up in Defence of real Christianity, such as used in primitive Times (if we may believe the Authors of those Ages) to have an Influence upon Men's Belief and Actions: To offer at the restoring of that, would indeed be a wild Project . . .*

In *Gulliver's Travels,* Gulliver praises the use of gunpowder for blowing people into shreds (treating the bad as good), and offers to teach the King of the Brobdingnagians how to make it. The King, however, refuses the offer, whereupon Gulliver thinks very critically indeed of the King's provincial stupidity. Here, the King's moral humaneness, which is good, is treated by Gulliver as though it were bad.

The preceding example suggests two additional conclusions. The first concerns the mediocre and the good as subjects of satiric evaluation. Satire aims at correcting bad things. The mediocre and the good are not bad; in themselves, therefore, they are not really objects of satire, things to be satirized. However, if people do not understand the mediocre or the good—if they regard the mediocre as very important, or if they do not recognize the good—then these erroneous attitudes are indeed objects of satire. The technique employed will be the "mock-demonic," mock-heroic, or ironic denunciation of goodness.

The second conclusion to be drawn from the example of Gulliver's offer of gunpowder to the King of Brobdingnag, which moved quickly from treating the bad as good to treating the good as bad, is that the devices may be combined in the same work. Indeed, far more often than not, the same work will use, in rapid succession, most of these techniques. This typology is not a classification of works, but a classification of methods.

In summary, then, satire is an attack on human vices, aimed at improving them; it may proceed by showing the bad as bad, in generally hyperbolic vituperation or in allegorical

---

* *Satires and Personal Writings,* ed. William Alfred Eddy (London: Oxford University Press, 1932), p. 4.

equation of the object of satire with something worse; it may treat the bad as mediocre, either understating or allegorically equating the object of satire with something trivial; it may treat the bad as good, in ironical praise of vice. Satire may show a fictional person treating a mediocre subject as bad; it cannot treat the mediocre as mediocre; but it frequently treats the mediocre as good, in mock-heroic. That satire which treats good subjects must almost of necessity show them as bad, operating ironically.

In conclusion, I wish to point out a complication. The complication involves the fictional persona, or speaker employed by the satirist. Usually the satirist speaks in a dramatic guise which is not the real author at all. In Swift's essay, *A Modest Proposal for Preventing the Children of poor People in Ireland, from Being a Burden to their Parents or Country; and for making them beneficial to the Publick,* in which he explores with great patience and in exhaustive detail the advantages of eating the children of poor people, he really doesn't mean half of what he says. But the fictional author of the essay does. Swift is *posing* as a man who really thinks that cannibalism is an answer to the social problem of poverty. This adoption of a fictional persona, this playing of a role, complicates matters tremendously. (It has led some to equate Gulliver with Swift, and thereby to misconstrue *Gulliver's Travels.*) In this quicksand of satirical irony, shifting fluidly from one kind of irony to another, everything that is said is suspect. How, then, do you know what to believe?

The only answer I have to offer is questions. In addition to the questions on p. 39 dealing with irony, the following should be asked:

1. *Are there at least a few clear disparities between evaluation and true worth?* (If there are none, the work is probably not satirical.)

2. *What moral evaluations are expressed by the characters in the work, including the narrator?* (The answers will identify whether things are treated as good or bad.)

3. *With which of these moral attitudes do you agree? With which do you think the author agrees?*

4. *By combining the first two questions, decide which of*

the six major methods (three types collapsed, remember) are employed.

5. *If you have trouble with the preceding question, check for self-contradictory elements in the evaluations the characters make. Do they, in their very praise, express what is wrong with what they praise?* (As Flecknoe does, for example, in Dryden's poem, in phrases such as "mature in dullness.") *Do they, in their very criticism, express the virtues of what they condemn?*

6. *Are some of the evils presented or implied by the work rectifiable?* (If they are not rectifiable, at least in individual cases, the work is probably not satiric, but ironically tragic.)

7. *Is the style too lofty for the subject?* (If yes, the work or passage is mock-heroic.)

8. *Does the style seem inappropriate?* (If so, the work or passage is probably parody.)

9. *Is there any allegorical symbolism?* (Talking animals are almost undoubtedly allegorical; once the work has been established as satirical, any specific references to historical events imply there may be some concealed references, that is, allegorical references.)

10. *Is the tone biting* (Juvenalian) *or bland* (Horatian)?

11. *What is the real object of the satire? That is, what actual vice or folly is the satirist ultimately attacking?*

12. *Do you find any lines or passages treating the good as good?* (Although showing the good as good is not per se satirical, sometimes direct affirmations of values the author holds are presented in satirical works.)

11. Tragedy

A newspaper account of a passenger boat accident in the Savithri River, 200 miles south of Bombay, states: "Unofficial reports placed the death toll in the tragedy as 140." The word *"tragedy"* in that context means any catastrophic event. This is not the literary sense of the word, for two reasons. First, tragedy as a literary form does not refer to history, to what has really happened; it is fictional, an art form, with its own structural patterns. You are not supposed to react to the death of Hamlet's father the way you would react to the death of your own. Secondly, even though you might be tempted to call the deaths "tragic," you probably would not mean it; the figures are remote statistics, with no strong emotional impact. The numbers of deaths defy imagination. Such a horde cannot be understood in human terms, which are essentially terms of the individual. In this respect, tragedy differs not only from statistical reports, but also from comedy, which tends to be socially oriented and to have a more crowded cast of characters.

One of the Russian novelist Dostoevsky's characters poses the dilemma: Should you buy eternal salvation for the entire human race, if the price were the eternal damnation of one innocent child? If you unhesitatingly answer, "It is worth the price," then you are not a tragedian.

If a tragic event must involve individuals rather than crowds, consider another possibility. The lead to a newspaper article states: "Van Johnson Collapses After Cutting Finger." Tragic? No; in spite of the fact that he collapsed, the accident is too trivial, and furthermore it is hard to believe that Mr. Johnson's finger hurt that much. Or how about the ninety-five-year-old who dies in his sleep? Death is certainly serious. But such a death is not tragic for the same reason that Mr. Johnson's cut finger is not tragic: not enough suffering. The man passed away quietly in his sleep, and his next of kin cannot have been unprepared for the loss of one so old. In this respect, too, tragedy differs from comedy, for the problem in humor is to limit suffering.

Consider another example. The essayist James Thurber tells of a town character with a most annoying habit. Every time anything went right for Josh, he would say, "Something just told me I ought to do that." This constant repetition of the claim that not luck but his own doing brought good things to him wore down his friends' tolerance until, when he died, no one really minded. His death was quite—so to speak—striking: walking down the street, Josh passed an acquaintance, went on six steps, stopped, turned, went back two steps, and was decapitated by an 18-pound meteorite. It was a decent interval of about three days later that Josh was given his epitaph, during a lull in barbershop conversation: "Well," mused one of Josh's ex-friends, "I guess something just told old Josh to go back two steps."

Indeed a striking death; but once again, not tragic. Josh of course did not suffer. And, not only did he not suffer, he did not even know what happened to him. The tragic victim must have some idea of what is going on. As a matter of fact, he ought to have a chance of learning something from his suffering.

One more example, and then I will turn to tragedy itself. Archibald MacLeish's play *J.B.*, like its prototype, the Book of Job, shows a wealthy, happy man smitten by continuous undeserved misfortunes. If you know the play, you may have wondered between Acts I and II how on earth MacLeish could write a second act to follow the horrible catastrophes of the first act. What more could possibly happen? What had to happen was that the play turn into a tragedy, for the first act was not truly tragic. J.B. was a single man, an individual;

he suffered—really an understatement; he knew that he was suffering, and he was beginning to learn, for by the end of the first act he at least knew that the world was not his oyster. But throughout the first act he does nothing; he is a passive sufferer, not a tragic victim, but a pathetic victim. *Pathos* is not tragic. In the second act, he begins his struggle, and in the second act the play becomes a tragedy.

A tragic event is one in which an individual suffers greatly; one in which he suffers self-consciously, aware of his plight and perhaps learning from it; and one in which he struggles against his suffering and its causes. I propose now to analyze several significant critical definitions of tragedy, specifically, those of Aristotle, Arthur Miller, Francis Fergusson, R. B. Sewall, and Friedrich Nietzsche. All of these men incorporate suffering, learning, and struggle into their definitions, in one way or another.

In his *Poetics*, Aristotle identifies six elements in drama; these terms may be applied with varying relevance to other genres as well: "plot," "character," "thought," "diction," "melody," and "spectacle." "Plot" and "character" are treated as separate topics elsewhere; "thought" is discussed as a subdivision of "theme."

Of the remaining three terms, "spectacle" means what we would now call "staging" or "production." Aristotle is referring to the simply visual impact of a play presented upon a stage. As such, the term has relevance to drama, movies, and television, but not to other forms of tragedy. It is discussed in the chapter on "Drama," particularly with reference to dramatic convention (and see also p. 24, under "Scene").

"Melody" may also be dispatched rather hastily; a better translation might be "music." Like *Carousel, Porgy and Bess,* and *West Side Story,* Greek drama was musical: there were dance numbers and songs. (See the discussion of the role of the chorus in the chapter on drama.)

"Diction" meant pretty much what it means today, except that Aristotle puts a rather heavy emphasis on metrics, a subject more of scholarly than of general interest today. The concept of diction is still useful in relation to poetry, and is discussed on p. 181.

Aristotle suggests that the protagonist be of noble station; so many worse things can happen to a rich king than can happen to a diseased beggar. Granting the contemporary insignificance of royalty, J.B. would probably satisfy Aristotle quite well on this score, for he is rich, successful, happily married, with a nice family, envied and admired by all. The bigger they are, the harder they fall. The best tragedy thus has a plot in which a noble character moves from good fortune to bad.

The value of art has been variously identified as the true, the good, and the beautiful or valuable-in-itself, which may also be called "the pleasant." Aristotle attributes all three of these to tragedy. It is true, it makes you good, and it is pleasant.

For Aristotle, tragedy is true because of its unity of plot. The plot of a tragedy must proceed according to the laws of probability or necessity. The events of the plot must be related as cause to effect, each arising out of the one before. (The *deus ex machina,* or completely fortuitous ending—Hurrah! Here Come the United States Marines!—is a terrible flaw.) If the events are related as cause to effect, then none can be removed without destroying the whole plot structure.

Tragedy, therefore, is "truer" than history, in which things frequently happen by chance. As in a science fiction story, once given the initial premises, everything should follow with reasonable probability, no matter how impossible those initial premises may be.

The truth of tragedy is that it imitates the universal in the particular: it shows what history would be if there were no accidents. It imitates the true form of things, rather than their accidental appearance. You will of course note that this is a doctrine of art as selective, refining imitation, not a cheap literalism. This doctrine has numerous modern adherents, among them a third-grader described on television by David Brinkley. This young aesthetician, in an art class, painted a landscape with a large blank space between the blue sky and the green earth. His teacher led him to the window and pointed. "Look out there, Johnny," she said. "Do you see how the sky touches the earth?" "Yes," said Johnny. "Then, dear," asked teacher. "why don't you paint the sky touching the earth at the horizon?" "Because I've been there," said Johnny, "and it doesn't." Like Aristotle, Johnny thought art must imitate the true nature of things, and not just their appearance. And the true nature of things, for Aristotle, is the necessary or probable consequences of a given combination of people and circumstances.

The second value of tragedy, according to Aristotle, is that it makes you a better citizen; it has a moral effect. The key word here is "catharsis." Catharsis means purgation. It is a medical term, and Aristotle applies it to the emotional release the audience gets from witnessing a tragedy. The specific emotions that are aroused are pity and fear which are purged or drained off so that the audience departs ready to face life again, in effect, purified. Aristotle is directly answering Plato's charge that tragedy stirs up a lot of undesirable emotions. It does, says Aristotle, but only to effect a catharsis of them.

The final value of tragedy is its real purpose: pleasure. For some reason, not only the recognition of truth, but also the arousing and purgation of the emotions of pity and fear is pleasant; and this particular pleasure (not just any old pleasure) is what tragedy is for.

To Aristotle, the cause of the catastrophe, *hamartia,** is a flaw, defect, or mistake. Presumably, it would have been better for the hero to have had no *hamartia*, and not to have gotten entangled in fate, blood, and destruction. Arthur Miller, the author of *Death of a Salesman*, thinks differently. For him, what leads to destruction is not a flaw but a virtue.

The following quotes are from a newspaper article by Miller, frequently reprinted:

As a general rule, to which there may be exceptions unknown to me, I think the tragic feeling is evoked in us when we are in the presence of a character who is ready to lay down his life, if need be, to secure one thing—his sense of personal dignity. . . . Tragedy, then, is the consequence of a man's total compulsion to evaluate himself justly. . . . For, if it is true to say that in essence the tragic hero is intent upon claiming his whole due as a personality, and if this struggle must be total and without reservation, then it automatically demonstrates the indestructible will of man to achieve his humanity.†

* See "Character," p. 10.
† "Tragedy and the Common Man," *The New York Times,* February 27, 1949, sec. 2, reprinted in *Tragedy: Plays, Theory, and Criticism,* ed. Richard Levin (New York: Harcourt, Brace, 1960).

You will note that Miller's essential tragic hero needs no mistake, no *hamartia*. Miller is offering an undefined substitute for Aristotle's pity and fear; perhaps a fearful awe, certainly with much less pity. Incidentally, since he implicitly rejects Aristotle's insistence on pity and fear, he is also convinced that common men make just as good tragic heroes as outstanding nobles: his emphasis is not on the long fall, which Aristotle thought most effective in arousing pity and fear, but on the personal affirmation of individual integrity. The main point is that Miller's tragic hero embraces catastrophe in order to define his own worth. Thus, the salesman Willy Loman commits suicide not as a sacrifice, but to show that he is a successful provider, in the economic terms that are all he understands. He kills himself for his insurance money, and thereby proves that he is worth $20,000.

Miller is concerned with character; Francis Fergusson is more like Aristotle, primarily concerned with plot. In place of the word "plot," which Aristotle said was the soul of tragedy, Fergusson speaks of "the tragic rhythm of action." He defines this essential quality of tragedy in an excellent book available in paperback, *The Idea of a Theater*. His formula for the tragic rhythm is purpose, passion (or suffering), and perception.

> This movement, or tragic rhythm of action, constitutes the shape of the play [*Oedipus the King*] as a whole; it is also the shape of each episode, each discussion between principals with the chorus following. . . . It is this tragic rhythm of action which is the substance or spiritual content of the play, and the clue to its extraordinarily comprehensive form.*

Apparently, the three "moments of tragic rhythm" may be experienced by different characters; thus, one man's purpose may produce another man's perception. All that is necessary is that they bear a causal relationship to each other, rather a la Aristotle. But often, particularly in a work as a whole, all three will be found in the central character.

There is a parallel between purpose, passion, and percep-

---

* Francis Fergusson, *The Idea of a Theater* (Garden City, N.Y.: Doubleday Anchor Books, 1953), p. 31.

tion, and the beginning, middle, and end that Aristotle insists upon in the plot. Indeed, there is a sense in which Fergusson's three terms are Aristotle's plot terms applied to character or the human psyche. This parallel is further strengthened by Aristotle's remark that character is the source of action. You will note that for passion to follow purpose there must be some conflict, some opposition, some difficulty, which prevents the accomplishment of the original purpose, and produces a new understanding of the total situation, perhaps a new definition of the original purpose. A series of such conflicts, causally related, would begin to resemble an Aristotelian plot.

Another way of looking at tragedy is found in Richard B. Sewall's *The Vision of Tragedy.** Tragedy, for Sewall, involves the relationship between evil, suffering, and values. The basic questions Sewall uses to test a work of literature for tragic stature are:

1. Is there a protagonist confronted with evil?

2. Does he choose to act, and persevere in opposing the implications of the initial situation?

3. Does he suffer, and thereby in some sense learn?

4. Does the work as a whole maintain the coexistence of evil and good, affirming the value of good without denying the existence of the evil?

To the extent that these questions may be answered "yes," a work is tragic.

Sewall's concern is theme rather than plot, the tragic vision of the universe rather than the tragic rhythm of action; he differs from both Aristotle and Fergusson in this respect. He does not, of course, think that tragedy is philosophy, for the theme is expressed in action rather than in philosophical statement. But he remains primarily interested in what kind of world the play seems to affirm, with a strong subordinate interest in the tragic hero and his deeds as a means to affirming something. His emphasis on the perseverance of the tragic hero is rather like Miller's insistence that the tragic hero assert his own dignity at any cost. Like Miller, he sees the essence of tragedy as

* New Haven: Yale University Press, 1959.

involving the affirmation of value. They differ in that Sewall looks for the affirmation of value in the universe at large, whereas Miller looks for it in the individual protagonist. Thus Miller emphasizes character, whereas Sewall emphasizes theme.

Still another view of tragedy is offered by Friedrich Nietzsche, the nineteenth-century German poet and philosopher, whose idea of the superman was perverted and adopted by Hitler. Nietzsche does not write precisely, and seems totally uninterested in clarity. In his long essay *The Birth of Tragedy,* he dabbles in the mythic origins of Greek tragedy. I quote:

> . . . art owes its continuous evolution to the Apollonian-Dionysiac duality . . . until at last, by the thaumaturgy of an Hellenic act of will, the pair accepted the yoke of marriage and, in this condition, begot Attic tragedy, which exhibits the salient features of both parents.*

The basic concept Nietzsche offers for the understanding of tragedy is the Apollonian-Dionysiac duality. Apollo, in Greek mythology, was the god of the sun, of prophecy, and of such human arts as music and medicine and archery. Dionysus, not an Olympian god, was the god of wine and intoxication, and a symbol of birth, death, and rebirth, in alternation. His worshipers were thought to be possessed. Around these two symbols, Nietzsche clusters two contrasting groups of ideas. The Apollonian cluster includes reason, order, light, dream, perfect form, restraint, the principle of individuation. Around Dionysus are clustered will, chaos, darkness, reality, action, rapture, loss of identity in union with nature.

In his metaphor of the marriage of Apollo and Dionysus, Nietzsche is trying to say something about the origin of Greek tragedy. He is not actually describing a characteristic of all tragedy; he is stating how tragedy came to be, stating the psychological impetus that caused the Greeks to start writing tragedies. However, the dichotomy between the ordered-and-comprehensible and the chaotic-and-irrational has a good deal of relevance for literature, from individual Greek tragedies to modern existential fiction. It is relevant in two ways. First,

---

* Friedrich Nietzsche, *The Birth of Tragedy and The Genealogy of Morals,* tr. Francis Golffing (Garden City, N.Y.: Doubleday, 1956), p. 19.

the protagonist may be pitted against a universe that is totally unlike his conception of it. He could be a Dionysiac hero in an Apollonian universe, or he may be an Apollonian hero trying to understand rationally a Dionysiac and therefore incomprehensible universe. Secondly, there may be an internal conflict within the protagonist himself, between Apollonian and Dionysiac elements of his character.

The latter case, internal conflict, is expressed in the following quote from Nietzsche:

> As a moral deity Apollo demands self-control from his people and, in order to observe such self-control, a knowledge of self. And so we find that the esthetic necessity of beauty is accompanied by the imperatives, "Know thyself," and "Nothing too much." Conversely, excess and hubris come to be regarded as the hostile spirits of the non-Apollonian sphere. . . . *

With this quote, we are moving back toward Aristotle once again, for the Apollonian ethic of self-knowledge, restraint, and nothing in excess is characteristic of Aristotelian ethics. The Nietzschean dichotomy between Apollo and Dionysus, although basically a matter of theme, may thus be applied to character.

In conclusion, I suggest some questions for you to consider in relationship to tragedy. In effect, I ask you to try to apply these ideas to the tragedies you read, and decide which one or which ones fit them best.

1. *Does the protagonist suffer?* (If he does not suffer at all, then the play is not a tragedy for any of the critics.)

2. *Is the protagonist good?* (The answer is important for Aristotle because it affects audience response to his suffering; it is important for Sewall if the goodness is affirmed in the face of some evil; and it is important for Miller if the kind of goodness is that expressed in question #12 below.)

3 *Is he bad in any way?* (Virtually the same comments apply here as follow question #2. The answer to this question may also be the answer to question #4.)

4. *What is the protagonist's hamartia?* (The term is Aris-

* *Ibid.*, p. 34.

totle's and the answer should make the protagonist's fall acceptable to the audience. Insofar as *hamartia* makes the protagonist deserve his fall, the world presented is Apollonian rather than Dionysiac.)

5. *Does the protagonist deserve what happens to him?* (If he does, is it because he acted in a Dionysiac way in an Apollonian universe, or because he acted in an Apollonian way in a Dionysiac universe? This is the Nietzschean equivalent to questions #3 and #4.)

6. *Is the protagonist in any sense a sacrificial victim?* (Dionysiac revels usually involved a bloody sacrifice.)

7. *Are the characters consistent?* (If they are not, then the play will lack the truth—inevitable development—that Aristotle sees preeminently expressed in tragic plots: see the next question.)

8. *Are all the events of the plot related according to the law of probability or necessity, or do any of them happen by chance?* (The probability or necessity of the plot's development is the truth of tragedy, for Aristotle; it also helps to make the hero's suffering acceptable. Chance suffering is merely a flaw, in dramatic truth and in audience psychology, for Aristotle; for Nietzsche, however, chance suffering may imply a Dionysiac universe.)

9. *Does the protagonist express an initial purpose?* (For Aristotle, this could be the initial action or beginning of the play, although he does not insist that the protagonist be the one to start things; for Sewall, this should be the protagonist's opposition to some evil inherent in the initial situation; for Fergusson, this purpose should move through passion to a new perception.)

10. *Identify the major conflicts.* (For Aristotle, this question is part of a plot analysis; in answering question #8 one would also answer this question. For Sewall, the answer should involve the protagonist's perseverance in opposition to evil. And for Fergusson, the answer should identify the passion by means of which new perception is achieved.)

11. *Identify any internal or external conflicts between reason and will, between restraint and frenzy.* (This is the way Nietzsche might put question #10. The answers identify Apollonian and Dionysiac aspects of character.)

12. *Does the protagonist assert himself courageously at the end of the play?* (If he is being true to his own sense of values, then the play satisfies Miller's concept of what produces tragic awe. If he is persevering in opposition to evil, then two of Sewall's requirements for tragedy are satisfied. For Aristotle, all that is necessary is consistency.)

13. *Does the protagonist learn anything?* (For Aristotle, he will discover facts of identity, or recognize people, as part of the development of the plot; for the other critics, however, the learning should involve a more profound understanding of the nature of things. Here one would identify Fergusson's "perception"; here in part Sewall's affirmation of the value of good without denying the existence of evil; here Miller's willingness to pay the ultimate price in order to be true to oneself.)

14. *To what extent does the play as a whole affirm the co-existence of evil and good?* (To the extent that it does, the play expresses Sewall's tragic vision.)

15. *To what extent is the world of the play rationally understandable?* (The answer to this question identifies Apollonian aspects of the world.)

16. *To what extent is the world of the play mysterious, irrational, and incomprehensible?* (The answer to this question identifies Dionysiac aspects of the world.)

I have used the word "play" throughout these questions simpy because it is more convenient than "art work" or "piece of literature"; partly, too, because tragedy is more often thought of as a dramatic form. The same questions, however, apply to tragic epics and novels. All of the above questions are simply applications of the basic terms with which this definition of tragedy began: the individual (the protagonist), what he suffers, how he struggles, what he learns. In their most generalized form, the questions relevant to tragic form resolve into these:

1. What is the protagonist like?
2. What does he struggle against?
3. What does he suffer, and why?
4. What does he learn?

12. Allegory

An *allegory* has four basic characteristics: first, it consists of many elements of meaning; second, each element has one, and only one, meaning; third, the relationships among the elements parallel the relationships among the meanings; and fourth, it expresses the abstract (the meanings) in concrete terms (the elements).

Consider Canto I of the First Canticle of Dante's *Divine Comedy*. The First Canticle of *The Divine Comedy* is *Hell;* or, as it is sometimes called, *The Inferno.* The first canto may be summarized as follows: A man halfway through life loses his way and finds himself in a dark wood. As he is about to despair, he sees the sun rise and, shining over the crest of a hill, light the way up the hill. The man tries to climb out of the wood up to the hill, but is driven back at each effort, by a leopard first, then by a lion, then by a she-wolf, and he is forced to remain in the dark wood. The ghost of the Roman poet Virgil then comes to tell him that because he is not on the road, he will have to take the long way around in order to climb the hill; that is, he must first go down through hell and come up on the other side.

72

That is an allegory. It is an allegory because it has all of the four defining characteristics listed above.

Consider the first quality of allegory, its many elements of meaning. In Dante's first canto, the man, the road, the dark wood, the sun, the hill, the leopard, lion, and she-wolf, the ghost, and hell are all elements of meaning. To understand the allegory, you must understand what each element means.

The plurality of elements in allegory sets it apart from such a poetic device as the single metaphor. A metaphor calls an object something it isn't, and has one unit of meaning. Thus, Shelley says, "O wild West Wind, thou breath of Autumn's being," and the single unit of meaning, breath, really means the West Wind; and Shakespeare describes a woman's sex appeal: "Age cannot wither her, nor custom stale/ Her infinite variety: other women cloy/ The appetites they feed, but she makes hungry,/ Where most she satisfies." The basic metaphor here is a single equation of meaning: Cleopatra equals a perfect appetizer. But allegory has many elements of meaning, and many equations.

This brings up the second characteristic of allegory: each allegorical element has one, and only one meaning. Logically, the possible kinds of relationship between elements and meanings are one-to-one, one-to-many, many-to-one, and many-to-many. I will consider these relationships in reverse order. The possibility in which, in a single meaningful situation, many elements all have many meanings, is usually chaos. More common is the use of many elements with one meaning. The many-to-one relationship characterizes mixed metaphor. Mixed metaphor is usually derided and is often funny. A former vice-president of the University of Chicago enlivened the administration building periodically with such phrases as, "Let's nail this custard pie to the wall," and, "We've got to pull ourselves up by our own bootstraps and get a running start!" But Shakespeare uses mixed metaphors, with many meaning-elements all meaning one thing, in such famous lines as these from *Macbeth*, Act V, Scene 5:

> Tomorrow, and tomorrow, and tomorrow,
> Creeps in this petty pace from day to day
> To the last syllable of recorded time,
> And all our yesterdays have lighted fools
> The way to dusty death. Out, out, brief candle!

Life's but a walking shadow, a poor player
That struts and frets his hour upon the stage
And then is heard no more: it is a tale
Told by an idiot, full of sound and fury,
Signifying nothing.

In this passage, time is treated as an animal, for it is said to creep; and also as a book entry, in the phrase "syllable of recorded time." This is a mixed metaphor, in which animal motion and clerical record both represent time. A more striking example in the same quotation is the number of elements all of which mean *life:* candle, shadow, actor, and actor's part ("Out, out, brief *candle!/* Life's but a walking *shadow;* a poor *player* . . . it is a *tale/* Told by an idiot . . ."). The relationship of elements to meaning is many-to-one.

The one-to-many relationship is characteristic of symbolism (discussed in the next chapter). The one-to-one relationship, the last of the four possibilities, is the allegorical. In the summary of Dante's Canto I a simple series of equations explains the allegorical meaning of all the elements of the story in one-to-one fashion: the man is any Christian; the road is a good Christian life; the dark wood is human error; the sun, divine guidance; the hill, salvation; the animals, three types of sin; the ghost, human reason; hell, knowledge of sin. These are the main elements of meaning in the allegory, with the meanings to which they bear a one-to-one relationship.

The third characteristic of allegory is not an equation but a proportion. The relationships among the allegorical elements correspond to the relationships among their meanings. Thus, in the first canto of the *Divine Comedy*, the sun is to the man as divine guidance is to any Christian; and more elements can be added and the proportion still holds. Just as the sun shows the man the way out of the wood up the hill, so divine guidance shows any Christian the way from error to salvation. And still more: just as the man trying to climb the hill from the wood instead of the road finds his way blocked by beasts, so a Christian trying to attain salvation from a state of error rather than from a good Christian life finds his effort impeded by sin. And still more: just as the ghost of Virgil tells the man he must go through hell before climbing the hill, so reason tells any Christian (in a state of error, remember) that he must come to understand sin and evil before he can attain salvation.

Contrast this allegorical correspondence of relationships with a list of similes, in which the units of meaning, the individual similes, are not related to each other in the same way as the things they mean. This passage is from the first five verses of the fourth chapter of the Song of Songs:

> Behold, you are beautiful, my love,
> behold, you are beautifull
> Your eyes are doves
> behind your veil.
> Your hair is like a flock of goats,
> moving down the slopes of Gilead.
> Your teeth are like a flock of shorn ewes
> that have come up from the washing,
> all of which bear twins,
> and not one among them is bereaved.
> Your lips are like a scarlet thread,
> and your mouth is lovely.
> Your cheeks are like halves of a pomegranate
> behind your veil.
> Your neck is like the tower of David,
> built for an arsenal,
> whereon hang a thousand bucklers,
> all of them shields of warriors.
> Your two breasts are like two fawns,
> twins of a gazelle,
> that feed among the lilies.

The relationships among the various similes do *not* correspond to the relationships among the parts of the beloved's body. For example, lips are not to teeth as a scarlet thread is to a flock of shorn ewes that have come up from the washing, all of which bear twins, whether they are bereaved or not. Contrast this nonallegorical interrelationship with the complex but perfectly precise proportionality of Dante's canto: (1) man is to (2) road is to (3) dark wood is to (4) sun is to (5) hill is to (6) animals is to (7) ghost is to (8) hell AS (1) any Christian is to (2) a good Christian life is to (3) human error is to (4) divine guidance is to (5) salvation is to (6) sin is to (7) human reason is to (8) knowledge of sin.

Finally, the fourth characteristic of allegory is that it embodies or expresses the abstract in concrete terms. Thus, the rather nebulous concept of a state of error (moral, spiritual, or intellectual), is translated allegorically into the simple, concrete, dark wood.

Sometimes allegory will serve notice that it is rendering the abstract in concrete terms; that is, sometimes allegory will name its elements with the abstractions they personify. Thus John Bunyan, when writing *Pilgrim's Progress,* named his hero Christian, and describes his fight with the giant named Despair. Bunyan describes the death of one of his virtuous characters in this often-quoted passage:

> When he understood [the summons], he called for his Friends, and told them of it. Then said he, I am going to my Fathers, and though with great difficulty I am got hither, yet now I do not repent me of all the Trouble I have been at to arrive where I am. *My Sword,* I give to him that shall succeed me in my Pilgrimage, and my *Courage* and *Skill,* to him that can get it. My *Marks* and *Scars* I carry with me, to be a Witness for me, that I have fought his Battles who now will be my Rewarder. When the Day that he must go hence, was come, many accompanied him to the River side, into which, as he went, he said, *Death, where is thy Sting?* And as he went down deeper, he said, *Grave, where is thy Victory?* So he passed over, and the Trumpets sounded for him on the other side.

On the basis of this description, what would you have named this man? Rather than call him Hubert, Bunyan named him Mr. Valiant-for-Truth. Of course, such explicit labeling is not necessary.

In applying the technical concept "allegory" to literature, ask these questions:

1. *Do the names of characters and/or places suggest abstract meanings?* (If they do, there is a good chance the work may be an allegory. It may, however, be allegorical even if the answer is no.)

2. *Does a completely literal interpretation of the story*

seem incomplete? (If so, test for the four characteristics of allegory.)

3. *Are there many single items that stand for something else?* (Naming these will be naming the elements of meaning.)

4. *Does each of the many elements of meaning seem to have a clear single meaning?* (The answer should be yes in allegory. Sometimes the allegory may have several levels of meaning, but at each level the meaning of each element should clearly be one thing.)

5. *Do the relationships among the elements of meanings, the literal relationships of people, places, things, and deeds, correspond to the figurative relationships of the abstractions symbolized?* (The answer must be unequivocally yes. Stating the relationships at the abstract level will spell out the *theme* as it is allegorically presented.)

6. *Are the various elements concrete, and do they express abstractions?* (Again, of course, yes if the work is allegorical. The possible exception is allegorical *satire*, in which specific people and historical deeds may be allegorically represented.)

13. Symbol

A literary *symbol* is both literal and figurative, and must be distinguished from several other concepts.

You are probably familiar with the first stanza of William Blake's "The Tiger":

> Tiger, tiger, burning bright
> In the forest of the night,
> What immortal hand or eye
> Could frame thy fearful symmetry?

In this poem, the tiger is a symbol. I use it to illustrate three things a literary symbol is not. A literary symbol is not a linguistic symbol; it is not a simile; and it is not a metaphor.

First of all, "Q," "the," and "disintegration" are all linguistic symbols; but none of them (and none of their meanings) is a literary symbol. The *word* "tiger" is a linguistic symbol, just as all words are; not a literary symbol. Suppose Blake's poem were translated into French; suppose, for example, that it began, *Tigre, tigre, brûlant fort.* . . . The linguistic symbols would have changed, for "tiger" and *"tigre"* are not identical, even in print; but the literary symbol is identical. From now on, I will use "symbol" to mean literary symbol.

The second point this poem may indicate about the literary symbol is the distinction between literary symbol and simile. Suppose the poem read:

> Spirit of evil, growing stronger,
> You certainly are like a tiger,
> Although the tiger's tail is longer,
> Especially when seen at night in Niger.

I offer this revision not as an improvement on Blake's original; posterity will decide that question. I offer it as a simile, in which a comparison is explicitly stated between the tiger and the core meaning. Such a simile is not a symbol.

A symbol is not a linguistic symbol; it is not a simile; and, third, it is not a metaphor. I try my hand again on Blake's poor badgered poem.

> Spirit of evil, with growing claws,
> Prowling through the moonless present,
> With striped flank and silent paws,
> You are fantastically unpleasant.

In this metaphor, the spirit of evil is talked about as though it were a tiger. This is metaphorical, but not symbolic.

The reason a symbol is neither a linguistic symbol, nor a simile, nor a metaphor, is that a symbol must be a thing in its own right. Thus, in the metaphorical example, there was no real tiger in the poem—I use the word "poem" carelessly—there was no actual tiger at all, and you knew it. Metaphors are not intended literally. But in the Blake original, there is an actual tiger, as the explicit and literal subject of the poem. That tiger is something more than the ordinary garden variety of tiger, but it is at least that. The symbol is in the poem not only at the figurative level, but also at the literal level.

Having indicated some of the things a symbol is not (linguistic, simile, metaphor), I have offered a positive statement about symbols: A symbol is meant literally as well as figuratively. A symbol may be literally a thing, a deed, or a combination of the two.

The tiger in Blake's poem is, of course, a thing, a creature. But sometimes a symbol will be a deed. In the medieval tale *Tristan and Iseult*, for example, Tristan fights a duel with a powerful villain. After Tristan rows to an island to fight the duel, and the villain rows there in another boat, Tristan casts his boat adrift. In this act he symbolically enacts the outcome of the duel: death for one. You cannot explain this act simply by saying only one boat will be needed, because even the medieval knight doesn't throw away everything except what he needs. Deeds can be symbols, as this example shows.

We might note at this point that a deed does not symbolize its motive. Suppose a teacher shoots a student whom he hates for being unprepared. The shooting does not symbolize the teacher's hatred of the student. It evidences his hate; it expresses his hate; it may relieve his hate; but it does not symbolize it. Romain Gary's novel *Roots of Heaven* provides another example. The hero devotes his life to stopping the slaughter of elephants. His career, which he pursues single-mindedly even into outlawry, is interpreted symbolically by most of the other characters in the book. For example, they see his defense of elephants as a protest against cruelty, as a defense of freedom, as dramatization of the need to preserve natural resources, as an attack on the doctrine that efficiency is all that matters. The hero is quite clear on his motive: his motive is to stop the slaughter of elephants. He literally intends that elephants should live. To say that his action symbolized his desire to save elephants would be ludicrous. His actions are symbolic, but what they symbolize is not his motive.

Sometimes the very fact that an action is unmotivated is a hint that it is symbolic. Tristan's only motive in casting the boat adrift, for example, is to make a symbolic assertion. Another example from the same tale is an unmotivated deed whose only significance is the symbolic use of an object. Tristan has run off with King Mark's wife, Iseult. For a year and a half, they have fornicated in the forest. One night, as they lie down, Tristan puts his unsheathed sword between them. That very same night, King Mark finds them. Misled by the sword, he concludes that they have not committed adultery; he therefore does not kill them, but simply removes Tristan's sword and, without awakening them, leaves his own as a symbol of his right to his wife, Iseult. This symbol thus combines thing (sword) and deed (replacing Tristan's with his own). Tristan's action in sleeping with his sword was completely unmotivated. It provided the occasion for King Mark's symbolic act (and might itself have a sexual significance, if the sword is taken for a phallic symbol). The unmotivated action is thus a clue to the presence of a symbol.

Now, Tristan could have had a motive; he could have wanted to keep himself from rolling over in his sleep. If he had had that motive, however, the sword would have been an expression of the motive, but not a symbol of it. I have said that a symbol may be a thing, a deed, or a combination of the two, and in discussing these symbols I have attempted to distinguish between what the deed symbolizes and the motive for the deed.

The first characteristic of a symbol, discussed thus far, is that it is both literal and figurative. The second characteristic of a symbol is that it bears its meaning in a single element. This singleness characterizes all the examples cited thus far. The tiger, the casting off of the boat, the defense of elephants, the substitution of King Mark's sword, all are single elements.*

The third characteristic is that the symbol has many meanings. Symbol and meanings thus stand in the ratio of one-to-many. All of the examples cited have multiple meanings. The tiger may be evil, or destructiveness, or the inexorability of natural processes, or even divine punishment. Tristan's casting the boat adrift means that only one will survive; that he is ready to gamble, or puts his faith in the outcome (his boat is given to the control of the sea); that death is preferable to some ways of living (such as running if he begins to lose); that he is committed. The symbolic meanings of the defense of elephants are listed above. Symbols of sex seem to be the most single in meaning, and in their mere anatomical sense they are. In the case cited, however, from the medieval romance, the symbolism is also associated with guilt, responsibility, and memory. All of these single symbols thus have multiple meanings.

Questions to ask when applying the technical concept "symbol" to literary analysis include the following:

* The elements of meaning in allegory (see p. 72) are usually called "symbols" for this reason—they are single elements of meaning. The ratio of element to meaning in allegory, however, is one-to-one, not one-to-many.

1. *Are there any objects, or deeds, or both in combination, that seem to stand for more than their literal meaning suggests?* (If the answer is "yes," this significance beyond the literal is their figurative or symbolic meaning.)

2. *When the figurative meaning is stated, is there a literal meaning that still applies?* (If the answer is "no," the item in question is probably a metaphor or other such figure of speech.)

3. *Is more than one meaning possible for each of the symbols identified?* (If there are a number of symbols, check the possibility that the work is allegorical; if not, each symbol should suggest a number of meanings.)

4. *A cautionary question: Are the multiple meanings suggested in answer to question #3 contradicted by any of the other facts of the work analyzed?* (Overinterpretation, or reading meanings into a work, is the greatest danger in symbolic analysis.)

5. *Are any symbolic meanings explicitly stated within the work?* (The minor characters in *The Roots of Heaven* stated the symbolic meanings of the protagonist's crusade to save elephants. Implicit symbols, or symbols whose meaning is not stated, are harder to identify. Note that questions #1 and #2 are about recognizing symbols, questions #3 and #4 about finding their meaning. Question #5 involves both spotting the symbol and finding its meaning, since the explicit interpretation says simultaneously "this is a symbol" and "it means so-and-so." For suggestions as to other methods of identifying symbols, see the discussions under the various genres.)

6. *Is the figurative meaning something within the work itself or something outside, beyond the work?* (The less clearly the symbolic meaning is tied to the work itself, the more your interpretation is apt to be fanciful or in error.)

II. Literary Genres

1. A Survey of the Genres

The present chapter systematically defines the types of literature, the literary *genres*. It thus serves as an introduction to the individual discussions that follow. The basis of distinction between the genres is twofold, presentation (the relationship between author, work, and audience) and structure. Since the difference in presentation is harder to understand, much more time is spent explaining that distinction than explaining the typical differences in structure. Since these differences will be repeated and illustrated in the following chapters about genres, it is not absolutely necessary to read this chapter of general classification before proceeding to the discussion of the individual genre. The overview, however, will probably help.

The classification to follow, although systematic, does not produce a tidy bin of completely separated literary types. A certain blurring of the classification is inevitable when what is being classified is art, for art is more like living nature than like the grocer's sorted and labeled vegetable remains. Like living nature, art does not stand still; it develops and changes. Artists, like any force that produces mutation and evolutionary change, are constantly seeking novelty and variety. Thus, no sooner has a critic defined a difference between two kinds of literature (or any other art, for that matter), separating them neatly from each other, than an upstart artist hurries to see what he can create that falls between the kinds, defying classification, or, at least, making classification much harder and less tidy. Just as nature seems constantly to expand, filling every available niche with some kind of life, varying in order to take every possible opportunity for living the environment offers, so all artists as a group seem constantly to expand their efforts, apparently trying to develop every possible kind of art work. Some children, when they go down a sidewalk, play the game of never stepping on a crack. The artist tries to step on them all. The classification that follows, although in broad outline almost universally accepted, suffers all the consequences of the inconsiderate artist's concern for the individuality and uniqueness of his own work.

In spite of this difficulty, critics go on classifying works, adjusting older understandings to newer forms, refining their concepts and sharpening their tools. Their motive is not perversity (or at least usually not); it is the desire for understanding. There is so much literature that, without some classifications, the reader is lost in a welter of random books. The critic feels this need most urgently, since he is professionally concerned, and probably knows more works than the avocational reader (which is what most college students are). But even the occasional reader's understanding will be increased if he sees not only the single work whose pages he now turns but also some relationship between it and the ones he has already read. Moreover, many authors have worked self-consciously in terms of classifications such as the ones to follow. Knowing the differences in genres, therefore, is part way toward knowing what the author intended.

Literary genres include drama, the short story, the novel, poetry, the essay, and the epic. Each is distinguished by a characteristic relationship of three elements: the author, the audience, and the art work itself.

Although each of these three terms presents some difficulties, "author" provides least. Except for the special cases of anonymous and traditional literature, especially oral literature, when "the author" is mentioned everyone knows who is meant. The word "audience" is less satisfactory, for it implies hearing; and usually forms such as the short story are not heard, but read on the printed page. In what follows, "audience" is assumed to cover such cases and to include all of those who in fact encounter the literary work of art. The words "art work" or "literary composition" unfortunately blur the issue when the work itself contains the author speaking in his own person. The alternative phrase, "what the author presents," is stilted; perhaps "contents" is better. Usually, what is presented is characters in some kind of situation who do and/or say something. This is what is meant by "art work."

The basic distinctions among genres may then be set forth in the following table:

Genre	Audience	Author	Work
drama	group	absent	performed
epic	group	present	recited
short story	private	concealed	read
novel	private	concealed	read
poetry	ignored	present	recited (or sung)
essay	private	implied	read

This table may be restated as follows: drama is performed objectively before an audience, the actors being presumed to be the fictional characters themselves, not spokesmen for the author; it is seen and heard. The epic is recited to an audience by the author or a spokesman for him; it is heard. The short story and the novel are marked by the absence of the author and any actor or expositor; they are read. Since they do not differ in this respect, both may be called simply "fiction." Poetry is recited by the author or a spokesman for him, but not to the audience; figuratively, it is overheard.

These characteristics are normal, or typical, rather than universal. Thus, fiction is normally read by a single individual alone in his armchair. A father, of course, may be joined in his armchair by children, to whom he reads aloud, or a performer may give a public reading from a novel or short story. But these are departures from the norm, and are not typical.

The situation is clearest with drama. Plays are obviously and traditionally designed to be performed, and the author is almost never one of the characters. The distinction between fiction (novel and short story) and drama, the distinction between what is performed and what is read, is perhaps the easiest and clearest.

The epic * is somewhat out of date, and, because less familiar, perhaps harder to grasp. Indeed, the vast majority of genre courses ignore it. Some "beat" verse resembles the epic genre, because it is intended to be delivered orally by a spokesman (either the author or someone speaking for or as the author) to an audience.

When distinguishing genres the basic quality that defines poetry is not versification (rhyme, meter, stanza). The basic quality of poetry as a genre is most clearly seen in the lyric poem, a songlike outpouring of feeling and belief. Oral delivery is essential to poetry in this generic sense. Indeed, most textbooks clearly recognize this oral-aural quality of poetry explicitly, urging students to read every poem aloud. In the typical situation, however, the poet does not address an audience but speaks spontaneously to himself or the universe, or perhaps an absent lover. In this sense, the audience (of whose presence he is of course aware when he recites) is presumed not to be around at all. The audience thus may be considered to overhear the poem, rather than to be addressed by it, as in epic.

The fact that most poems are presented on the printed page does not make their typical form any the less oral, just as the printing or recording of a play does not make it any the less a typically dramatic, presented, enacted form. Drama is drama insofar as it is to be performed. Similarly, a poem differs from fiction, epic, and drama insofar as it is to be heard by an audience to whom it is not addressed.

Of the many alternative ways of defining poetry "versification" is an obvious possibility. In a fairly sophisticated form, this definition of poetry as versification is restricted to literary art, thus eliminating philosophy or science expressed in rhyme and mnemonic rhymes such as "Thirty days hath September" or "Red sky at morning, sailors take warning; red sky at night, sailors' delight." But poetry as versification may well be found in the drama, usually in the epic, and even in fiction, although the last is more rare. Therefore, when poetry is differentiated

---

* Northrop Frye, in *The Anatomy of Criticism*, prefers to use the word "epos" in order to include lesser works that envisage narration to a live audience.

from drama and fiction, the basis for the distinction must be like the one just stated.*

Most genre courses also include the *essay* as a literary genre. The essay is something of a borderline case largely because its purposes tend to be expository, informational, discursive, rather than artistic. That is, whereas literature exists for the sake of the experience, for its own sake, other uses of language aim at informing or persuading, and do not exist for their own sake. The goals of literary art are intrinsic, the goals of other uses of language are extrinsic.† Sometimes, therefore, the essay is used primarily as a foil, to make the nature of literature clearer by contrast. But many types of essay are largely if not wholly artistic, predominantly if not entirely valuable in themselves without reference to practical action or information. The principal characteristic of the essay as a literary genre is that although read (just as fiction is read) rather than heard or seen, it is assumed to be a communication from the individual author, as a person, to the audience (the reader). The author will, typically, identify himself as one addressing the audience. The persuasive or informational essay, in contrast, does not exist for its own sake, for the value found in the experience of reading it, and is not a communication from any individual. This kind of impersonal essay is nonliterary.

At this point, it might be helpful to set up the table of genres again, with a few modifications. First, of course, short story and novel will be combined into one label, fiction. Secondly, instead of starting with the genres usually taught (short story, novel, drama, poetry, and essay), adding only the older form, epic, let us this time consider all the logically possible relationships between author, audience, and work.

* The analysis to this point is based predominantly on Northrop Frye's classification.

† In this century, psychologists and others concerned with mental health have found self-expression to be a valuable extrinsic use of language. An angry man may write out a letter expressing his rage and then find he does not need to send it. The value of the letter is not communication or persuasion, for no one but he sees it; nor is it artistic, for the real value is not in the man's experience of the rage revealed in the letter but in his getting rid of the rage by writing it.

The question is, Who is "present" at the moment of the artistic experience? The actual writing of the work will be ignored, since that presumably is a means to the end that others may read, hear, or see it, and is thus not itself the artistic or literary experience.

The possibilities are:

1. The audience alone is present.

2. The work alone is present.

3. The artist (author) alone is present.

4. Audience and work are present.

5. Audience and artist are present.

6. Artist and work are present.

7. Audience, artist, and work are all present.

Now some of these logical possibilities seem ridiculous. However, there is a type of human activity related to art that corresponds to each of the above situations, even though every art work is created by an artist, has an independent existence, and is experienced by an audience. The difference is in the way they are experienced.

The audience alone is "present" in the case of *fiction*. The reader, of course, holds the novel in his hand. But he does not experience the novel as something hand-held, nor as something looked at. He experiences the novel as events and emotions that he participates in himself. Plays, too, may be read; but the play is experienced as events that are observed, as the reader imaginatively produces and stages the play in his mind's eye. Fiction typically presents experience as something to be lived through by the audience, not as something witnessed from outside by the audience. The reader-audience participates vicariously in fiction in a way that he does not in other genres. When reading a poem, one imagines a speaker; when reading a novel or short story, one does not.

The second possible case, in which the work alone is present, is not really art; it is ritual. Ritual is not performed for an audience; everyone present is presumed to take part. (Holy Communion involves such group participation, as its name implies.) Moreover, ritual is presumed not to have an author, but to be the performance of a pattern of words and actions meaningful in themselves. Ritual certainly has aesthetic or artistic qualities, but from the point of view of a student of literature it is peripheral, however central it may be to his religious life.

The third case, in which the artist alone is present, is also not really art. Both dreams and happenings fall into this category. In both, there is neither an audience (in theory, at least) nor a product that has objective existence. The "happening" (which, of course, some do call art) is supposed to be a spontaneous mutual experience generated by those who live through it. In theory, a group gets together and something unplanned, unstructured, uninterpreted, simply happens. For example, in a happening staged in London, a group played in garbage, and then "painted" a nude woman, on top of a car, with spaghetti. The focus of the happening is entirely upon the experience of the participants who create the events. If there is an audience, they are encouraged to participate, e.g., to call for spaghetti to be thrown upon them, too. To the extent that they are expected to participate, they are not intended to be an audience. And, of course, when the happening is over, everyone goes home, and there is no record—beyond a few news photographs—to give any objectivity to what has happened, to give it existence as an art work. The emphasis in the happening is thus entirely upon the "creative experience" of the artist.

The fourth of the seven possible combinations of artist, work, and audience involves the presence of work and audience. The artist, the author, is absent. This genre is the familiar situation encountered in the theater. A play is performed as an objective occurrence witnessed by the audience. The author must skulk in the wings, wringing his hands in concealment from the audience, until the final applause tells him whether his work has succeeded or failed. Drama thus is the objective genre, involving the presence of audience and work.

In the fifth case, audience and artist are present. The emphasis here falls upon communication. The literary form is the essay. There are printed pages, but no work to be objectively presented, as in drama. Instead, essays are read from the printed page. The real content of the work, therefore, is not objectively present. This is also true of fiction, but we said the author was absent in fiction; how is the author "present" in the case of the essay? Literally, of course, he is not crowding the reader out of his armchair. Imaginatively, however, the typical essay is thought of by the reader as a communication from the author to himself. Here lies the essential difference between an autobiographical familiar essay and a short story in the first person. The essay, like conversation, is a verbal contact between two people; the short story is an imaginative experience. In this sense, then, the essay involves the presence of the audience, the reader; a playing down of the work itself; and the assumption of a real person, the author, who as a real person is communicating to the reader his own thoughts and experiences.*

In the sixth case, artist and work are present, but not the audience. This is the typical form of lyric poetry. The lyric is not addressed to an audience, no matter how many people the author really hopes will ultimately hear or read his work. The poem itself is allegedly the outpouring of the author, whether in his own or fictional guise. The lyric poem, is, as Frye says, "overheard." The work is present not because it is written down but because it is offered as a formal entity, as a product, rather than as pure self-expression. The lyric poet is perfectly aware that he is not merely exclaiming "ow!" or groaning. He is (for example) writing a love song; or (as Shakespeare says in many of his sonnets) creating a monument that may be appreciated by posterity, although not addressed to them.

The last case requires the presence of all three: audience, artist, and work. This genre, now rare in its literal form, was common when narratives were recited to an audience by a bard. The narrator (or performer) regarded himself as the author (whether he was in fact or not). Frequently, as in the *Iliad*, he expresses his own views on the meaning of what has happened. These remarks presume the presence of an audience with whom the narrator-artist is communicating. Unlike the essay, however, the epic form lays great emphasis upon the objectively created story. The author regards himself

---

* In pure expository prose all three—work, audience, and author—are virtually ignored. Such prose should be transparent as to its meaning, and is not art since it does not exist for the sake of the experience itself.

as creating something independent of his own attitudes and beliefs. Thus, the epic frequently has a mythic or partly historical base, and a poetic form. Modern descendants of this form include the novel in which the reader is addressed, but even this form of address has tended to fade with the disappearance of the literally present narrator-author. As the narrator-author disappears, the objectivity of epic turns into the subjectivity of the novel. The genre of fiction is born when public narration, the genre of epic, has died.

The preceding discussion classifies genres in terms of the presence or absence of the author, of the work as an objective entity, and of the audience. The significant categories for the student of literature are fiction, in which audience alone is present (#1); drama, in which audience and work are present (#4); essay, in which audience and artist are present (#5); and lyric poetry, in which artist and work are present (#6). Of the other forms, two [ritual (#2), dreams and happenings (#3)] do not appear in the typical literature course for obvious reasons. Epics (#7) are usually studied in world literature courses or courses concerned with a particular historical period, not in introductory courses organized by genres.

At this point, if you have read much literature, your mind is bubbling over with memories of marginal cases. Many works that you may have read tend to combine characteristics of several genres. That is unquestionably true. "Drama" may perhaps seem the most clear-cut genre. But even in the case of drama, there are plays that were not written for presentation on a stage, such as those of Seneca; drama in which the author addresses the audience, as in the so-called *"parabasis"* of ancient Greek comedy; and the essaylike prologues and stage directions of George Bernard Shaw's plays. If these exceptions or borderline cases occur in the case of drama, how much more confused the issue becomes when the genre is "poetry." As noted above, poetry as versification is frequently found in drama, almost always in the epic, and sometimes in other narrative forms. For this reason, to indicate that not "versification" but the genre of poetry was being defined, I used the label "lyric poetry," emphasizing the songlike, presentational aspect of the typical form. In addition to distinguishing poetry from versification, the label "lyric" helps us to remember that many poems are not poetry in this sense, the sense of the lyrical genre. That is, special forms bordering on drama, such as Browning's monologue "Ulysses" or Shelley's unperformed verse drama "The Cenci" or Frost's dialogue "The Death of the Hired Man," and special forms bordering on fiction, such as Walter de la Mare's "The Listeners," although they are poems, are not poetry in this sense. The list of borderline and hard-to-classify works could be expanded at great length for each genre. Why, then, bother with a system of classification that has such blurry boundary lines?

The answer to this valid question is twofold. The first, based on the nature of art in general, was made at the beginning of this section. Although all classifications of art will have blurry dividing points, if the central distinctions are clear, a classification will increase understanding. Borderline cases may then be seen as experiments, so to speak, in which the author tries to write poetic fiction or dramatic poetry.

The second reply to the question, "Why classify works by genre?" is based on the nature of literature in particular. In fact, works of different genres tend to differ not only in the relationship between author, work, and audience but also in structure. Classification by genres is important, and not arbitrary, because it distinguishes structural types.

The four basic genres usually encountered in the introductory course in literature, as already stated, are drama, fiction, poetry, and essay. Each of these four has a distinctive structural base. Thus, drama is usually structured in terms of *plot*. Fiction, structured in terms of chronology in such early novels as *Moll Flanders,* is increasingly structured in terms of consciousness, that is, of character. The emphases on stream of consciousness in the novel and on point of view in the short story are examples of structuring in terms of consciousness. Poetry, of course, is typically structured in terms of tone, involving both sound and mood. The essay, finally, is most characteristically structured in terms of theme.

Structure means the relationship among the parts. The "structural base" means what defines a part. The parts of a poem, for example, are typically defined in terms of sound and patterns: line length, rhyme scheme, stanza, etc. In contrast, the parts of a novel such as Faulkner's *As I Lay Dying* are distinguished from each other in terms of point of view, of the character whose consciousness is presented. Each short chapter of the novel reveals the thoughts and experience of one of the characters. The novel proceeds chronologically, and tells a straightforward story; but the parts are not defined in terms of chronology, nor in terms of story or plot; the parts are distinguished by the varied consciousnesses of the different characters.

All four structural bases—tone, character, plot, and theme—will probably function quite significantly in all works in each genre. However, each genre is most typically structured in terms of one of the four. In each case, the typical structure derives from the presentation that defines the genre. Poetry is heard; its structural base is sound and what sound expresses, mood; the two together are tone. Drama is witnessed; its structural base is event, the building blocks of plot. Fiction is vicariously experienced; its structural base is consciousness, the realm of character. The essay is communicated; its structural base is the message to be understood, theme.

The following chapters explain each of the major genres. In each case, first the defining characteristics of the genre, both in presentation and in structure, are illustrated. Then, a certain concept particularly relevant to the genre in question is explored in detail; for example, the chapter on "Fiction" explores point of view, and the chapter on "Drama" explores various theatrical conventions. In the course of these discussions, use is made of the general technical terms defined in Part I. (If you encounter an unfamiliar technical term you should refer to the index and check the definition in Part I before proceeding.) Finally, further ways of analyzing a work in this genre are illustrated, combining technical questions that use literary terms and purely methodological questions that do not use any technical terminology.

The method of approaching the work may be expressed generally in terms of the question: What questions should be asked? The questions to be asked are of two kinds, technical and methodological. A technical question applies a literary term (defined either in Part I or perhaps in the specific genre chapter), such as "plot" or "subjective point of view" or "irony," to the work: What is the plot? Is the point of view subjective? Is there any irony? Such questions are found in Part I at the end of each major entry. A methodological question does not use a literary term, but applies such general concepts as "repetition" or "the unexpected" to the work: Are any words repeated? Are any events repeated? Does anything I encounter startle me? The answers to the methodological questions frequently provide significant leads to the answers to the technical questions. Out of the combination of the two should come increased understanding of the work being studied. The goal of this book is to suggest these ways of understanding.

2. Fiction

A. Presentation

Fiction has been described * as presuming the presence of an audience—the reader—while placing no emphasis on the author or the work—the novel or story—as an entity in itself. There is in fact an author, and there is in fact a work. But when fiction in its most characteristic form is read, the reader imaginatively lives through the presented experiences as though they were his own. The author does not, typically, address the reader in his alleged own person; nor does the reader of fiction persistently notice a formalized, independent structure which would make the story as an art work somehow independent of its content.

In these terms, fiction is essentially vicarious experience. Unsophisticated readers frequently require of fiction characters with whom they can easily identify. Such readers do not like to identify with people who have very obvious faults, and so they tend to reject novels and stories in which there is any moral complexity or ambiguity to the major characters. I have noticed in my own reading preferences a shift, through the

* See p. 87.

years, in the kind of naïve fiction—"mere" entertainment, or escape literature—that I can enjoy. Whereas I used to want a protagonist or at least a deuteragonist (second most important character) who was in his early teens, now I am comparatively uninterested in characters under thirty. Think how many children's books, even those about adult worlds, have a child as an omnipresent wanderer through the action. Dorothy in the *Oz* books frequently is unnecessary for the story, but provides an easy identification for the young reader.

The more sophisticated reader is capable of greater leaps of the imagination. He need not identify himself with people of his own age, or own profession, whether present or future, or own nationality, or own race, or even his own imagined morality. He finds an increased meaningfulness in fiction that offers genuine insights into other ways of thinking, experiencing, and deciding, precisely because they differ from his own.

There is a big difference between the first-person point of view in a novel and the first-person point of view in an essay. The essay is characteristically a conversation; one-way, but still a conversation. The author, the "I," talks to the reader, and his words are received as coming from someone else. The "I" of fiction, however, merges with the reader. It is through the narrator's eyes that the action is seen, and the narrator's reactions are experienced by the reader as though his own. In fiction, instead of looking *at* the narrator, one looks *with* the narrator.

B. Structure

It was also suggested, in the general discussion of the literary genres, that fiction tended to have its own distinctive principle of structure, i.e., character. Since fiction is basically vicarious experience, the difference between the characters' experiences is most naturally the principle by which the parts of fiction are defined and ordered. One of the radical modern developments in fictional technique, the interior monologue, which presents the stream of consciousness of a character, orders all the contents by the sequence in which they are thought.

In its most sophisticated form, this technique may combine various levels of consciousness, ranging from fully self-conscious reflection to wholly subliminal repressed attitudes.

Faulkner's *The Sound and the Fury* employs this technique in several variations. First, the major sections of the novel include several interior monologues, of different people, to some extent covering the same events. The basic organization of the novel thus includes a shift from Benjy's consciousness to Quentin's consciousness to Jason's consciousness. Second, the characters vary greatly in their modes of thought. Most strikingly, the first interior monologue is that of an idiot, Benjy. There are limits, of course, to how fully most people can experience idiocy. And Faulkner exploits these limits: thus, Benjy does not understand the words he hears, but the reader does. Although Faulkner does not expect the reader to be totally immersed in the thought processes of an idiot, he does much to suggest the extreme naïveté of idiotic experience. For example, Benjy perceives his own reflex actions—such as yanking his hand away from a hot stove—as though they were performed by someone else; and, having no sense of time, Benjy does not distinguish between fragmentary memory and the present moment of experience. His section therefore consists of snippets of past and present experience, jumbled together in no overall order, each one linked to its successor by random association.

Quentin, whose stream of consciousness is provided in the second interior monologue, is much more sophisticated. Living through the inner workings of his mind includes reasoning; general reflections on the meaning of life; decisive present action; conscious memory; disturbing fragmentary memories of traumatic experiences, memories which he tries to avoid, but which keep popping distractingly into his mind; and finally a long passage which may be totally subconscious, reliving the worst of the repressed experiences.

In older fiction, the presentation tends to be more straightforwardly narrative than in such modern works as the one just described, and the organization is more typically chronological. In such early novels as Defoe's *Moll Flanders* and *Robinson Crusoe*, the chronology covers a whole lifetime. Such a novel has clearly been conceived as the experiences of an individual, for unity of character is the only unity such books may have.

It could be argued that any work of literature that has gone beyond pure fable, any work of literature that has real people as its characters instead of puppets, is in a sense more concerned with experience than with mere event. This assertion is, in fact, true, and applies to all genres. But fiction, read in privacy, offers the clearest opportunity for imaginative identification. The dramatic hero is regarded with awe, pity, or amusement; if his fate makes us fear for ourselves, we still remain quite aware that we are not the dramatic hero, not in his plight.

Many novels, even large ones, develop not simply in the cause-and-effect evolution of plot but in terms of a transformation of the central character, who develops significantly during the course of the novel. Such a novel is called a *Bildungsroman,* (a German term meaning a novel of education or character development). In this kind of novel, the experience of maturing is the basic structural principle. Even in escape literature, which of all fiction tends to put the heaviest emphasis on pure event, the hero usually undergoes at least the development of discovering that he is in love.

Of course, the bigger the novel, the greater the number of organizational devices which must be used to make possible some perspective on the whole; in longer fiction, plot becomes more important as an ordering principle. However, even in novels of epic proportions, the reader tends to share the events rather than merely witness them. Conversely, the shorter the fiction, the less room for a chain of events, the more unitary the structure will tend to be. The basic difference between the novel and the short story is thus one of complexity. The novel is, so to speak, a moving picture; the short story, a slide. Lengthy plot, varied scene, subplots, developing characters, all are much rarer in the short story than in the novel. The length of the novel requires development if it is not to bore the reader; the length of the short story makes development (whether of plot, or character, or theme) necessarily slight. The short story thus tends to be a one-part work, the novel a work of many parts.

Since this difference is one of polar tendencies—novels tending one way, short stories tending the other—there is here, as with most other literary categories, no sharp dividing line between one subgenre and the other. But a distinction, in terms of a difference in structural complexity, remains loosely valid if it is not pushed too far.

C. Point of View

Thus far in the discussion of fiction, we have reviewed the definition of the genre in terms of presentation (the presence of the audience and relative absence of author and work), and looked hurriedly at several examples of structuring in terms of the inner experience, or consciousness, of the characters. Interior monologue has already been suggested as a technical term especially relevant to fiction. It is a special case of point of view, the basis of fictional structure.

Since fiction is the imaginative experience of character, and since "point of view" identifies the locus of the experience— that is, whose experience it is—"point of view" is clearly a relevant term, perhaps the most relevant single critical concept for fiction.

How is it applied? You ask yourself: "What is the story's point of view?" Sometimes an author may employ several different points of view. Once in a lifetime you may find the point of view identified for you as explicitly as in F. Scott Fitzgerald's *Tender Is the Night:*

> . . . It was characteristic that after greeting Rosemary and her mother he waited for them to speak first, as if to allow them the reassurance of their own voices in new surroundings.
> To resume Rosemary's point of view it should be said that, under the spell of the climb to Tarmes and the fresher air, she and her mother looked about appreciatively.*

The student too might well be appreciative when the author provides the analysis himself. But even if the general question "What is the point of view?" does not produce a literal answer from an obliging author, you do have some more specific terms (like "objective," and "omniscient") to back up your original question.

Some texts provide an apparatus that consists not only of introductory sections but also of study questions to help in

* New York: Charles Scribner's Sons, 1934, p. 28.

analysis. One such text * includes James Thurber's story "The Catbird Seat" in the chapter on point of view. The story may be summarized as follows: The firm for which the quiet and withdrawn Mr. Martin works has hired Mrs. Barrows, a loud, vulgar, bossy woman. Mrs. Barrows, presently on very good terms with the boss, threatens to reorganize Mr. Martin's department. He decides to kill her. He takes a pack of cigarettes to her apartment to leave one as a false clue (he does not smoke), and accepts a drink to get her out of the room while he selects a weapon (he does not drink). Instead of killing her, he says nasty things to Mrs. Barrows about their employer, refers to heroin, uses the slang expression "sitting in the catbird seat," and leaves. The next day Mrs. Barrows indignantly reports his misconduct to the boss; Mr. Martin denies it, as the boss expected; and the boss has the indignantly raving Mrs. Barrows dragged away.

At the end of the story, the editor, Laurence Perrine, has provided these questions (among others):

1. How is suspense aroused and maintained in the story? What is the story's principal surprise?

2. Through whose consciousness are the events of the story chiefly seen? Are there any departures from this strictly limited point of view? Where in the story are we taken most fully into Mr. Martin's mind? For what purpose?

3. At what point in the story do Mr. Martin's plans change? What happens to the point of view at this point? What does Thurber's handling of the point of view here tell us about the seriousness of the story's purpose? †

Note that questions #2 and #3 apply the terms we are concerned with, point of view, to the story. (Suspense and seriousness of purpose have been presented earlier by Perrine as semitechnical terms.) This excellent series of questions should lead the reader to the following conclusions: The story's point

---

* Laurence Perrine, *Story and Structure* (New York: Harcourt, Brace, and World, 1966).

† *Ibid.*, p. 219.

of view is basically from over Mr. Martin's shoulder, with insight into his thoughts. For the first quarter of the story, we
see him mulling over the decision to kill Mrs. Barrows:

> Sitting in his apartment, drinking a glass of milk, Mr.
> Martin reviewed his case against Mrs. Ulgine Barrows, as
> he had every night for seven nights. . . . The woman
> had appalled Mr. Martin instantly, but he hadn't shown
> it.[*]

At the moment when Mr. Martin decides not to kill Mrs.
Barrows, however, the point of view is changed: we stop
seeing what Mr. Martin thinks.

> Somewhere in the back of his mind a vague idea stirred,
> sprouted. . . . The idea began to bloom, strange and
> wonderful. [†]

But the reader is not told what Mr. Martin's idea was. Suspense, therefore, is maintained by not telling Mr. Martin's
new plan, setting up the surprise ending with Mrs. Barrows
dragged frothing from the office, fired.

Have you learned anything significant about the story by
applying the concept of point of view to it? As Perrine suggests, you should be clear that the story is not an attempt
at a great art work, for this shift is an inconsistency whose only
purpose is to keep you guessing; the story is comic, and consistency of form is sacrificed for the sake of the joke.
Analyzing the treatment of point of view therefore has helped
to classify the story as light comedy and to identify it as
entertainment rather than story-with-a-message.

If you are not using a text, or are using a text with a
different approach, you will lack the guidance of the study
questions quoted above. In *The Worlds of Fiction*,[‡] for example, the same story is included basically as an example of
comedy, and the story's point of view is not mentioned. If you
already have the concept of point of view in your critical

[*] *Ibid.*, p. 212.

[†] *Ibid.*, p. 216.

[‡] T. Y. Greet, Charles E. Edge, and John M. Munro (Boston:
Houghton Mifflin, 1964).

armory, however, you may bombard the story with point-of-view questions even if no one suggests it to you. And if you trace the point of view throughout the story, you should notice that the change does occur; then you ask why.

As a matter of fact, a mere summary of the story may lead you to ask the relevant question "What is the point of view?" If you look back at the above summary, you may note that no reason was given for Mr. Martin's not killing Mrs. Barrows. You see him making the first plan; you see in detail why he made the plan; suddenly the plan is abandoned. Surely you must ask yourself, why? and immediately, how come I know the first plan but don't know the second? The answer lies in the manipulation of point of view, and defines the story's basic purpose (entertainment). The handling of a story's point of view can thus be seen to affect other aspects of the story, including the significance of the story as a whole.

Consider a longer work, the short novel *The Stranger*, by Albert Camus. In analyzing this novel, one might begin by applying the concept of point of view. What is the point of view? Answer: Subjective; the protagonist is the narrator. This does not take us very far into the novel. Suppose, however, that we try to be more precise. Behind the technical concept of point of view lies the generalized idea of the consciousness to be shared by the reader. What is the protagonist's (Meursault's) consciousness like? Answer: He is almost totally devoid of emotions, until near the end of the novel, and records only sensory experiences. Since he becomes emotional at the end of the novel, and begins to express decisions and motives, he is clearly a developing character. Indeed, this same conclusion might have been reached simply by applying to the novel various questions derived from character as a technical term: What decisions does each character make? Do any of the characters develop?

To get further toward the center of the novel one might try a methodological approach that does not use technical literary concepts. What parts is the novel divided into? At a perfectly literal and straightforward level, the novel is divided into two parts. How are they related to each other? In the first part, Meursault describes his mother's funeral, his affair with his girlfriend, his casual association with the procurer Raymond, and his apparently unmotivated shooting of an Arab upon the beach. In the second part, Meursault is questioned and tried; the events of the first part are gone over by the defense, prosecuting attorneys, and various witnesses; and, in the last chapter, Meursault is sentenced to death and awaits execution.

The relationship of the two divisions of the book is thus cyclical, or repetitive: a series of events that lead up to murder is recounted by Meursault; the same series of events is reviewed by the state and leads up to execution. Technically speaking, the point of view remains apparently the same. Narration is first person, by Meursault, in both parts. As can be seen in this summary statement, however, the consciousness or awareness of what happens changes. In the first part, Meursault narrates the events as they happen to him. In the second part, Meursault watches as other people narrate the same events. The two versions look completely different. Meursault's account stated no emotion on his part, neither love, nor hate, nor condemnation, nor fear. Both the prosecution's version and the defense's version, however, as well as the attempted accounts by most of the witnesses, attribute all kinds of emotions to Meursault during the events he described unemotionally. Thus, in the first part we have an inside view of the events and see nothing of Meursault's feelings; in the second part we have outside views of the events and are offered many contradictory feelings for Meursault.

There is a final development in the novel that is not reflected in this summary, a development that is crucial to a complete statement of the theme of the novel: Meursault becomes extremely emotional about his conviction that the universe is "benignly indifferent." The approach just illustrated has thus not exhausted the meaning of the novel. However, it shows that by combining the methodological question "What are the divisions of the novel?" with the technical concepts "point of view" and "character" we can get at the underlying structure of the novel in terms of the character's consciousness and experience, and begin to formulate a theme: someone else's actions cannot be morally judged, because his inner experience cannot be known.

Point of view is frequently relevant to theme. Joseph Conrad, for example, frequently manipulates point of view in such a way as to create a framework surrounding the story's narrative, as he does in *Heart of Darkness*. This story is transitional in length between what is clearly a short story and what is clearly a novel. Usually it is called a short novel or novelette. *Heart of Darkness* is narrated on board a cruising yawl in England by Marlow, the protagonist, to an anonymous character from whose point of view the whole story is told. That is, Mr. Anonymous begins the story in the first person, a subjective point of view; he reports his conversation with Marlow, which consists predominantly of Marlow's account of a trip up the Congo. Most of the actual narrative, therefore, is Marlow's words in quotes. Mr. Anonymous and the English yawl function simply as a framework within which the bulk of the story is contained. Every once in a while, Marlow's narrative of his river adventures is interrupted by a comment made by Mr. Anonymous.

Now, why should Conrad choose such a framework? He could very easily have used a subjective point of view, perhaps have treated Marlow's narrative as a diary entry if he wished to enable Marlow to make reflections more appropriate to a later recall of the events than to a person who is living right through them. Marlow does make interpretive comments to Mr. Anonymous on the meaning of his experience, and clearly Conrad wanted him to be able to do so; but the diary or account written long afterward would have enabled him to make such comments just as well as the device of narrative within narrative. The diary format would also have permitted Conrad to scramble the chronology of his account as he in fact does scramble it. Is some other purpose served better by the conversational than by the diary framework?

The answer is yes; the purpose is to emphasize the theme. Conrad's theme in *Heart of Darkness* is that moral darkness dominates the universe. The framework gives him two different situations—one in Africa, one on the English yawl—in which his theme can be demonstrated; it also gives him more characters, more witnesses, to testify that his theme is true. If the point of view were a straightforward first-person narrative by Marlow, the evidence for Conrad's theme would be: "My experience in the Congo shows that moral darkness dominates the universe. I, Marlow, testify to the truth of this theme." However, by using the framework device, Conrad expands his evidence: "Marlow tells me that his experience in the Congo shows that moral darkness dominates the universe. He testifies to the truth of this theme. In addition, I,

Anonymous, can see by looking around at the world from this English yawl in the Thames River that the theme is true; I add my testimony to Marlow's." The point of view of *Heart of Darkness* thus establishes a greater universality for Conrad's specific theme.

To see the relationship of one critical concept to another, to get from point of view to theme (which, as a statement of meaning, is the more significant), one asks not simply "What is the point of view?" but also "Why is the point of view what it is?"

One could also reach the same conclusion with a slightly different question: What happens at the beginning and end? For frequently the beginning and end are particularly significant. In this case, looking at the beginning and end focuses attention immediately on the framework device as a shift in point of view, and should lead toward the same conclusions. Moreover, Marlow's very first words—the first words of dialogue in the story—state that the Thames River "has been one of the dark places of the earth," * and in the last sentence of the story the anonymous narrator says the Thames seems to lead "to the uttermost ends of the earth . . . into the heart of an immense darkness." †

The technical question "What is the point of view?" thus can be combined with the methodological questions "Why was it chosen?" "What are the novel's divisions or parts?" and "What happens at the beginning and end?" to produce significant analysis. These three questions can be combined with another methodological question—"What is repeated?"— to good effect when analyzing *Gulliver's Travels*. The point of view is subjective—Gulliver's—throughout. The satire is divided into four parts; each part begins with Gulliver's setting out on a voyage and ends with his returning home; the beginnings and endings are thus clearly repetitive.

Now, the other side of the question "What is repeated?" is the question "How is each repetition different from the first statement?" Each part begins with a voyage to an unknown land. How do the voyages differ? Answer: They differ

---

* Joseph Conrad, *Heart of Darkness and The Secret Sharer* (New York: New American Library of World Literature, 1960), p. 59.

† *Ibid.*, p. 142.

primarily in the means by which Gulliver arrives. In Part I, he is shipwrecked; in Part II, he is abandoned ashore by his shipmates when they flee the giant Brobdingnagians; in Part III, he is set adrift by pirates; in Part IV, he is marooned by mutineers. The progression intensifies the moral faults, starting with natural accident, and passing through frightened selfishness and the cruel enmity of strangers to culminate finally in betrayal. This worsening is directly related to the satiric purpose of the book. It is also related to the structure of the work as fiction. The structure of the work depends upon Gulliver and his point of view. For as each part opens with a worse aspect of human character, Gulliver's reactions at the end of the part (Part III is a possible exception) show a development of his mode of thinking. The ends of the parts involve a repetition of event—the return home—with a significant variation. Increasingly, Gulliver wants to stay in the foreign, nonhuman land. At the end of the first part he leaves deliberately; he leaves Brobdingnag in Part II accidentally, carried away by a giant eagle; and he must be thrown out of Houyhnhnm-land and virtually forced to return to his English home at the end of Part IV. The structure of the work is thus a development in character: the education of Lemuel Gulliver to a knowledge of the true evils of human society.*

The way Gulliver sees things, his moral evaluations, thus develop; and this development is the structure of the *Travels*. The way Gulliver sees things is also part of the structure of the *Travels* in another sense, which is a change in a kind of nontechnical point of view. In Part I, people are seen as small (the Lilliputians); in Part II, they are seen as huge (the Brobdingnagians); in Part III, they are seen kaleidoscopically —as crazy sky-dwellers, as fantastic earth-wasters, as ghosts of the past, and, in the immortal Struldbruggs, as ghosts of future old age; in Part IV, they are seen stereoptically, as beastly passion (the Yahoos) and calm reason (the Houyhnhnms). Gulliver in each case views the creatures from a more or less normal human vantage point. With him, therefore (apart from occasional satiric tensions and ironies), we

---

* The fact that this development is itself satirically ironic is irrelevant to the present discussion. John Middleton Murry argues that Part III fits this progression, in *Jonathan Swift: A Critical Biography* (New York: Noonday Press, 1955).

look through one end of the telescope, we look through the other end, we shake it around past a wild succession of distorted images, and then find true binocular vision of evil and apparent good. *Gulliver's Travels* as a whole thus has a four-part rhythm that changes the protagonist's "viewpoint" while preserving his point of view, thus educating him as a developing character to the satirist's vision of human sin. When the right methodological questions are asked, the technical concept of point of view is thus deepened into a vision of the world, and the fictional structure of the particular work is made clear.

Thus far, fiction, including both short story and novel, has been explored primarily in terms of point of view, the critical concept most distinctively relevant to fiction. The rest of the chapter touches briefly on the relevance of other basic technical concepts to fiction.

D. Other Technical Concepts

Irony in fiction generally is not presented as self-conscious—the speaker (whether character or narrator) saying one thing and meaning the opposite. Most frequently, fictional irony contrasts the point of view of a character with the reader's (and the author's) convictions. A nonobjective point of view makes possible a contrast between what is said or thought by the character telling the story and what is accepted or thought by the reader.

Whenever a story is in the first person, the reader must judge how accurate are the opinions, standards, and judgments of the narrator. When these opinions, standards, and judgments seem to contrast with what any reasonable person would think, this contrast is ironic. In Ring Lardner's story "Haircut," the point of view is subjective, through the eyes of a barber, who talks as he gives a haircut. He tells about Jim Kendall, a practical joker. Jim, the barber reveals, is on bad terms with his wife, who would divorce him if she had any chance of getting alimony; he was fired from the only steady job he had; he spends what money he earns on liquor; he was an adulterer; on one occasion, he attempted to rape a young woman who rejected his advances; he played cruel practical jokes, such as having his children meet him in front of the circus to go in and then never showing up, and such as writing anonymous letters to husbands away from home accusing their wives of infidelity. Now, it seems pretty clear what would be the reader's evaluation of such a man. But the barber does not tell the story quite this way. He does not use words like "cruel" or "adultery." He recounts the events, and what they imply is clear to everyone but him. He constantly excuses Jim. "I said I thought he was all right at heart, but just bubblin' over with mischief." * The difference between the barber's laughing admiration—"He certainly was a card" —and the author's precise although indirect sketch of a drunken, immoral, irresponsible, fornicating, vindictive bum, is ironic. The barber says one thing, but the reader understands another.

Conrad uses his unnamed narrator in *Heart of Darkness* ironically, getting in a wry comment on his own work:

> We looked on, waiting patiently—there was nothing else to do till the end of the flood [tide]; . . . we knew we were fated, before the ebb began to run, to hear about one of Marlow's inconclusive experiences.
> "I don't want to bother you much with what happened to me personally," he began, showing in this remark the weakness of many tellers of tales who seem so often unaware of what their audience would best like to hear. . . . †

In *Heart of Darkness*, plot and story are deemphasized. Many exciting actions occur, but the excitement is played down, and they are narrated in an offhand, out-of-order chronology that makes it hard for the reader to concentrate on event. This, of course, is deliberate on Conrad's part. He is not trying to write an adventure story that comes to a clear conclusion with the hero defeating the villain and marrying the heroine. Rather, he is interested in the thematic implications of the whole situation. The unnamed narrator is thus being used by Conrad to warn the readers that this tale is going to be an "inconclusive experience."

Obviously, there is an ironic contrast between the unnamed

---

* Ring Lardner, "Haircut," reprinted in *The Pocket Book of Short Stories,* ed. M. Edmund Speare (New York: Pocket Books, 1957), p. 175.

† Conrad, *op. cit.,* p. 61.

character's criticism of Marlow's storytelling style and Conrad's evaluation of it, the evaluation he surely hopes the reader will share. After all, Conrad is writing both what the unnamed narrator says and the tale that Marlow tells. If he really thought Marlow's tale pointless and dull, he would not have written it or would have written it differently. Here, then, is an instance of dramatic irony, brought about by the play between different points of view, in this case, three—that of Marlow, who does not know what people would best like to hear; that of the unnamed narrator, who knows what people would best like to hear, and thinks that is the only thing to give them; and that of Conrad, who knows that Marlow's tale is not in the most popular vein, but hopes the sensitive reader will think it worth the telling.

Irony in fiction thus most characteristically involves a tension between what is said or thought from one point of view and the standards and expectations of the reader. This tension keeps the reader from identifying with the character whose opinions conflict with his own. The quality of the vicarious experience therefore tends toward a greater distance, especially if there is no one else with whom one easily identifies. For example, in "Haircut" the reader is for all practical purposes sitting in the chair, listening to the barber talk; the experience is not a direct experience of the events the barber recounts, but the experience of meeting such a person and hearing such a tale. In *Heart of Darkness*, for another example, the experience is that of being one of the listening group, with a privileged view into the thoughts of the unnamed narrator.

Both of these stories are still fiction and not some other genre. In neither case is the narrator to be regarded as the supposed author of the story (as would be the case in the genre of epic, or near-epic fiction in which the reader is directly addressed by the author himself). The irony of these stories is not a conflict between what the speaker says and what he means, as it would be if the voice were the author's; the conflict is between what the character says and thinks and what we are willing to accept and agree to. The author's own voice remains unheard.

Character in fiction has, of course, been extensively referred to in the preceding discussions of point of view and fictional structure. The two basic aspects of character—morality and personality—are both subject to very full development in fiction. The possible points of view, with the sole exception of the objective point of view, offer clear opportunities for character delineation: if the point of view is subjective or omniscient, the character's inner thought processes are exposed to the reader, and in the latter case may be evaluated or summarized by the narrator. In the case of the limited omniscience of a minor character, that character may still comment and interpret the character of the protagonist at length, although of course his views must be regarded more suspiciously than would a direct statement by an omniscient author.

In the case of subjective point of view, repetition as a methodological concept may be applied in the questions: "What thoughts is this person constantly thinking? What is he preoccupied with?" The character of Jason in *The Sound and the Fury* is clearly defined by this methodological search for repeated content. A very cursory examination of his stream of consciousness, the third section of the novel, identifies him as a constant hater and self-pitier. He hates everybody and everything: he hates his niece; he hates his servants; he hates his car; he hates his boss; he hates his assistants; he hates Negroes; he hates Jews; he hates the local telegraphers; he hates New York financial experts; he hates pigeons; and— most telling of all—he hates Babe Ruth. Anybody who hates Babe Ruth must be all bad.

Such an approach to the character of Jason establishes him as a choleric comic humor: he is walking anger. The only response he knows is anger. He is the kind of man who, if tapped on the shoulder, turns around swinging. The rigidity of this response mechanizes him, and makes him laughable in Bergson's terms.

The methodological question "What occurs at the beginning and ending?" strengthens this character analysis. Jason's very first words are, "Once a bitch always a bitch, what I say." * That is a hating thought. Moreover, it is a thought that stereotypes and refuses ever to relinquish the stereotype—an affirmation of rigid mechanical response. And, finally, it shows the egomaniacal satisfaction with his own opinions ("what I

* William Faulkner, *The Sound and the Fury* (New York: Random House, 1946), p. 198.

say") necessary for complete indifference to the reality of others' feelings. On the last page of his section, Jason is thinking the same thought, and the very words are repeated. Looking at the beginning and the end of his section thus shows Jason to be a static character, and suggests the comic inflexibility that his steadily repetitive section shows throughout.

"What is unexpected or unexplained?" is a methodological question frequently relevant to character. Whenever a character does something that seems unmotivated, or that you wouldn't expect, the author is probably giving a clue to some new or fuller understanding of what makes him tick. Camus' use of a totally unexpected reaction—casual—to the death of a mother is the initial basis of his characterization of Meursault in *The Stranger,* and must be understood if either the character or the theme is to be understood. Faulkner uses unexplained laughter in two of his novels in contexts that can identify the characters' basic motivation. In *The Sound and the Fury,* Quentin laughs at a piece of newspaper he passes on the road. Faulkner does not comment (the point of view is subjective), but the inquisitive reader will remind himself that the paper was carried by a little girl Quentin has just been accused of attacking sexually; and such a reader will recognize that Quentin is laughing bitterly at having been accused of the crime he detests most of all. For it is his own sister's sexual sin that he cannot stand.

In *As I Lay Dying,* the character Darl is attacked by his brothers and sister. He says, "It's not that I—" and then bursts into laughter. Why? A few pages later, at the very end of the book, Darl is clearly crazy. He thinks of himself as two people: "I" and "Darl." In retrospect, one sees the word that drove him into laughter: "I." He laughs because he is schizophrenic, because he has no identity.* Throughout the book, he has been seeking to establish meaningful family relationships. In his failure to relate to the family, he loses his identity; and his otherwise unexplained laughter becomes intelligible as recognition of his loss of self.

Plot is usually rather insignificant in short stories, as stated in the general comments on the genre of fiction. Short stories are just too short to involve much action, especially if any

---

* Faulkner, *As I Lay Dying* (New York: Random House, 1946), pp. 526-527.

attention is paid to character and theme. Brooks and Warren, in their analysis of Hemingway's "The Killers," have pointed out that the story lacks both a beginning and an ending. Killers come to a small town to kill Swede; at the end of the story they have not yet killed him. No reason is given for their murderous intent; nor do we see the end of the plot, the actual killing (although there is no doubt that it will occur). The focus of this short story is not the plot, the action, but the reactions of the various characters, in particular the young protagonist, to being confronted by evil, in the person of the killers. Attention to the methodological question about beginnings and endings obviously helps clarify the plot, since plot is precisely the causal connection leading from beginning to ending. Also, asking "What is unexplained?"—in the case of "The Killers," the beginning and ending of the plot itself— may lead to understanding of the issues to which plot has been subordinated.

In novels of any length plot is more important. Directly applying the technical questions—what is the crisis, are there subplots, etc.—may reveal a basis for order in the long novel.

Since we tend to assume order, the *absence* of plot may show up as a series of unexpected, perhaps unexplained, events. Joseph Heller's *Catch-22* presents a hodgepodge of events partly as a satiric attack upon the established order, partly as a thematic insistence upon the need for human freedom in an unpredictable world. In this case, the technical question "What is the plot?" becomes the methodological question "Why is there no plot?" that is, "Why are there so many unexpected and unexplained events?"

Even if the novel or story as a whole has a perfectly clear plot, any events or contents that do not seem required by the plot itself are worth noting. Thus, Graham Greene, at the end of "The Fallen Idol," a story about a young boy's failure to support his one friend in that friend's moment of greatest need, suddenly leaps in the last paragraph to the boy's deathbed scene many years later. Unrequired by the plot, this final scene drives home the theme of the story, that withdrawal from involvement is the death of love and the end of the life of the soul.

Comedy and satire both present a problem in their fictional forms: insofar as both imply the reader's separation from the characters, insofar as both minimize empathy, they work against the natural tendency of the genre. It has often been commented that comedy is social in nature. The fact that people laugh more easily when watching a play than when reading a novel is cited as proof of the social nature of comedy. The same fact is also evidence that fiction as a genre encourages empathic identification whereas drama as a genre tends to discourage or minimize such identification. Therefore, the audience in the theater can laugh *at* the people on the stage more easily than it can laugh at the characters it reads about at home.

If the most characteristic irony in fiction contrasts the attitudes of a character to the attitudes of the reader, satire goes further, to suggest that the attitudes of the reader are wrong. The suggestion that the reader is wrong begins to introduce the author as the standard of rightness. Satire in fiction, therefore, frequently tends to border on those genres in which the author speaks in his own person, particularly the essay. Frequently, for example, in *Gulliver's Travels*, one loses Gulliver's humorless, reasonable, agreeable voice, and hears that of Swift himself speaking out against the reader.

In contrast, satire that *is* pure fiction tends to be indirect, to be allegorical, perhaps a beast-fable such as Orwell's *Animal Farm* or a mock utopia such as Huxley's *Brave New World*. Such indirect fictional satire frequently loses its satiric punch, its corrective tone, and tends toward comedy or tragedy. In *Animal Farm*, Orwell has tried to control the humorous tendency of the beast-fable by keeping his limited-omniscient point of view with the exploited animals, rather than with those that exploit them. The technique of indirection is less effective in Orwell's *1984*. Reading this depressing portrayal of successful totalitarianism, one lives through the agonies of the government's victims. The objectivity of judgment, either the reader's or the author's, may be lost, and with it the satiric effect; the result is tragic irony. Some intrusion of the author's voice (as in *Gulliver's Travels*) is thus required for fiction to be really satirical.

Comedy in fiction generally is not very laughable (in contrast at least to comic drama). Fictional comedy tends toward romance and stressing the happy ending, rather than emphasizing the blocking characters. When a comic character such as Jason in *The Sound and the Fury* is presented, the reader's temptation to empathize with his victims is so strong that he may find nothing amusing in his first encounter wtih Jason. Faulkner therefore takes great pains to see that Jason fails at everything. He tries to cheat a mother of seeing her daughter, to steal the money the mother sends her daughter, to keep the daughter from the man she wants, to insult his hired help and customers, and to keep a servant boy from going to the carnival. He fails in every one of these efforts, even the hired help besting him in verbal exchanges. When seen in this light—that is, as the failure of a villain whose "victims" are not really victimized—Jason can be laughed at.

Some people, having gotten beyond sympathizing with Jason's victims, swing past the comic attitude to sympathize with Jason himself. This is not the place to argue the validity of such sympathy (there is textual justification for it). What should be noted is that comedy's requirement that people who are to be laughed at must not be sympathized with, makes it difficult for fiction, as a genre which encourages empathy, to be as funny as comic drama.

Two very funny passages illustrate this tension between the nature of the genre as vicarious experience and the nature of laughable comedy. One is the description of the escaping horses in Faulkner's story "Spotted Horses," the other the court-martial scene in *Catch-22*. The first, however, describes animal antics, and although part of the humor is the futility of all efforts to recapture the spotty equine dynamite, the horses themselves are funny as overstatement, as horsy vitality carried to a ludicrous extreme. The reader laughs more easily, since his normal sharing in the experience of fiction does not have to be violated. That is, the reader does not imagine himself as one of the horses in the first place, and therefore laughs much more readily than he otherwise might.

The second laughable passage I wish to cite is the court-martial of Clevinger in *Catch-22*. I have laughed harder at this passage than at any other I can now recall. In addition to the fact—which I cite because I think it typical, not because it happened to me—that I laugh louder when reading this passage aloud to others—thus pushing it toward a different genre—than when reading it to myself, the scene as printed is presented in a nonfictional way. Heller presents it as pure dialogue. That is, reading it is virtually the same experience as reading a play. Again, it is easier to laugh out loud because the humor is not typically fictional. Typical comedy in fiction tends to be the comedy of happy endings rather than the comedy of uproarious laughter.

A special form of comic novel that frequently has satiric aspects is the picaresque novel. Named for the Spanish word for rogue, *picaro,* picaresque novels deal episodically with the travels and adventurous scrapes of a rogue, a protagonist who is neither villainous nor respectable, living by his wits. *Huckleberry Finn* is a well-known American example of this novel. Huck and Jim are both outside the law, and Huck at least has an unconventional morality. Their journey down the river involves them in a variety of adventures (some of them heavily satirical), but they manage somehow to scrape through each situation, regaining their balance in the manner prescribed by Miss Langer.

Tragedy in fiction focuses on character, using the advantages offered by the various possible points of view to explore closely the inner experience of the tragic protagonist. Many approaches to a fictional tragedy are possible, including of course the contrast of ending to beginning both in plot and in character. Presumably, the situation at the end of a tragic novel will be worse (at least for the protagonist) than at the beginning, and the protagonist himself presumably will be different, perhaps in knowledge and increased understanding, and thus a tragic developing character. The short story may use its condensation to present a tragedy in embryo, perhaps a tragic hero who is not shown experiencing a full-fledged tragic plot; such is, I think, close to the case in "The Fallen Idol," although the little boy does make a significant decision. The reason it is embryonic, rather than fully developed tragedy, is that his failure functions as foreshadowing of his failure throughout life at least as much as it functions as tragic in its own right. The concluding deathbed scene, many years later, confirms the lifetime failure. Thus, in this case, too, the methodological question about beginnings and endings helps apply the technical concept of tragedy.

Identifying the protagonist's tragic motive may result from any of the methodological approaches suggested thus far. For example, the question "What is repeated?" applied to the end of Quentin's section in *The Sound and the Fury* should point immediately to his last memory, the conversation with his father, and specifically to the words "and i temporary" which occur over and over. (The absence of punctuation and capitals identifies the words as part of his stream of con sciousness rather than narrated event. Normally punctuated, the words would be: "and I [said,] "Temporary!") His father has told Quentin that in time everything ceases to matter; that Quentin's concern for his sister's sin is purely temporary. This Quentin will not accept, as his horrified repetition of the word "temporary" shows. He therefore kills himself, so that he will die still caring, and so that his father's statement that he will stop caring will not come true. Attention to what is repeated thus leads directly to the tragic motive, the commitment to his own standards of value that Quentin tries to affirm by killing himself.

The unexplained can also reveal tragic motivation. Smerdyakov, in a sense the villain of *Crime and Punishment*, kills himself. The reader is not told why. But the night before his suicide, he dreams three disgusting dreams, each of which is introduced at first as though it is really happening, and none of which is explained. But they all express Smerdyakov's disgust with his own conduct and a sense of guilt, and they tell the reader that Smerdyakov kills himself because he accepts moral responsibility for his crimes.

Novels and longer fiction may combine personal tragedy with some national catastrophe, such as war, as in *Gone with the Wind;* or may blend happy and unhappy endings by combining a number of plots dealing with many characters. Evaluating the novelist's vision of the universe—is it a tragic vision, or a comic vision?—thus requires great care and a complex total evaluation.

Scene is frequently very important in fiction. Details that refer specifically to some actual region or area are called "local color," and may be used to increase verisimilitude, to make the experience more real, or simply for the sake of their own interest. One of the most interesting vicarious experiences is encountering new places, and much fiction takes advantage of this natural human interest. The description of whaling techniques in *Moby Dick* develops scene for its own sake, as a new and interesting experience in which the reader may share.

Scene in the broadest sense, as the world-presented, still appeals to this interest in novelty. Fictional travels (such as Gulliver's, Robinson Crusoe's, and Tarzan's) and accurate historical novels satisfy such interests. Attention to the unusual should immediately reveal use of scene for its own sake, as long as you are the audience the author had in mind. Sometimes a detail not intended as local color or historical characteristic becomes such to the later reader. Thus, Gulliver comes back from Houyhnhnm-land detesting people, and nauseated at the necessity of wearing a borrowed shirt that has actually touched—ugh!—a human being. So he washes his shirt every day. Swift intended this fact to show Gulliver's obsession with cleanliness; but it becomes a commentary to the modern reader on eighteenth-century standards of cleanliness. Generally, however, attention to scene for its own sake will be immediately obvious simply because what is described is new and unfamiliar. Having noted such an interest, the reader may then simply enjoy it. But if the novel is a great novel, the details of the scene may themselves develop symbolic or thematic significance, and should be explored for such possibilities.

Some novelists, indeed, have expressed their themes by working continuously within a specific region. Appropriately enough, they are called "regionalists." Faulkner is one such, having created a mythological county with the jawbreaking name "Yoknapatawpha," which is the site of all his novels. Many of the major characters of one novel appear in other works as minor characters or are alluded to in passing. The mythological county is quite similar to the Mississippi county in which Faulkner lived and wrote, even though the characters and events are by no means autobiographical (as they are for Thomas Wolfe, another regionalist). Faulkner thus is not simply telling tales, but exploring in detail the immediate world in which he lived, offering in fiction an interpretation of the nature of the society around him. Discussion of the scene of Faulkner's novels thus quickly uses the word "world," and shortly becomes indistinguishable from a discussion of his sociological themes about the problems of the South. One of his novels (*As I Lay Dying*) is used as a text in sociology courses concerned with primitive rural areas. "Scene" here has been broadened to include patterns of behavior peculiar to one historical time and place.

Attention to scene in such a case reveals not pure entertainment, but real thematic significance.

Theme is as important for fiction as for all the genres, although not the distinctive structural basis of fiction. Repetition is perhaps the most important methodological clue to theme.

Repetition of an incident strongly implies that the author regards the incident as typical. When Faulkner shows, time after time, descendants of the southern aristocracy being defeated by brash, hard-minded businessmen emerging from the lower classes, the reader should conclude that this is one of Faulkner's themes, and look for other expressions of the same conviction.

Repetition serves as a clue to the theme of Stephen Crane's short story "The Open Boat," which states its theme explicitly twice. Based on an actual experience of the author, the story describes the efforts of four shipwrecked men to get their small boat safely ashore on the storm-wracked Florida coast. After describing several days of bitter exposure and grueling labor, Crane states his theme:

> When it occurs to a man that nature does not regard him as important, and that she feels she would not maim the universe by disposing of him, he at first wishes to throw bricks at the temple, and he hates deeply the fact that there are no bricks and no temples. Any visible expression of nature would surely be pelleted with his jeers.
>
> Then, if there be no tangible thing to hoot, he feels, perhaps, the desire to confront a personification and indulge in pleas, bowed to one knee, and with hands supplicant, saying, "Yes, but I love myself."
>
> A high cold star on a winter's night is the word he feels that she says to him. Thereafter he knows the pathos of his situation.[*]

A few pages later, the same conclusion is restated more briefly:

> [a wind-tower visible on the shore] represented in a degree, to the correspondent, the serenity of nature amid the struggles of the individual—nature in the wind, and nature in the vision of men. She did not seem cruel to

[*] *In The Rinehart Book of Short Stories,* ed. C. L. Cline (New York: Rinehart, 1958), p. 143.

him then, nor beneficent, nor treacherous, nor wise.
But she was indifferent, flatly indifferent.*

The fact that the idea is repeated shows its importance.
To emphasize it further, Crane repeats particular words. Halfway through "The Open Boat" occurs the following:

> As for the reflections of the men, there was a great
> deal of rage in them. Perchance they might be formulated
> thus: If I am going to be drowned—if I am going to be
> drowned—if I am going to be drowned, why, in the
> name of the seven mad gods who rule the sea, was I al-
> lowed to come thus far and contemplate sand and trees?
> Was I brought here merely to have my nose dragged away
> as I was about to nibble the sacred cheese of life? . . . But
> no; she [Fate] cannot drown me. Not after all this work.†

Five pages later come these words:

> If I am going to be drowned—if I am going to be
> drowned—if I am going to be drowned, why, in the name
> of the seven mad gods who rule the sea, was I allowed
> to come thus far and contemplate sand and trees? Was I
> brought here merely to have my nose dragged away
> as I was about to nibble the sacred cheese of life?

And again, three pages later:

> If I am going to be drowned—if I am going to be
> drowned, why, in the name of the seven gods who rule
> the sea, was I allowed to come thus far and contemplate
> sand and trees?

The answer to this repeated question is the theme of Crane's
story: Nature is indifferent. The long explicit statement
of theme, first quoted, immediately follows the third posing
of the question. In this case, repetition is virtually a signpost
to the theme.

* *Ibid.*, pp. 146-147.
† *Ibid.*, p. 135.

Repetition of words also suggests a theme in Faulkner's short story "The Bear." The words "not even" or some equivalent to them are used continually. The ultimate implication of this simple repetition is a metaphysical theme that Faulkner returned to over and over again, just as he repeated the words again and again: the ultimate nature of reality, including the mystery of human personality, is inscrutable; and the proper attitude toward that mystery is wonder. In his constant reiteration "not even" Faulkner expresses the constant violation of human expectation by reality.

A methodological gimmick that sometimes leads to identifying the themes is attention to names. Both titles and the names of characters may be relevant to theme.

The Sound and the Fury, like many titles, makes an allusion to earlier literature which helps identify its theme. In this case, the allusion is to *Macbeth,* Act V, Scene 5:

> Tomorrow, and tomorrow, and tomorrow,
> Creeps in this petty pace from day to day
> To the last syllable of recorded time,
> And all our yesterdays have lighted fools
> The way to dusty death. Out, out, brief candle!
> Life's but a walking shadow, a poor player
> That struts and frets his hour upon the stage
> And then is heard no more: it is a tale
> Told by an idiot, full of *sound and fury,*
> Signifying nothing.

In addition to opening with a long interior monologue from the point of view of a literal idiot, the novel's theme generally is the decay of values and the problems of adjusting to the passage of time (even the shadow image is carried over, as Quentin tries to avoid seeing shadows that are cast by the sun and which thus indicate the time).

To use a more contemporary example, the most striking qualities of the hero of Camus' *The Stranger*—his isolation and estrangement—are suggested by the title.

Names of characters too are often very suggestive. This applies most obviously to allegories like *Pilgrim's Progress,* in which characters have names like "Christian" and "Valiant-for-Truth." Even in nonallegorical works, however, names are frequently meaningful. Shirley Jackson's chilling story of a ritual stoning to death in a contemporary setting, "The Lottery," includes as one of the stoners a Mrs. Delacroy. The name is an anglicization of the French "de la Croix," which means "of the Cross." Mrs. Delacroy, like the cross on which Jesus was hung, is a means to a sacrificial offering. (The comparison is ironic, since the victim of the stoning dies meaninglessly.) As the crowd start to throw stones, Steve *Adams* goes first, accompanied by Mrs. *Graves.* These names imply that the original sin of Adam, a spiritual death which causes literal death, is still with us; and perhaps also that old religion has lost its meaning to the modern world, the cross of Jesus now the blindly destructive Mrs. Delacroy. Another example is Nathaniel Hawthorne's short story "Young Goodman Brown." The wife's name is "Faith," and when Brown exclaims, "As long as I have my Faith, all will yet be well," the reader should recognize that Faith is more than just a woman.

Symbolism is used extensively in fiction, perhaps more in modern fiction because of the popularity of Freudian theories among writers and critics alike. (An interesting extension of Freudian symbolism is found in novels like Alberto Moravia's *Two Loves,* in which sex is not symbolized, but itself becomes symbolic of other meanings and thematic interests.)

Recognizing symbols is frequently difficult. Probably, it is safer to under-interpret than to over-interpret, safer to miss a few symbols than to spot hallucinatory symbols that aren't really there. But there are some fairly clear indications of symbolic intent. For example, Heller's *Catch-22* includes a bizarre hospital episode involving a mummified patient. At least, there may be a patient inside the swath of bandages; he is never seen. Two bottles are at his bedside, one feeding (presumably intravenously) into him, the other draining (presumably from his excretory organs) out of him. He never moves or gives any indication of life. When the top bottle empties and the bottom bottle fills up, they are simply switched. This situation, and the switching of the bottles, is completely improbable. In spite of the fact that during an interview Mr. Heller maintained that it was literally possible, there is no reason (certainly none offered in the novel) for anyone to set up such a grotesque situation. The hoax of the empty bandages is completely unmotivated. Such an act, one that stands out as unexpected and seems unmotivated, is frequently symbolic. In this case, Heller may have meant that the superefficiency of a complex organization, such as a hospital, tends to function pointlessly, for the sake of its own functioning. The nurse takes the temperature reading each morning, balancing the thermometer on the lower edge of the oral cavity of the bandages; and the bottles are switched; and the hospital routine goes on working over empty bandages. Organization itself is counter to humanity.

The unusual and the unmotivated may have been included for symbolic reasons. A different methodological clue to symbolism is repetition.

Joseph Conrad uses repetition as a clue to symbolism and theme in "The Secret Sharer." In this story, a young captain, given his first command, takes a fugitive on board, hides him in his cabin, and finally risks his ship by sailing close enough to shore to allow the fugitive to slip overboard and swim to shore. The fugitive had committed the murder, almost unconsciously—he does not recall the actual crime—of a sailor whom he thought to be endangering his ship. At the end of the story, when the young captain has successfully helped the fugitive to escape, the captain for the first time feels at one with his ship and secure in his command of her. The theme of this story will involve responsibility, law or command, and instinctive violence.

In order to state that theme accurately, one essential fact of symbolism must be grasped: the fugitive is the captain's alter ego; the fugitive stands for the unbridled impulses of the captain's subconscious self, which must be recognized and set aside if command is to be exercised responsibly. Conrad takes great care to make it clear that the fugitive and the captain are one, by constantly repeating the phrases "my double," used twelve times (not counting two uses of "double captain"); "my other self" and "my second self," used five times each (not counting a third-person reference to "his other self"); "secret sharer," used three times not counting the title; and " my secret self," used once. This constant repetition of phrase and idea drives home inescapably the identity of the two.

The reader who notices this identity should look for further evidence, evidence of how the identity affects the young captain. Such a reader will then notice such lines as these:

... I was almost as much a stranger on board as himself, I said ... we, the two strangers in the ship, faced each other in identical attitudes.

... our eyes met—the eyes of the only two strangers on board.*

Note the repetition of the fact that both the captain and the fugitive are strangers. This may remind the reader of the young captain's earlier statements, before the fugitive came on board:

... my position was that of the only stranger on board. ... But what I felt most was my being a stranger on the ship; and if all the truth must be told, I was somewhat of a stranger to myself.

The fugitive and the captain are both strangers on the ship; how does their identity affect the captain?

... the dual working of my mind distracted me almost to the point of insanity. I was constantly watching myself, my secret self, as dependent on my actions as my own personality. ...

I had become so connected in thoughts and impressions with the secret sharer of my cabin that I felt as if I, personally, were being given to understand that I, too, was not the sort that would have done for the chief mate of a ship like the *Sephora* [the fugitive's ship]. ...

... something in me that ... suggested a mysterious similitude to the young fellow ...

I was not wholly alone with my command; for there was that stranger in my cabin. Or rather, I was not completely and wholly with her. Part of me was absent. That mental feeling of being in two places at once affected me physically. ...

And it was as if the ship had two captains to plan her course for her.

* This and the following quotations from "The Secret Sharer" are in Conrad, *op. cit., passim.*

Clearly, the secret sharer has a bad effect on the young captain, isolating him even more from his ship. (The captain's relationship with his crew, who begin to think him crazy, bears out this conclusion.) He cannot concentrate on his command; he is only half a captain.

How, then, in view of these repetitions, should the theme of "The Secret Sharer" be stated? First, the major symbol must be identified: the fugitive is a symbol of some aspect of the captain himself—since he is an unconscious murderer, an outcast before the law, he probably represents some primitive and lawless passion buried deep in the captain, who at the beginning of the story is "a stranger to himself." It was, says the captain, "as though I had been faced by my own reflection in the depths of a somber and immense mirror." Secondly, the theme itself may be stated: A person in command must come to recognize his baser elements—a process that may interfere with his command while it goes on—and set them aside (put the fugitive ashore) before he can command effectively. The next-to-last sentences in the story confirm this theme:

> And I was alone with her. Nothing! no one in the world should stand now between us, throwing a shadow on the way of silent knowledge and mute affection, the perfect communion of a seaman with his first command.

Repetition (both in itself and as a clue to symbolism) and symbols serve to identify theme, as close reading of "The Secret Sharer" has shown. Before leaving this story, one final point should be made about symbols: frequently they mean more than one thing. Thus, the fugitive in that story primarily represents the dark side of the captain's self. Also, however, he is, in his own right, a person whom the captain pities and tries to help, not only putting him ashore, but also giving him some money and a hat for protection from the sun. This hat too becomes a symbol. Risking his ship by putting in too close to shore in order to insure that the fugitive can swim to safety, the captain cannot tell in the still waters whether his ship is moving or not. But the hat he gave his other self floats into view, and serves as a mark of the ship's progress.

And I watched the hat—the expression of my sudden
pity for his mere flesh. It had been meant to save his
homeless head from the dangers of the sun. And now—
behold—it was saving the ship, by serving me for a
mark to help out the ignorance of my strangeness.

As another person, the fugitive deserved humane treatment.
The very fact that the young captain treated him humanely
actually helped him save his ship from the danger into which
he had brought her, and helped him overcome his strangeness. The hat, which "expressed his sudden pity," symbolizes
that pity (we are told several times it is a white hat against
black water); and when the hat saves the ship one may
understand that pity saves the ship. The theme should, then,
be restated in a more complicated form: In order to command
well, a person must come to recognize his baser elements and
set them aside; *but* only by acting humanely will he command
effectively.

The fugitive thus represents the captain's baser self and
is a person in his own right, and the fugitive affects the meaning of the story in both his roles, as a symbol of subconscious
evil and as a literal character. To some extent, too, he also
symbolizes all of the young captain and not just his worst
elements. Thus, both are strangers to the vessel, a fact which
is true not just of the captain's subconscious self but also of
his conscious self. And finally, when the captain thinks of
the fugitive striking out, "a free man, a proud swimmer striking out for a new destiny," one should understand that the
young captain himself is striking out for a new destiny.

In concluding our discussion of symbolism and theme in
fiction, we may note that the good reader will be on the look-
out for thematic statements or implications; that he will expect the theme to require some qualification; and that by
looking for repetitions and possible symbols, marking them
as he goes and reviewing for further relevance of these repetitions and possible symbols to the events of the story, he may
accurately state its theme.

In general, the analysis of fiction should proceed by a
combination of technical questions and methodological approach. Critical concepts are applied to the work; which ones
fit? how? At the same time, the methods of looking closely at
repeated or unexpected material and the other methods sug-

gested in this chapter are used to bring out what might otherwise be overlooked. You cannot know in advance which way to begin for the best results. Start with what occurs to you, and work from here.

3. Drama

A. Presentation

Drama has been described as involving the presence of work and audience.* In this basic sense drama is perhaps the easiest of all the genres to understand. Plays have audiences, groups of watchers who are literally present, and they are enacted or performed right there on the stage for everyone to see. The word "theater" has Greek roots that mean a seeing or viewing place.

Drama is still objective when it is read in an armchair. Of course, it is much harder to read a play than to see it, because the imagination must construct all kinds of details that are not provided. A good reader of plays is producer, stage manager, director, voice coach, casting office, costumer, makeup artist, and practically everyone else associated with the play. Except the author and the actors.

The reader does not imagine himself the author, because in drama the author is not present. The script of the play is independent of the author; his voice is not to be heard. The

* See pp. 87ff.

play-reader does not get instructions, advice, interpretations from the author as individual. Stage directions should be as transparent as possible, as neutral as the instructions in a recipe or the description of a scientific experiment, objective accounts of pure fact.

Nor does the reader imagine himself to be the actors, that is, to be enacting the part himself, living through it. "The method," by which actors are taught to identify themselves wholly with the role they are playing, to feel it in themselves, is a technique for acting, not for reading. Some empathy may be appropriate, depending on whether the play is comic or tragic, the character good or bad. But never in drama does the aesthetic distance dwindle to the degree of identification that typifies fiction. Drama is not vicarious experience, but witnessed event.

The point of view of drama is thus irrevocably objective. True, various expressionistic attempts to represent the inner thoughts of a protagonist may be fairly successful as border-line cases. Thus, Willy Loman in *Death of a Salesman* wanders in and out of his memories and his present experi-ence, the lights going up on a scene from the past as he steps into a representation of a hotel room, then dimming there to brighten another part of the stage as his wife calls him onto the back porch. The medieval allegory *Everyman* might be regarded as a representation of internal conflict between alle-gorical figures that literally inhabit the mind. But in both the medieval and the modern presentation of experience, what happens is that the inner experience is so objectified that it, too, is witnessed, not seen from within.

Only the movie has really produced a subjective drama, which although literally witnessed is witnessed as though the experience of the audience itself. Unfortunately, the examples are not artistic successes. The camera as the eye of the pro-tagonist is not convincing for long. But the illusion of sub-jective point of view may be achieved temporarily. Usually, this temporary success is precisely during those moments when the emphasis falls on what the protagonist is seeing rather than on what he is thinking or feeling. The effect is still objective. The most effective temporary successes in camera-eye subjectivity are the cineramic representations of rapid motion, such as a roller-coaster ride, airplane flight, or train crash. These exceptions are entertaining, but have little literary and not even much cinematic significance.

Both English and Greek drama derived from religious rituals. Indeed, Greek dramatic festivals were religious celebrations, and an altar was a prominent part of the theater. In both cases, the history of the development of drama as distinct from rite is the history of the separation of the audience from participation in the event. Thus, the development is the transition from taking part to witnessing, or the emergence of the audience from "the work" as a communal celebration.

B. Structure

The basis of dramatic structure has been identified as plot. Drama is witnessed, and what is witnessed is action. Actions related purposefully are a plot. That plot is the basis for structuring plays follows logically from the definition of drama as a genre.

The primacy of plot also follows from an inductive look at how plays are built. Even in ritual, the ancestor of drama, action—event, or doing something—is primary. The importance of ritual may be called its theme, the meaning behind what is done. But this belief about ritual is at best a half-truth, as substituting direct prose statement for ritual enactment shows. The total value of ritual is by no means contained in summary statements of the ritual's meaning. The real strength of ritual is the enactment itself, the process of doing.

Drama inherited this primacy of action from ritual. Action without plot, of course, is pure spectacle. Circus parades, Armed Forces Day shows, are witnessed events, but events without structure. The ordering of the events through plot turns a mere show into literature, a spectacle into a play.

Because plot is human actions, the links of cause and effect binding the events of plot are human motives and purposes. Discussion of plot therefore involves reference to character, which is largely defined by motives. Thus, one excellent introductory text and anthology of drama is entitled *Character and Conflict*. The title implies the primacy of plot, for characters in conflict *are* plot.

The Greek dramatist Euripides generally provides a prologue, in which the action to come is anticipated by a god, and a *deus ex machina* at the end, who tidies things up. Such a framework might be expected to minimize the importance of motivation for plot, since what a god has ordained presumably happens for that very reason and needs no other explanation. But actually, in spite of the framework of divine determinism and beyond the motivations of the gods themselves (who seem too human in their jealousies and rivalries), Euripides in fact explores motivation with an almost psychoanalytical interest in character as the source of action.

Consider the following bare summary of events (I omit the prologue, in which the goddess Aphrodite explains everything that is to happen). Theseus brings home a wife, Phaedra. She falls in love with his son, Hippolytus. Phaedra's nurse sees that Phaedra is moping. The nurse lures Phaedra into revealing that she loves Hippolytus. "Tell Hippolytus," says the nurse. "No!" says Phaedra. The nurse tells Hippolytus. Hippolytus rebukes Phaedra, threatens to tell Theseus, but says he won't. Phaedra kills herself, leaving a note accusing Hippolytus of accosting her. Theseus calls down a curse on Hippolytus, and sends him away. The curse is fulfilled as Hippolytus crashes to his death. A goddess (Artemis, not Aphrodite) tells Theseus what really happened.

Even the barest summary includes some reference to aspects of character. This play is unintelligible without reference to Phaedra's love for Hippolytus. Moreover, even when events or actions can be stated without explicit reference to decision and motivation, both are clearly implicit as the connecting links that carry one event on to another. For example, the nurse's love for Phaedra combines with her rather coarse philosophy—she thinks it's all right for a son to have an affair with his stepmother—to produce the decision to tell Hippolytus of Phaedra's love with the motive of getting the two together and making Phaedra happy. Ironically, she produces the opposite effect from what she intended. This ironic reversal of intention occurs because the nurse's motivation, a product of her moral character, bumps into Hippolytus' strict morality, which she did not adequately take into account. Where there are different motivations and opposed decisions (such as the nurse's and Phaedra's, the nurse's and Hippolytus', and Hippolytus' and Phaedra's), conflict inevitably arises and must be identified in the plot summary.

Note that the making of a decision may itself involve a conflict if there are conflicting motives. Phaedra's refusal to tell Hippolytus involves an internal conflict between her feelings for Hippolytus on the one hand and her feelings for Theseus and decency on the other. In fact, the way she tells the nurse suggests her ambivalence, hinting that she secretly hopes the nurse may tell Hippolytus of her love.

To the bare summary of events given above, then, must be added identifications of motive and of conflicts. Then, when all of the motives have been stated—including Phaedra's frustration, shame, and desire for revenge; including too Theseus' righteous anger at his son—then the events of the plot will be seen as a causally related sequence with each one naturally arising out of the one before, given the initial circumstances and the nature of the people involved. This plot has a beginning (the stepmother Phaedra's love of Hippolytus), an extended middle, and an end (the death of Hippolytus).

But at the very end of the play, after the action has apparently come to an end, the goddess Artemis descends to tell Theseus that his righteous indignation was based on a mistake. This event is not really caused by what went on before, and is a *deus ex machina* in all senses of the phrase. Euripides apparently used it in this instance largely because he wanted to make the ending of the play as unhappy as possible, and did not want to leave poor old Theseus even the consolation of thinking that he had at least avenged the wrong committed by the guilty party. So the goddess tells him that the son he killed (through his curse) was actually the innocent victim. The goddess makes it clear that Theseus has failed, and brings him and the audience to full realization of his failure.

This discussion of Euripides' *Hippolytus* has ignored Aphrodite, the goddess of love who appears at the beginning of the play and foretells everything, which she says she will make happen because she is jealous of Hippolytus' attention to the goddess of chastity, Artemis. A methodological attention to beginnings and endings would certainly emphasize the thematic contrast between the two goddesses, Aphrodite and Artemis, and explore the religious implications of *their* behavior and motivation. But my concern at the moment is with plot. The preceding analysis showed, I hope, that even in a case where plot seems to be minimized—after all, everything is laid out from the very beginning—even in such a case, an exploration of how events are linked to each other by the

cause and effect of human motivations in conflict establishes
the structure of the play.

It is popular nowadays to minimize the importance of plot
and to emphasize other elements, such as character and
theme. Character, of course, is as important to plot as plot is
to character. And theme, as ultimate meaning, may dominate
the other analytical concepts. But drama retains enough of its
primitive ritualistic quality to communicate essentially by
demonstration in action. The stated theme, rather than the
enacted theme, is rarely the heart of a play. And plot is the
vehicle by which theme is enacted.

Greek drama makes very little use of subplots. For Shakespeare, however, the subplot is a major structural device. It
illlumines character, and it strengthens theme. And in connection with the main plot, Shakespearean subplots define the
structure of the play.

One critic* notes the use of subplots to define character in
Hamlet, calling them "reflections" of the principal action. The
basic situation is that Hamlet's uncle has killed his father,
married his mother, and then taken the throne. Told of this,
Hamlet delays his proper revenge. Two subplots nearly dupli-
cate the situation: Fortinbras is leading an army to reclaim
lands that used to be his father's, in contrast to the inactive
Hamlet's failure to pursue the throne; and when Hamlet
mistakenly kills Polonius, Polonius' son Laertes raises a mob
to storm the palace, demanding revenge. The vigorous decisions of both Laertes and Fortinbras, in their subplots, thus
delineate Hamlet more sharply by contrast.

The same subplots strengthen one of the play's themes,
again by contrast. The play shows that a country ruled by an
evil man suffers, almost independently of any of his policies.
That is, a country with an evil king is sick, even if the king
tries to rule as well as he can. The main plot shows the suffering, both personal and national, produced by the uncle-
king's efforts to find out what Hamlet really knows. In the
first subplot, Fortinbras' actions are unknown to his uncle;
but when the uncle learns what Fortinbras is doing, he re-
calls the young man, who obeys. The uncle is deceived about
his nephew, just as Hamlet's uncle is deceived about him,

* Francis Fergusson, in *The Idea of a Theater* (Garden City,
N.Y.: Doubleday Anchor Books, 1953), pp. 114-124.

but in the case of Fortinbras (whose uncle is not a murderer) the problem is easily solved without catastrophe. The parallel and contrast to Hamlet are clear. Moreover, in the other subplot, Polonius "spies" on his son Laertes, to find out how he is doing at the university, just as Hamlet's stepfather is spying on him. The difference, however, is the difference between a fairly normal conflict between generations in the subplot and the abnormal and diseased conflict between a murderer and the victim's survivors in the main plot. The contrast between the healthy misunderstandings of the subplots and the diseased misunderstanding corrupting the kingdom strengthens the royal theme.

The subplots also function structurally, as plots. All three unite at the conclusion, when Hamlet's uncle arranges a fight between Hamlet (the protagonist of the main plot) and Laertes (the protagonist of one subplot) that leads to the death of all three, thus terminating the main plot and the subplot, and the throne is claimed by Fortinbras (the protagonist of the other subplot), who thus solves his own affairs and terminates any further strife over the throne of Denmark. All three plots thus come together at the end, with the same events functioning in several plots at once.

The technical terms applied in this analysis of the plot structure of Hamlet are simply plot, character, and theme. The method depends first upon identifying the various plot lines, that is, the chains of cause and effect; these I simply stated. Next, to establish the relationship of plot to character and the relationship of plot to theme, the methodological question implicitly asked was: "What is repeated?" More concretely, "Do the subplots repeat the main plot in any way? And as a corollary to this question, "How do repeated things differ?" More concretely, "Do parallel subplots contrast to the main plot?" To establish the plot structure of the play, the methodological question could have been, "What happens at the end of each plot?" Locating the end of each plot thus identified a focusing of all the action (appropriately enough) in the last scene of the play, as the same events wind up all of the plots. The same statements about the structure of the last act of *Hamlet* might have come from the question, "What events are actually part of more than one plot?" or, "Where do plot lines cross?"

Let me illustrate the convergence of plot lines by reference to *King Lear*. The initial event of the play is Lear's division of his kingdom between two of his daughters, and his banishment of the third. Why Lear does this is a question that belongs to a discussion of character (he wants to keep the honor of kingship without the responsibility, and banishes his daughter Cordelia because she won't flatter him); that he does it is the first fact of the play, and the beginning of the main plot. The rest of the action will stem from these actions.

The two evil sisters react immediately. Lear "always lov'd our sister most; and with what poor judgment he hath now cast her off appears too grossly," says Goneril to Regan, speaking of their sister's banishment; "Such unconstant starts are we like to have from him as this of . . . banishment," * is Regan's reply. With the power Lear gave them, and because he did what he did, his two less charitable daughters plot the play. Throughout the first two acts, they shuffle Lear back and forth, countering his indignation with stricter and more humiliating demands, until driven by his own pride as well as by them, he exits to the sound of an approaching storm and the madness of the third act. Granted the character of the sisters on the one hand and of Lear on the other, no other outcome of his initial act could reasonably be expected. One of the unusual things about the structure of *King Lear* is that the crisis of the main plot thus occurs in the very first act.

While the main plot is occupying about three-fourths of the first two acts, a subplot that parallels the main plot develops quickly. Gloucester is tricked by his bad son Edmund into disinheriting his good son Edgar, just as Lear has disinherited his good daughter in favor of the bad ones. Edmund's character and his decision to trick his father are expressed in a speech that shows the clear connection between the two, beginning "Thou, Nature, art my goddess," and concluding, "Now, gods, stand up for bastards!" † Edmund's scheme is to forge an incriminating letter from his legitimate brother Edgar; and to trick Edgar into a phony fight with him, which

* William Shakespeare, *King Lear* (Arden Edition), ed. Kenneth Muir (Cambridge, Mass.: Harvard University Press, 1957), Act I, Scene 1, lines 290-292; 300-302.

† *Ibid.*, Act I, Scene 2, lines 1-22.

he explains one way to Edgar and another way to their father.

The lack of control that Gloucester manifested sexually by begetting his bastard son Edmund shows itself intellectually in his inability to remain in doubt. As soon as Edmund accuses Edgar (whom he has persuaded to hide from their father), Gloucester can't remain in doubt long enough to check the story. He believes immediately. (Edmund also plays on his father's superstition, hinting that Edgar was putting a curse on Gloucester.) Gloucester's character (both morally and in terms of his superstitious personality) thus leads him to accept the evil son, Edmund. He then commits the fatal error of putting himself in Edmund's power by confiding that he is communicating with a foreign power (actually France, the country to which the banished Cordelia fled).

Edgar, in contrast to his brother and his father, is a complete blank as a character throughout the first two acts. Why does he believe Edmund? Why does he hide when Edmund says hide, and fight when Edmund says fight? Well, there is more than one way to skin a cat, and more than one way to handle the motivation of action. When a character's actions clearly and significantly are related to what he is, Shakespeare lets him reveal himself, as Gloucester and Edmund do; when his action is irrelevant to his character, the playwright gags him. In this case, the demands of the plot overrule interest in character. Edgar has no speech of more than ten words in the first two acts, except one of sheer plot business—we must know how he plans to disguise himself if we are to recognize him when he comes on impersonating a madman. Later, Edgar will reveal himself as a man of compassion, faithfulness, and ability; but since these qualities have nothing to do with his being fooled, for the moment we are shown none of them.

Our immediate interest in *King Lear* is the structural relationship between the main plot and the subplot. Thus far, the two plots have paralleled each other. But the timing has been different. The focus in the main plot is upon the gradual working out of the consequences, once Lear has made his mistake, banishing Cordelia and giving Goneril and Regan power; in contrast, the subplot in the first two acts gradually develops by the steps outlined above toward the situation that the main plot reached in the very first scene: the fathers in the power of the evil children. Although the crisis of the main plot occurs at the beginning, the crisis of the subplot does not occur until Act III.

The similarity of the two plots, with their contrasting pace, constitutes the structure of the first half of the play. In the first two acts, there is still no crossing of the lines. Not Edmund, nor Gloucester, nor Edgar has any effect yet upon the action that concerns Lear; nor has there been any effect upon Edmund's scheme by the characters of the main plot. (Although Regan and her husband Cornwall support what Edmund says of Edgar, and offer their help in tracking him down, Gloucester has already accepted the story, and Edgar is already an outcast.) These are two separate series of actions, each following its own chain of cause and effect, its own inner logic. It is in Act III that the two combine, and with a vengeance.

The action of the main plot in the third act is that Lear goes mad; the action of the subplot is that Regan's husband Cornwall blinds Gloucester. Here, the two plot lines cross. First (except for scene 1), Lear scenes and Gloucester scenes alternate. Scenes 2, 4, and 6 are Lear scenes; 3, 5, and 7 are Gloucester scenes. This, of course, does not mean that the two plots are affecting each other, but it does concentrate attention upon the relationship between them.

Secondly, in both of the major events, the two plot lines do interact. Lear goes mad because Edgar reminds him of his daughters, in a process carefully traced out before our eyes (scene 4). And Edgar is there to remind Lear of his daughters because Edgar has been driven from home by Gloucester, at Edmund's instigation. The subplot here causes results in the main plot.

In the next-to-last scene of the act (6), Lear is crazy enough to talk to a stool as though it were his daughter, and by the next scene the subplot too has reached the central catastrophe, and catches up with the main plot. Here, in the last scene of the third act (7), Gloucester pays the consequences for his mistake, as Lear has now come to pay for his. This double climax is matched by the focusing of the two plot lines. For the immediate cause of Gloucester's blinding is the help he gives to Lear, his words that incite Cornwall to pluck out his eyes being a defense of Lear. The final cause, of course, is Edmund's plan; but Edmund strengthens his case by citing Gloucester's intervention in Lear's affairs, which Regan and Cornwall will not tolerate. Lear is affected by the Gloucester plot; Gloucester is affected by the Lear plot; and, as Cornwall blinds Gloucester with the words "Out, vile jelly!" Gloucester joins Lear at the nadir of their fortunes.

The plot structure of *King Lear* is complicated. To carry this analysis on through the last two acts would require at least as much space as has already been devoted to the first half of the play. The general points concerning plot, however, have already been illustrated. The organization of drama is plot. When there are subplots, not only the internal order of the main plot, but also the relationship of main plot to subplots constitutes the form of the play.

The analysis could have proceeded by asking questions that apply the technical terms: "Where is the crisis of the main plot? Where is the crisis of the subplot? What are the events in each plot line, and what events are part of the cause-effect chain of both plot lines?" The basic methodological question concerns the division of the play into parts. The act and scene divisions, even though not always Shakespeare's, may in fact correspond to divisions of the structural units of the play. This lead would have been most significantly helpful in the alternation of main plot and subplot in Act III. In general, Shakespearean plays do have a typical pattern of plot, corresponding to the act divisions: exposition and complication in the first two acts; crisis and/or climax in the third act; unraveling of the implications for society, the kingdom, in Act IV; and final catastrophe if a tragedy and unraveling of the implications for the protagonists in Act V.

Some modern dramas are apparently antiplot. In the theater of the absurd, plays violate all one's expectations of intelligibility and structure. They may be plotless or irrational. Two points should be made concerning the relationship of such plays to the typical plot structure of the genre. First, they are basically satirical, attacking the rationalistic point of view. As such, they succeed precisely because the audience expects an intelligible plot structure. Secondly, they frequently are structured in terms of connected actions, even though the motives offered are ridiculous For example, Ionesco's *The Chairs* shows a couple setting out chairs for an arriving audience who come to hear a speech. The play builds simply toward the entrance of the speaker, as more and more of the audience arrive, until the stage is crowded with chairs and the couple are bumped and jostled by the horde. The speaker arrives and makes his talk. This is a very simpleminded structure, but it is a structure in terms of related events. At the climax of the play, the events are virtually pantomimed, as the couple are jostled and crowded in their hurrying efforts to accommodate the multitudinous audience. The plot is somewhat episodic, since various arrivals constitute little incidents by themselves; but as in the *Iliad,* each such episode is clearly placed within the overall plot structure: the arrival and seating of the audience to hear the speech. The absurdity comes from the fact that there is no audience at all; the total cast is three—the couple who prepare, and the speaker who finally arrives to talk utter nonsense. But even though the satirical point of the play is irrationality, which does not fit well with Aristotle's law of probability and necessity, the play is dramatic, because it presents events; and even in this instance, the relationship between the events is the structuring principle.

C. Convention

So far, this discussion of drama has focused on the structure of drama, on who is seen doing what and why—that is, on plot and on character as it contributes to plot. But as Kenneth Burke said, "every act requires a scene in which it takes place." Scene in the sense of setting usually refers to the fictional location within which the plot occurs. But scene is more distinctively important in drama, which after all is intended to be literally seen, rather than imaginatively experienced as fiction is. The literal setting of an enacted play thus is not simply the spectacle of the scenery, the painted flats, drops, and props. The complete setting literally is the theater in which the play is performed.

Trivial? Not really; because theaters differ. They differ not simply in the number of seats per row, but in more significant aspects that affect the lines the author writes and the impression made on the audience. Differences between the theaters of different periods are matters of dramatic convention. Out of shared habit, audiences and playwrights agree that certain aspects of the presentation will be taken for granted. These include the physical characteristics of the theater itself.

For example: Greek drama was written for an open amphitheater, set into the side of a hill, seating perhaps 17,000 people. Elizabethan drama such as Shakespeare's was written for an enclosed courtyard, with both part of the audience and part of the stage under the roof of the enclosing structure. The nineteenth-century stage (developed from the Italian Renaissance) is separated from the audience by a proscenium arch, through which the audience, sitting in the dark, looks at the actors as though through a picture window. More recent productions may make use of the "theater-in-the-round," in which the stage is entirely surrounded by audience.

How do these physical characteristics of the theater operate to affect the quality of the plays written for each? Consider first the Greek drama. The large audiences, which might include the whole citizenry of a town, make casual informality and delicate subtleties of expression or movement ineffective. The style therefore is formal and perhaps even ritualistic in tragedy, broad and obvious in comedy. As part of the total dramatic convention of Greek theater, the actors wore masks to convey some basic aspect of their role even to the most distant spectators, and padded their shoes and robes for greater size. Consequently, rapid and violent actions were difficult and inappropriate. Partly for this reason, acts of violence were performed offstage and reported by a messenger, as in *Oedipus;* or perhaps after offstage mayhem the corpses might be wheeled onstage through the central door, as in *Medea*, when the title character displays the bodies of her children, whom she has killed.

One of the most distinctive conventions of the Greek theater is the chorus. In the case of the chorus, it is the history of the drama that affects the shape of the theater, rather than vice versa. Greek drama developed out of the performances of religious choirs, so to speak. First a single leader emerged, singing back and forth antiphonally with the group; then gradually more characters were distinguished, and the typical pattern of Greek drama—an alternation of plot scenes with choral songs—took shape. This conventional pattern produced a theater that had both a stage for the scenes with individual characters, and a large floor in front of and below it on which the chorus sang and danced in very slow stately fashion. (This dance area, called the orchestra, roughly corresponds to the main floor seating area in a normal modern theater of the type you are probably used to.)

The chorus, literally standing between the actors and the audience, also came to stand between them functionally. Thus, the chorus might from time to time ask questions the audience might be supposed to be wondering; it might tell the audience the meaning of the action; it might share the emotional state of the actors in the plot scenes on the stage above, encouraging the audience to do the same with a choral number—a sort of mood music; and at times it might function simply as additional characters in the play, as do the citizens at the end of *Agamemnon* who threaten to attack the regicide Aegisthus.

The plot controls the chorus, whose odes are in all of these ways about the plot. The alternation of plot scene and choral song therefore should not be described as "nonsong, song, nonsong, song, . . ." but as "plot, nonplot, plot, nonplot. . . ." Or, better yet, "plot, comment, plot, comment." My point is the dominance of the plot as the structuring factor in the Greek dramatic pattern of alternating scene and song.

In general, this dancing, chanting group, which not even the classical Greek would expect to encounter on the street, is accepted by convention. Unless the audience is willing to accept the convention, the Greek chorus is as bizarre as the singing and dancing young hoodlums in *West Side Story*. They, too, must be accepted as part of a convention, the convention of the musical. New York "hoods" are seldom seen dancing and singing through the slums, and should not be so depicted, according to the standard of realism. What is thus overlooked is the dramatic necessity that some conventions be employed. The shifting point of view of the movie itself must be accepted conventionally as much as the dancing and singing of the musical, for a twenty-foot-high face is not only unrealistic itself, but does not suddenly change to a three-foot-high distant figure. The conventions we are accustomed to we overlook. We reject different conventions which we should learn to accept.

The Shakespearean stage was much more intimate than the large Greek amphitheater. A typical attendance might approach as many as two thousand, seated in three-level balconies around the back and sides and standing shoulder to shoulder in the central, unroofed pit area. The open front of the stage that protruded out into the courtyard, called the apron, might actually serve as seating space for wealthy patrons who were willing to pay for good and prominent seats. In such circumstances, the aside and the soliloquy developed easily and naturally. The aside is an explanatory comment made directly to the audience by one of the characters on-stage. By convention, the audience assumes that it is not heard by the other characters on the stage. The soliloquy is a combination of thinking out loud and addressing the audience, occurring when a character is alone onstage. Since the Elizabethan audience now occupied the central floor area (used by the chorus in the Greek theater) and stood right beside the stage, it was possible to establish the convention of such remarks directly addressed to the audience.

The Greek theater did, in fact, make use of devices that accomplished much the same as the soliloquy. The leading character, the protagonist, might use the chorus as a sound-ing board for his own ideas and emotions, formally engaging them in a sort of dialogue, but not really expecting them to react to what he said the way real people would react—expecting instead that they would simply help him think through whatever was bothering him, and then forget about it. Like the soliloquy, this device* enables the audience to know what the character is thinking, thus breaking faintly through the barrier that dramatic form imposes on interior insight: the barrier, that is, of a consistently objective point of view. In old comedy,† halfway through the play the chorus would stop acting and turn to the audience to deliver a speech to it on behalf of the author, frequently asking for a prize for the play. However, even though the audience is directly addressed in the *parabasis* of old comedy, the pur-pose is quite different from the soliloquy, for the thoughts revealed are the author's, not those of one of the characters; indeed, the content of this violation of the genre more often

---

* Sometimes in a special half-chanted poetic form called a *kommos*.

† Old comedy is a technical term for plays like those of Aristoph-anes: bawdy satires with a rigid, almost ritualistic form, and radical changes of mood. Since Aristophanes' are the only ones we still have, the number is limited.

than not had nothing to do with the play itself. The effect of both of these Greek devices is quite different from the close, rapid intimacy of the aside and soliloquy of Shakespeare's dramaturgy.

The nineteenth century was dominated by the form of stage with which you are probably most familiar, the window stage. This stage is at one end of a large room, separated from the audience by a proscenium arch ("proscenium" means "in front of the scene") and a curtain that closes after each scene. With the audience indoors, more or less in the dark, and the light (first, of course, candles, and later electric footlights and floodlights) concentrated on the stage, there is less distraction. The people in the next row are virtually invisible. Consequently, the actors do not have to declaim so vociferously or dramatically to claim the audience's attention. Plays written for such a theater can therefore be quieter, more restrained, more delicate in the effects they present. Moreover, the separation of the audience from the stage gives somewhat the feeling of looking through a window. Therefore, the people on the stage can behave the way they would in private, in their own homes, even in a bedroom, without seeming out of place. Shakespeare, in contrast, infrequently presents bedroom scenes. (When he does, he makes use of a curtained recess at the very back of his stage; this small area of the Elizabethan stage corresponds to the whole of the picture-window stage.)

Actually, the indoor theater developed almost contemporaneously with the Shakespearean. Indeed, it has been conjectured that some of Shakespeare's last plays were written experimentally with the possibility of indoor presentation in mind. By the end of the seventeenth century and on into the eighteenth, the drama was basically an "indoor" art, best represented perhaps by the comedy of manners. This sophisticated, witty form concentrates on the drawing rooms and salons of high society, focusing on polite after-dinner conversation and more-or-less casual flirtation. Later styles became more democratic in their concerns, paying more attention to the common man and less to the highest levels of society, but continued this quieter, more private tone that the window stage encouraged. The culmination of the progression toward domesticity was perhaps reached in the work of Henrik Ibsen, whose style was realistic and whose characters are ordinary, respectable, middle-class businessmen, teachers, and doctors.

In the twentieth century there has been much experimentation with the theater. The development of electric stage-lighting encouraged experimentation with peculiar lighting effects, particularly in expressionistic drama, which portrays inner states of mind rather than objective happenings. For example, Willy Loman in Arthur Miller's *Death of a Salesman* acts out his daydreams visibly before the audience. The people he remembers walk and talk with him, sometimes the same actors that are with him in the "present."

Other developments include a breaking-down of the barrier the proscenium arch presented between actors and audience. For example, in the plays of Thornton Wilder, Jean Anouilh, and (in *The Glass Menagerie*) Tennessee Williams a presenter may explain things to the audience, with varying degrees of role-playing; a character may even comment to the audience on how he is playing the role, or what kind of play he is in. This technique represents a breakdown of dramatic illusion. Shakespeare did something similar only in an occasional epilogue or prologue; but his asides and soliloquies (even when making topical allusions) are spoken by the actor as character, not by the actor as actor. The modern practice is itself, of course, a convention. When the actor speaks words written for him by the playwright, even if the words are presumed to come from him as actor, they do not in fact come from the man himself. He is now not just an actor playing a role, but an actor playing an actor playing a role. The breaking of the convention is itself a convention.

A popular contemporary theatrical design, the theater-in-the-round, is also partly a closer involvement of the audience with the action on the stage. A small theater-in-the-round lends itself to strong feelings of intimacy. I had the pleasure of seeing *Who's Afraid of Virginia Woolf?* in such a theater with only four rows of seats. Sitting in the first row, with my feet on the stage carpet, I had to uncross my legs to let the actors pass by as they roamed behind the sofa in front of me. The play concerns a vicious and bitter domestic quarrel enacted before several visitors. The small theater with no barrier between actor and audience encouraged a claustrophobic feeling of sharing in the action, and I found myself averting my eyes when the actors looked in my direction for fear they would notice that I was there and turn their stinging vituperation on me. The two significant factors here were the size of the theater and the absence of any physical separation between audience and stage.

These pages have been concerned with convention, and with a particular kind of convention: the physical nature of the theater itself. Without considering which causes which—whether the concept of drama shapes the theater or whether the theater shapes the concept of drama—one can be confident that the two are intimately related. The stateliness and formality of Greek tragedy, on an outdoor stage separated from a huge audience by an area for ritualized dancing and chanting; the fast-paced, richly poetic, action-filled drama of Shakespeare—with occasional asides to the audience, many of whom were standing and apt to be distracted if their attention was not held—presented in an enclosed courtyard; the witty comedy of manners, with its emphasis on conversation, and the domestic complications of Ibsen's bourgeoisie, both presented in an isolated intimacy of the actors among themselves, separated from the audience by the proscenium arch; modern experimentation with bridging the gap between audience and actors, as in the theater-in-the-round; all of these testify to the interaction of the theater in which the play is to be presented with the dramatic conception, in a broad sense, the style, of the play itself.

Convention affects drama more immediately and directly than it affects other genres. Convention affects drama because drama as a genre is witnessed event. The audience presumably is witnessing reality. Since what they see is objective, the obvious necessity that what they see differ in some way from literal event requires the audience's cooperation, their willing suspension of disbelief, to use Coleridge's phrase. The discrepancies between what they see and what they know to be normal, or real, or actual, are immediately obvious, and must be ignored. The platform stage itself does not exist except in the theater. The novel selects just as much as drama selects, but what it omits or alters is not immediately visible. For this reason, it is easier to read an old novel and not be startled than it is to watch a play using unfamiliar conventions and not be startled. The audience must conventionally accept the restrictions upon literal event within which the dramatist creates his illusion of reality.

The student who knows the major conventions of the historical tradition can anticipate what he will be asked to accept. The student who does not know the particular conventions of the play he watches (or reads) should be alert for the unexpected, for the obviously unreal. Such departures from what he expects may well be conventions he has not yet learned. A methodological question such a student should ask is, "Can things that I find unacceptable, that radically violate my expectations, be explained as conventions I am not used to?" In applying the concept of convention he can also ask, "How much of the physical theater am I supposed to see? What am I supposed to ignore? How is what I am supposed to see related to what I am supposed to ignore?" (The more what you actually see approximates what you are supposed to see, the more realistic the style and the fewer the conventions.) "How great is the aesthetic distance between the actors and the audience? between the members of the audience?"

In the last analysis, however, there is no methodological substitute for factual historical knowledge of the tradition within which the dramatist worked. This knowledge of convention is even more important when the play is read rather than seen, requiring mental staging by the audience-reader himself. Introductions are meant to be read; for the novice play-reader, they may be essential.

Sometimes the playwright may define his own conventions. One very recent comedy concerns a power failure and the consequent blackout.* The convention employed by the author is that when the lights are actually out, they are on in the play; when the lights are actually on, they are out in the play. Since they are "out" for most of the play, but really on, the audience can see the gropings, fumblings, and errors that the actors are presumed not to see. Such specific conventions usually define themselves clearly enough to pose little difficulty. With the historical convention, however, there is no substitute for knowledge.

D. Other Technical Concepts

Irony in drama most typically involves a contradiction between what one of the characters believes to be true and

---

* Peter Shaffer, *Black Comedy*.

what the action or plot shows to be true. Frequently what the character thinks turns out to be true in quite a different way from what he had originally meant. The audience, of course, must either know the character's error as he makes it, or be reminded of it in restrospect; otherwise the irony doesn't function. The typical irony of fiction was a conflict between the standards of the character and the standards of the audience. What is traditionally called "dramatic irony" is a conflict between the dramatic character's knowledge of fact and what the action of the plot reveals.

The tragedy *Oedipus* provides many examples of dramatic irony. For example, Oedipus promises to punish the killer even if the killer is a member of his own family; then the killer turns out to be himself. Oedipus curses the man who conceals information with exile; the direction of the curse is reversed when Oedipus, who is responsible for forcing the tale from unwilling witnesses, exiles himself, not the concealer but the revealer of information.

Another example of dramatic irony appears in *King Lear*, as the bastard Edmund falsely accuses the good son Edgar of betraying their father, Gloucester. Hearing Edmund's accusations, the intemperate Gloucester cannot stand uncertainty: "I would unstate myself to be in a due resolution," he says. That is, "I would give up my estate if I could be sure." And ironically enough it is by the loss of his estate to Edmund, who forcibly takes it, that Gloucester will become sure.

Reversal of intention is a form of dramatic irony, in which a character attempts to accomplish one thing and actually accomplishes the opposite. *Oedipus* furnishes a classic example. Tiresias has accused Oedipus of being the killer of Laius; Oedipus, naturally not believing the charge, concludes that Creon must have put Tiresias up to accusing him, Creon hoping to get the crown. Jocasta comes in to settle the quarrel. Learning its cause, she reassures Oedipus by telling him that prophets like Tiresias don't know what they are talking about, and frequently make stupid mistakes. To put Oedipus' mind at rest, and prove her point, she says that Laius was killed by strangers where three roads meet, and not by their son, as a prophet had said would happen. But when Oedipus hears the words "where three roads meet," he remembers that he killed a man where three roads meet. And for the first time, he begins to think that there might possibly be truth in what

Tiresias said. Thus, Jocasta's effort to calm Oedipus and convince him that prophets are wrong produces the opposite effect, reversing her intention, and actually upsets him and convinces him that prophets may be right.

The nearest thing to a methodological question for getting at dramatic irony is "What is unexpected?" But this question applies the technical concept itself, since the unexpectedness is the character's error that produces irony.

Just as dramatic irony involves a conflict with what the plot reveals, so too character must be defined largely with reference to plot. Although other characters may tell us what a character is like, dramatic character is usually externalized, and expressed in actions. Thus, the character Kent in *King Lear* is blunt and direct, honest to the point of rudeness. But since he tells Lear what Lear needs to hear rather than the flattery Lear wants, and then sticks with Lear in his misfortune even though Lear has banished him, the audience's sympathies are solidly on Kent's side. By the time he has cursed the villain Oswald unmercifully up and down the stage, he has become so sympathetic a character that Shakespeare can put a wickedly accurate characterization of him in the mouth of the least sympathetic character in the play, Cornwall, the future blinder of Gloucester, without reducing Kent in our estimation. Cornwall describes Kent thus:

> This is some fellow,
> Who, having been prais'd for bluntness, doth affect
> A saucy roughness, and constrains the garb
> Quite from his nature: he cannot flatter, he,
> An honest mind and plain, he must speak truth:
> An they will take it so; if not, he's plain. *

For all the accuracy of Cornwall's criticism, Kent's actions have already defined his true moral worth. Therefore, although it should be noted that even a villain may provide information about other characters, basically it is plot that defines moral character.

Character as personality may be defined in a number of ways, but often—particularly in comedy—it is defined visually, from the ridiculous masks of Greek old comedy, to the

* *King Lear*, Act II, Scene 2, lines 96-101.

crossed garters on yellow stockings worn by the gullible Malvolio in Shakespeare's *Twelfth Night*. In a more serious vein, Ibsen specifies that his sterile, life-opposing protagonist Hedda Gabler has thin hair, a visible symbol of her personality that is developed in the dialogue in contrast to the luxuriant hair of a productive, life-loving character. As with most serious drama and satire, however, character as personality here blends with character as morality.

The dominance of plot in drama perhaps makes it hard to distinguish personality from morality. A comedy of humors, which tends to be episodic and minimize plot, puts more emphasis on personality than on morality. Since plot depends upon motivation, and since morality after all means standard of choice, dramatic conflict almost always has moral overtones.

All of the technical questions suggested in the definition of character as an element of literature may be applied to drama except, of course, what the author himself directly tells us. Even this question may be asked when reading a play with long descriptive stage directions such as those of George Bernard Shaw.

But such lengthy descriptions as Shaw's are not possible when the play is presented. The emphasis falls upon what is seen, upon appearance and action. Since such character sketches often are not given even in stage directions, a methodological approach that may help is for the student to make a written character sketch himself. For example, sketches of the major characters in *Oedipus* might come out like this:

Oedipus: Concerned for welfare of city: asks what the crowd of suppliants wants; sends to oracle to find out how to get rid of plague; tries to follow oracle's instructions by finding killer of Laius, former king. Hot-tempered or quick-tempered: before start of play, had killed a man (turns out to be Laius, his father) for pushing him off the road, and killed five of his servants too—seems a bit extreme; gets furious with Tiresias; after accusing Creon of treason, won't listen to his defense; threatens to torture shepherd to make him talk. Smart: has already sent to oracle to find out how to lift plague before people ask; has already sent for Tiresias before the leader of the chorus suggests it; before play, solved riddle of Sphinx; accusation of Creon, though in fact wrong, is ingenious and reasonable. Optimistic: when hears he was a foundling, hopes he is a child of the gods—pride?

Jocasta: Dignified: treated respectfully by Oedipus; settles quarrel between him and Creon. Claims to be religious skeptic (challenges accuracy of soothsayers) but makes sacrifices to gods; inconsistency shows internal conflict, suggests possible theme about respecting gods.

Creon: Sensible, calm: defends himself against Oedipus' false charge of treason very reasonably—has power but not responsibility; reminds Oedipus at end that they should check with oracles before deciding what to do with him. (More evidence that Oedipus is hasty: unlike Creon, he decides immediately what should be done with him after he has blinded himself.) Creon maybe more pious than Oedipus. Religious theme?

Tiresias: Crusty old codger; just about as hot-tempered as Oedipus; although he says he won't tell Oedipus, when Oedipus chews him out he angrily tells him that he, Oedipus, is the killer (true), and hints that the victim is Oedipus' own father (true).

Chorus and *Choragos* (chorus leader): Very neutral. Sometimes react as though watching play—"what's going on? which character is right? what will happen?"—sometimes empathize with Oedipus, share his feelings, as when he hopes he is the child of a god; sometimes very pious in hoping oracles always turn out to be true, no matter what they say (even if they predict catastrophe!).

Oedipus clearly the protagonist: Onstage more of the time than any other single character; both the murderer and the detective, and therefore made or makes the major decisions that determine the plot of the play. Most of the conflicts involve him: he fights with Tiresias and Creon, disagrees with Jocasta, forces the shepherd to reveal the identity of the foundling baby (himself), and finally finds himself in conflict with himself, when as detective he discovers that he is the murderer and punishes himself.

Writing out such character sketches forces explicit analysis. They also lead directly into plot and theme.

The identification of character is a problem in drama, whether seen or read, at a very simple literal level. The name must be repeated often enough for the audience to know who is who; the reader is given the name for each speaker, but, if reading fast, may tend to brush past the names to get at the words. The dramatist frequently uses repetition, especially if there are very many characters, to fix names in the audience's memory from the beginning. In the first 53 lines of *Hamlet*, the names of four characters are repeated sixteen times: Francisco (who exits at line 18) is mentioned once; Marcellus, thrice; Bernardo, four times; and Horatio, the most important of the group, eight times. In Scene 2, when King Claudius first addresses Laertes, he names him four times in nine lines. Since Hamlet's name is in the title, it is naturally more memorable. Even so, of seven speeches addressed to him in his opening conversation, five give his name (the other two are one line apiece). This is, of course, a method used by the author, not by the student critic. When reading, as a substitute for the visual identifications that seeing a play gives, the student critic can copy out a list of names and relationships (it makes a good bookmark, too).

Through the dialogue when a character enters, the dramatist tries not only to fix names in the audience's mind but also, very frequently, to give an initial impression of what the character is. As a method of character analysis, therefore, looking at opening words, at the beginning of a character's life on the stage, frequently helps. Consider the opening speech of King Claudius, who first appears in Scene 2 of *Hamlet*:

> Though yet of Hamlet our dear brother's death
> The memory be green, and that it us befitted
> To bear our hearts in grief and our whole kingdom
> To be contracted in one brow of woe,
> Yet so far hath discretion fought with nature
> That we with wisest sorrow think on him,
> Together with remembrance of ourselves.

The syntactical convolutions of this complex sentence are extremely artificial. It begins with four lines of subordinate clauses, putting the independent clause off until line 5 ("discretion hath fought with nature"). Even then, the major idea of the sentence does not come until the last half of line 6 and line 7 ("we . . . think on him,/ Together with remembrance of ourselves.") The speech continues:

> Therefore our sometime sister, now our queen,
> The imperial jointress of this war-like state, . . .

At this point, the reader (or hearer) confidently expects the sister queen to be the subject of the sentence. But no; the sentence continues:

> Have we, . . .

and the reader is caught up by the realization that the sister-queen is not the subject, but the direct object. But the direct object of what? having? The speech puts off the rest of the verb:

> Have we, as 't were with a defeated joy,
> With one auspicious and one drooping eye,
> With mirth in funeral and with dirge in marriage,
> In equal scale weighing delight and dole, . . .

(This is still the same sentence, and all of these artificial parallel paradoxes do not tell us how he has the queen; but at last it comes:)

> Taken to wife. . . .

It takes him almost seven lines to say "Therefore we have taken the queen to wife." These grammatical postponements of information indicate a man with something to hide; and the syntactical deception as to whether the queen is subject or direct object of the sentence befits a liar and a cheat. Contrast Hamlet's opening speech (after three one-line remarks), which opens "Seems, madam! nay, it is; I know not 'seems,'" and continues as an attack upon pretense. By the style of the king's first remarks and the style and content of Hamlet's opening remarks their characters are set in direct opposition. They are in fact the protagonist and antagonist of the play. The method of looking at characters as they first appear— the beginning of their parts in the play—may produce significant analytical conclusions.

Last words frequently are significant, too. Although the words are more meaningful for plot than for character, it is fun to note that the last words of the Fool in *King Lear*— "And I'll go to bed at noon"—are spoken in the middle of the play; thereafter, he simply vanishes, as Shakespeare, having no further use for him, drops him with a clever, concealed exit line.

Comparison of last words and deeds with first words and deeds must be made to determine whether a character develops or not. For example, consider Cordelia's last words in the same play. (She and Lear are prisoners of his daughters, her sisters, and she next appears onstage dead, carried by Lear.)

> For thee, oppressed king, I am cast down;
> Myself could else outfrown false Fortune's frown.
> Shall we not see these daughters and these sisters?

The very last line expresses the same independence of spirit that led her in the first act to refuse to flatter Lear, even at the cost of her inheritance, when she said,

> Sure, I shall never marry like my sisters,
> To love my father all.

But her last speech expresses more: it is also an assertion that Cordelia is not unhappy for herself, but for Lear; that for him she is "cast down." She means "unhappy," but the words also apply to the plot. She is killed for Lear; otherwise she would not be licked by Fortune. Lear has no longer any place in the world; he has passed beyond it in the magnitude of his suffering. Lear must die. But what can kill him? Only one thing: the death of Cordelia. For Lear, therefore, Shakespeare kills Cordelia. This dramatic necessity may not make you happy; but in Cordelia's self-awareness, shown by her last speech, it becomes an affirmation of her dedication to Lear. She has learned since the first act, for she does what her sisters claimed to have done, and what she denied she would do—she marries, but loves her father all.

Cordelia is a developing character, and comparing her attitudes at beginning and ending reveals this development. Sometimes, critics attack characters who are not the same throughout, if they regard the development as too improbable. For example, Edmund at the end of *Lear*, as he lies dying, tries to save the lives of Lear and Cordelia. Some have criticized this change as improbable characterization. Ironically, others have criticized Shakespeare for having Edmund wait so long after he is fatally wounded before deciding to try to save Lear and Cordelia. Shakespeare certainly knew that it was not typical of Edmund to try to save someone, for he has Edmund himself say that he will do it "despite of mine own nature." In fact, Edmund's violation of strict consistency of character relates to a major theme in the play, freedom of choice vs. naturalistic determination. The comparison of end with beginning thus may lead beyond definition of character to more inclusive problems.

How much consistency must the dramatist show in his characters? Critics disagree. The developing character, like Edmund, poses one kind of test case; the complex three-dimensional character poses another. Hamlet is a famous example.

Hamlet is both a man of action who reacts quickly and violently, and a man of thought who delays and delays. Evidence can be piled up for both characterizations. As a man of action he pursues the ghost, stabs Polonius without even being sure who he is, saves his own life by framing two messengers (Rosencrantz and Guildenstern), and is the only man who boards the pirate vessel that attacks his ship. As a man of thought, his first reaction to learning that his uncle murdered his father is to write down a philosophical reflection; he in fact waits months before attempting anything; and over and over, in soliloquy, he tells the audience that he is delaying without any reason. Critics still argue what kind of man Hamlet is. Every now and then, one says he is too inconsistent to be real; but the consensus of most is that Hamlet is, in his complexity, one of the most fully realized characters in all literature.

Methodologically, one may get at a complex character by looking for the unexplained. Sometimes this will be the little detail that does not quite fit, and suggests other aspects to his character than those that are fully developed. Sometimes, as in the case of Hamlet, the unexplained may be pointed out by a character in the play, as it is by Hamlet.

> I do not know
> Why yet I live to say 'This thing's to do',
> Sith I have cause and will and strength and means
> To do 't.*

* *Hamlet*, Act IV, Scene 4, lines 43-46.

And sometimes, as in this same case, the unexplained may be the very core of the personality.

Modern drama may use deliberate inconsistency for thematic reasons, as in the theater of the absurd. Ionesco in *The Chairs* plays with such inconsistency, radically altering his characters' behavior and speech—for example, from sentimental reminiscence to baby-talk to lewd sexuality—as part of his thematic affirmation that reality is absurd. When inconsistency reaches these proportions, the question to ask is not "What is unexplained?" but "What is unexpected? What startles me?" In this case, the answer would lead through the inconsistency of the characters toward an understanding of theme.

"What is unexplained?" is also a good question to apply in connection with plot analysis. Since so much time was devoted to discussion of plot in the earlier part of this chapter, these remarks will be brief. Making a plot summary is a good study device, partly for the sake of analysis, partly for the sake of memory. It has other uses too. Having made a plot summary of a play, go back over the play and check which pages are covered by which sentences in your summary. If you find long sections of the play, whole groups of pages, that do not appear in your plot summary, then there is a good chance that you have overlooked something the author thought important. Probably, such groups of unexplained pages mean that you have not understood what the plot really is. Plays, like Chekhov's, in which characters do not communicate with each other but always talk at cross-purposes, and in which many decisions are negative—failure to take advantage of an opportunity or to meet a crisis—will often seem to have no plot. Similarly, French neoclassical tragedy, such as Racine's, in which characters talk about the situation in which they find themselves, will contain page after page that a simple plot summary will not include. In both cases, a more sophisticated concept of plot—plot as psychological rather than physical action—will provide the explanation of the unexplained pages.

Consider, for example, Goethe's *Faust*. Although the play bubbles over with events such as murders, seduction, an orgy, and spell-bindings, students frequently have difficulty with the spiritual conflict in Faust's own soul. That is, they do not realize it is there. A straightforward summary of the first scene "Night: Faust's Study" might read like this:

> Wanting knowledge, Faust magically conjures
> up an earth-spirit, who denies Faust's claim
> to be his equal, and vanishes; his servant comes
> in and doesn't understand Faust's conviction
> that he doesn't know enough; when the servant
> has left, Faust decides to take poison, but hears
> an Easter choir, and remembering his youth,
> decides not to kill himself.

In one translation,* this scene occupies pages 43 to 57. The spirit is called up on page 47, leaves on page 48; the servant enters at the bottom of page 48 and leaves at the top of page 51; Faust lifts the poison to his lips on page 55, hears the choir, and on page 56 decides not to kill himself. Now, even allowing for the fact that Faust first sees the poison in its container at the bottom of page 53, and thinks about killing himself on page 54, there remain two groups of pages, comprising about 40 per cent of the scene, that are not included in the summary: pages 43 to 47 and the top of 51 to the bottom of 53. The student who gets this far finds himself confronted with something unexplained.

By going back to the unexplained pages, the student may find out that there really is something happening, and that Faust's long soliloquies are not static. Instead, he is alternating between despair at his ignorance and optimistic aspiration toward a better condition. He goes through a succession of ups and downs, depending on whether he is occupied with the knowledge he aspires toward or with the ignorance in which he feels himself virtually trapped. The student who, on rereading, explains the opening pages of the scene in this way, probably will avoid the mistake that many hurried readers make when they come to the suicide. For the contemplated suicide is not an act of despair, but a courageous venture toward the unknown. His decision not to kill himself reflects not simply joy in life, but abandonment of the desire to become godlike in knowledge. Moreover, not only will the student who has gone back and explained these pages,

* Tr. Philip Wayne (Baltimore, Md.: Penguin Books, 1958).

omitted by his original summary, understand the ending of the scene; such a student will also be more likely to recognize the complex ebb and flow of despair and aspiration that is Faust's major characteristic and a basic theme of the play.

Much later in the same play occurs a scene of six pages entitled "Walpurgis Night's Dream or the Golden Wedding of Oberon and Titania, A Lyrical Intermezzo." The devil has tried to satisfy Faust by taking him to a Walpurgis Night (German Halloween) orgy of witches and demons. Faust sees a vision of his human love, Gretchen, in danger. Then comes the peculiar scene of the "Dream or Golden Wedding." Thirty-seven characters make forty-four four-line speeches. Now, explaining this scene will not spell out plot action within the scene itself, for the scene *is* plotless. At least, however, after noticing that it does not advance the plot, a good reader certainly asks "Why is it included?" With inspiration and good footnotes, he may realize that it is a scattering blast of satiric buckshot, aimed at everything. Then, backing off and looking at the scene in its entirety, checking what immediately precedes and what immediately follows the scene, the good reader sees that the scene as a whole does serve a function within the plot: it is a distraction, an entertainment, by which the devil tries to keep Faust from going to help his human love, who really is in trouble. First summarizing, and then checking to see what the summary has omitted, and then trying to figure out why the nonsummarized pages were included by the author, the inquisitive student may thus explain for himself passages the weaker student allows to remain unexplained.

Satire in drama, like fictional satire, suffers from the absence of the author's voice. Drama is objective. It is no coincidence that the word "objective" has come to mean not simply "impartial" but also "expressing no evaluations." Drama's objectivity tends to obscure the evaluations that are at the heart of satire.

Two brief examples: Shaw's *Pygmalion* is clearly a love story, and the logic of the story as pure plot strongly requires the comic ending, that Eliza marry Professor Higgins. Since, however, he was concentrating on other things, Shaw did not settle the issue by showing the two at the play's end in a curtain clinch. Nevertheless, audiences were virtually unanimous in concluding that the romantic ending was intended.

Shaw, who was a wicked old satirist if there ever was one, rubbed his hands and chortled with unholy glee, and promptly dashed off an epilogue in which he explained at great length and in great detail why Eliza did not marry the professor, but married a fathead named Freddy instead. He even wrote some scenes for the first movie version, to make Freddy more important in the play and give a little basis to his epilogue. (The producers betrayed his satirist's intent, however, by showing Eliza coming back to Higgins at the very end.) This epilogue is clearly an attack on the audience's romantic inclinations, but it required Shaw to speak in his own person. And ultimately, the play's objectivity and the audience's predilections defeated him again, for *My Fair Lady* makes the romance even more explicit. Without the voice of the satirist to control the judgments, they may not go the way he intended.

Jean Anouilh's modern play *Antigone* centers on a conflict between an idealist (Antigone) and a practical politician. The play was produced in Nazi-occupied Paris, and was taken by the audience (fortunately, not by the Nazis) as the author probably intended it, as an attack on the German occupiers and their political totalitarianism. Since then, some very moral people have reversed this judgment, believing that Antigone was actually wrong in her conduct, and that within the context of the play—that is, without reading in "Nazis in Paris in 1943"—the practical politician is morally correct, and represents a better and more ethical way of life. The status of drama as witnessed event thus invites the audience to make its own judgments, and handicaps the satirist's corrective evaluations.

The objectivity of drama, which hampers satire, makes comedy natural to the stage. Of course, characters can be presented sympathetically onstage as well as in fiction, and that sympathy tends to keep the audience from laughing. Shakespeare's *Merchant of Venice* is structurally a comedy, moving toward an idyllic last act in which all the young men get all the young women, and the money, too. Shylock, however, is presented so realistically as a three-dimensional character that many readers tend to see him as a tragic protagonist rather than as a comic blocking character, a *senex iratus* in relation to his daughter, a miserly "humor" with a strong choleric desire for rigid legality in the main plot. The difference between the comic villain and the tragic protagonist depends upon how real his suffering is and on the extent to which we sympathize with him when he is overthrown.

Of course, in all comedy of the Bergsonian type, the methodological question "What is repeated?" becomes virtually a technical question based on Bergson's definition of what provokes laughter. Thus, Shylock's repeated exclamations about his ducats make him ridiculous and show how his miserliness is virtually an obsession. If, however, we see his exclamations when he finds his money gone as bordering on madness, then the suffering is too intense, and we find it hard to laugh. Molière's *Miser* similarly borders on tragedy, as he goes nearly mad when his money is stolen. King Lear's madness, which is not intended to be funny, comes out of his obsession with his evil daughters and is communicated in his repeated statements that the beggar's (the disguised Edgar's) daughters must have impoverished him. Thus, repetition, to be funny, must occur within the comic limits of acceptable suffering.

Attention to the end, of course, also is important in establishing the comic status of a play. Here, as with repetition, a methodological concept (looking at the ending for special clues) is virtually part of the technical definition of comedy. For comedies should end happily, one way or another. One of the strongest arguments for calling the equivocal *Merchant of Venice* a comedy is that Shylock, the nearly tragic character, disappears at the end of Act IV. Act V is all music, laughter, and love.

"What does the title suggest?" is always a good methodological question, and sometimes may clearly imply comic intent. A title like "A Funny Thing Happened on the Way to the Forum" would be inappropriate for most tragedies. Even the fact that the merchant of Venice is not Shylock ought to make you cautious about identifying him as a tragic protagonist. If the title sounds funny but the play isn't, then a satiric contrast exists between title and work, and if the play is not satirical it is badly titled. You might perhaps be amused at the full title of Peter Weiss's *Marat/Sade;* it is so cumbersome, it is virtually a joke itself: *The Persecution and Assassination of Jean-Paul Marat as Performed by the Inmates of the Asylum of Charenton under the Direction of the Marquis de Sade;* but the joke is satirical, not gay.

The same thing applies to names. Characters named Sir Fopling Flutter or Abhorson must be comic or a very ironic satire.

Reading comic dialogue to oneself is often hard to do perceptively. If you encounter passages that seem pointless to you in a play you know to be comedy, try reading them aloud, seeking the right tone of voice, and perhaps you will discover that the witty sophisticate is teasing the country bumpkin. The lines may become actually funny, if you objectify them yourself by reading out loud.

Tragedy too, of course, is objectified in drama, but some degree of feeling for or with the hero is necessary in tragedy. That is, the objectivity and impersonality of drama are more necessary for comedy than for tragedy.

The simple methodological device of asking what the title refers to may sometimes produce significant results—or at any rate, significant problems. The title *Oedipus the King* poses no problems: the titular character is the tragic protagonist. But in Shakespeare's *Julius Caesar*, the titular character is killed in the middle of the play. Does the title apply to what happens in the second half of the play? Some sophisticated critics talk about "the Caesar principle," seeing him and the kind of rule he stands for represented by Mark Antony. Lines like "O Julius Caesar, thou art mighty still," long after his death, suggest that Shakespeare was not just being careless when he chose the title, but meant that in some way Julius Caesar dominates the whole play.

The title of Sophocles' *Antigone* raises a similar problem, for she too disappears long before the play is over. Some have argued that this tragedy is mistitled, and that in fact Creon is the tragic protagonist. The German philosopher Hegel implicitly agreed that the play was misnamed. He, however, would presumably have preferred the title *Antigone and Creon,* or even *Antigone vs. Creon,* for he thought the tragic quality of the play derived from the conflict between two standards of good conduct, Antigone's and Creon's, each of which was in its own way right, but which in the tragic dilemma turn out to be incompatible with each other. This kind of tragic conflict has been called "ethical tragedy," to distinguish it from the so-called "tragedy of fate," such as perhaps *Oedipus*.

Examining the title may genuinely lead to profound questions concerning the nature of the tragedy. Whether the title really does apply, as in *Julius Caesar*, or seems to be imperfect, as in *Antigone*, the methodological question "Why is the play named what it is?" deserves attention.

Comedy might be called making the best of a bad situation, whereas tragedy is the best made worst. In tragedy as with comedy, therefore, attention to the beginnings and endings, which is usually methodological, merges with the technical critical concept, "tragedy."

The discussion of tragedy in Part I pointed out that various definitions of tragedy may emphasize plot, or character, or theme. Any of the techniques and methods for analyzing these aspects of a play may be very relevant to the clarification of its tragic nature.

The word "scene" derives from drama, naming the part of the ancient Greek theater that constituted a background for the action. Convention largely determines what we expect in the way of scenery, as has been discussed earlier in this chapter. In Shakespearean dramaturgy, many scenes were not definitely located at all, and place and time might shift very freely, with little visible change—perhaps a prop or two—to indicate the changes in the locale that the dialogue required. When the dialogue required no particular location, the audience was not expected to think in terms of a particular location. The ease with which the audience assimilated this is reflected in *King Lear* in Scenes 2, 3, and 4 of Act II. Scenes 2 and 4 are identified in most editions by added stage directions, "without the gates of Gloucester's Castle"; Scene 3 is labeled "open country in the neighborhood of Gloucester's Castle." But on the Elizabethan stage, Kent, who was locked into the stocks by the castle gate at the end of Scene 2, would remain onstage—sleeping through Edgar's soliloquy in Scene 3—until Lear enters to begin Scene 4. Edgar has just fled the castle to save his life, and is not likely to be hanging around right outside its very doors. But because location on the Elizabethan stage is not identified by visual impression, the audience could see Kent out of the corners of its eyes and still not associate Edgar with any specific place.

At the opposite extreme, French neoclassicism generally

observed the three unities: unity of time, unity of place, and unity of action. (The three were commonly held to have been recommended by Aristotle, but actually only the last—unity of plot—is important to Aristotle. He mentions unity of time casually, and ignores unity of place.) Ideally, unity of time and place meant that the scene never changed, and that the presumed time of the play equaled the actual time in the theater. In practice, of course, such restriction was virtually impossible and the pragmatic compromise was to accept scenes within the same city, and time schemes up to 24 or even 30 hours. As recommendations to playwrights, these two unities are very naïve, since (as Dr. Samuel Johnson pointed out) a Londoner who can believe himself in Rome in Act I can just as easily believe himself in Venice in Act II. They also overlook the psychological flexibility of time. In fairness, one should note that the greatest French neoclassical tragedian, Racine, said very clearly that the three unities were tools, not rules; and that he followed them to produce an effect of intense concentration.

Usually, the parts of a play bear some relationship to changes in time and place. If time and place are important (as they sometimes are), attention to the act and scene divisions of the play will usually turn up place divisions, which may have broader significance. The alternation between scenes in Egypt and scenes in Rome in *Antony and Cleopatra* has thematic significance; the movement in the last act to the idyllic Belmont in *Merchant of Venice* helps establish the play as comedy, shifting literally from an inferior society to a superior one by leaving Venice behind.

In connection with the methodological question "What parts is the play divided into," we may note how Shakespeare could give the illusion of staging a battle. In *Henry V*, for example, or in *Richard III*, although Shakespeare's Globe would not encompass several tons of mounted steel, the battle is seen by his audience in the anticipatory dreams of the soldiers on the night before; in the marshaling of the forces as day dawns; and in descriptions of the progress of battle by participants scattered across the field. But his basic battle technique was the pacing of scenes: a series of rapid entrances and exits of armed men, shouting hurried commands of war, all in different parts of the field. For example, in the last 220 lines of *Troilus and Cressida,* a play that ends with a battle, there are 7 scenes, with 42 stage directions reading "enter" or "exit," involving 34 people (counting a man each time he is onstage, but not counting those identified simply as "Myrmidons" or "others"). There are also four sword-fights and one killing of an unarmed man in this same 220-line span, all onstage. For the rest of Shakespeare's battle supplies, a flourish here, a trumpet sounding there, and an occasional cannon shot (such as set fire to the roof during a performance of *Henry VIII* in 1613 and burned down the theater) round out his wars.

The relationship of scene to tone and mood, and therefore to audience response, should be obvious to anyone who has enjoyed a bright spring day after a dismal wintry one. The beginning of the play—either as seen, as described in the opening stage direction, or as revealed in the opening dialogue—should be closely examined for implications about the play to come. Ibsen decorates his stages carefully, both with explicit symbols and with more indefinite mood controllers (e.g., in manipulation of brightness, openness to the out-of-doors, etc.). Shakespeare too uses poetic descriptions of scenery and surroundings for both mood and thematic reasons. Francis Fergusson has argued persuasively that the opening scene of *Hamlet,* in which two guards enter from opposite sides, peering at each other through the night and not at first identifying each other, represents the ignorance and uncertainty in which all of the characters try to find out what the others really are; and, of course, the darkness (described by the dialogue) both sets an ominous mood and becomes symbolic in the second scene in Hamlet's black costume.

The unexpected or outstanding should be noted in this connection, for Hamlet's suit of inky black contrasts visually with the multicolored finery of the rest of the court of Denmark. Costuming may be considered a part of scenery for it both contributes to the sense of date and is part of the visual impact of the total spectacle. Hamlet's unusual costume should be noticed (in production, of course, it is more obvious than in reading), and explanation sought. It singles him out as the protagonist; it shows that he still mourns his father, which of course is explicitly why he wears it; it separates him from the falsehood of the court as a whole; it links with death he who will be responsible for the deaths of seven people besides himself; and in his dialogue with his mother, it becomes a symbol of the relationship of appearance to reality, as he attacks her use of the word "seems" and maintains his inward grief. This discrepancy in Hamlet's dress in contrast with the dress of others can therefore point the way to many other aspects of the play. The methodological question is, "What is unusual? How do I explain it?"

Frequently, the methodological questions illumine scene, including costume, by relating it to theme. The most important single method for getting at theme, however, is hunting for repetitions. Earlier discussions of plot have shown how Shakespeare duplicates plot situations, often with thematic implications. Evil or folly at the center of society is mirrored by evil or folly at the edges of society; if a king is evil, society is corrupt; if a duke is helplessly in love, the rustics are ridiculously in love.

Hamlet's anger when his mother even hints his mourning may not be genuine shows his hatred of pretended grief. The same theme appears when he comments on the traveling actor's semblance of grief, noting how he cries for a woman he doesn't really know ("What's Hecuba to him, or he to Hecuba,/That he should weep for her?"). It shows again when near the very end of the play Hamlet leaps into Ophelia's grave to outdo her brother's show of grief, ending contemptuously, "Nay, an thou'lt mouth, I'll rant as well as thou." The repetitions of protest at false grief imply a strong thematic interest in hypocrisy, which can, after more analysis, be related to the whole play—for example, to the peering through the mist of the opening scene, mentioned above; to the entry Hamlet makes in his notebook, when told his uncle killed his father: "meet it is I set it down,/That one may smile, and smile, and be a villain"; and to the false brightness of the court that surrounds the murderous King Claudius.

Every now and then a title will state a theme. A play by Pirandello bears the title *Right You Are, If You Think You Are*, which is the theme of the play: thinking something is true makes it true. The satiric title of the movie *Dr. Strangelove: or How I Learned to Stop Worrying and Love the Bomb* is a criticism of people who "love" the atom bomb instead of worrying about it. Their "love" is "strange"—their attitude perverted.

The end of a play is a good place to look, frequently, for

an explicit statement of a theme. In the Pirandello play just cited, each of the three acts ends the same way: the character Laudisi says ironically that they now know the truth, and the curtain falls as he bursts out laughing. This repetition at the end of each of the major divisions is clearly thematic. Throughout the play, the "truth" that the other characters pursue is the identity of Signora Ponza. She finally appears onstage, and in the next to the last speech—just before Laudisi once more crows triumphantly over the impossibility of establishing a public, objective truth—she says she is whoever they believe her to be.

Pirandello was preoccupied with variations on this theme, and another play of his—*Six Characters in Search of an Author*—ends with one group crying "Pretense!", a character protesting that it is not pretense but reality, and another character, in charge of the proceedings, giving up the whole thing as a waste of time.

Of course, what appears at the end of a play is not always the best or the most sophisticated or even a halfway decent statement of theme. Even Laudisi's comments ("now we have the truth") must be recognized as irony, meaning the opposite of what he says. But that is obvious from his laughter and the bewilderment of the people he addresses.

Sometimes, such final statements are merely plausible, not profound. Thus, *Oedipus* ends with this speech:

> Dwellers in our native Thebes, behold, this is Oedipus,
> who knew the famed riddle, and was a man most mighty;
> on whose fortunes what citizen did not gaze with envy?
> Behold into what a stormy sea of dread troubles he hath
> come!
> Therefore, while our eyes wait to see the destined final
> day, we must call no one happy who is of mortal race,
> until he hath crossed life's border, free from pain.*

Now, it is certainly true that Oedipus seemed to have it made, and that suddenly and unexpectedly his whole world collapsed horribly. No one who knew his life history up to the

---

* In *The Complete Greek Drama*, ed. Whitney J. Oates and Eugene O'Neill, Jr. (New York: Random House, 1938), vol. I, pp. 416-417.

end of the play would want to call the blind, beggared, exiled, incestuous patricide and regicide "happy." The action therefore confirms the thematic statement of the chorus, just quoted: call no man happy until he has died, for you never know what may come next. Many critics, however, reject this formulation of the play's theme, one (David Grene)* even saying that the main purpose of the chorus in Greek drama seems to be reducing the theme to its cheapest and most inferior expression. The problem in this case is one of complexity and importance. Most critics feel that *Oedipus the King* is about more important things than whether you can be sure a happy person will never suffer misfortune or reversal. And they are right. But if you at least recognize this part of the total theme of the play, you will have made a start; because at a simple level, the play really does show what the chorus says it shows. So look closely at endings for thematic statements; look carefully, and critically, but look.

Since symbolism is closely related to theme, you should expect repetition to be a methodological clue to it as well as to theme. For example, several images in *King Lear* are often repeated, including animal images and, perhaps more frequently, images of torture. One of the critical images is the image of seeing. Goneril says she loves Lear "Dearer than eyesight"; Lear banishes Cordelia from his sight, and Kent too: Kent retorts, "See better, Lear, and let me still remain the true blank of thine eye." Cordelia wants it known that she is banished for not having "a still-soliciting eye"; she says she leaves "with washed eyes." All of these are from the first scene. There is a lessening of the density of eye-metaphors in the remainder of the play, but it is more than compensated for by the emergence of a pervasive symbolism of blindness-as-ignorance vs. eyesight-as-knowledge. This symbolism begins with Gloucester's demand to see the letter he won't need his glasses for. It is developed further by Kent's disguise, which Lear cannot see through, as later no one sees through Edgar's disguise; it reaches a first climax when Lear descends into mental blindness, and Gloucester is precipitated into physical blindness; is reemphasized in the encounter between Lear and Gloucester; and is Lear's dying phrase: "Look there,

---

* In *Three Greek Tragedies in Translation* (Chicago, Ill.: University of Chicago Press, 1942), pp. 5-6.

look there!" The early repetitions of the eye-metaphor therefore serve as preparation for the symbolic concern with moral insight manifested later.

Sometimes, an unexpectedly emotional response may identify a symbol. When a character reacts with more than normal emotion to something fairly innocuous, he may be seeing a symbolic meaning in it; and if he does, we should too. At the end of one of the acts of *Hedda Gabler,* Hedda burns the only copy of a manuscript written by the man she jilted. The man wrote the manuscript with the naïve help and inspiration of a young woman named Thea; Hedda is jealous of Thea's power to inspire. As she pushes the pages of the manuscript into the fire, Hedda gloats exultingly to herself, "I'm burning your baby, Thea, burning your baby!" Now, besides deserving a little special attention just because it is at the end of the act, that gloating claim of infanticide is overemotional. But if you look more closely, you may see just what the nature of her abnormality is. You may remember that Hedda herself is pregnant, and hates being pregnant; she does not want a baby. Moreover, the manuscript is about the future. Babies are basically creatures of the future, like the manuscript; so the concept of futurity is repeated. By now, we have stated a symbolic meaning to the overemotional act: symbolically, Hedda is destroying not only her unwanted child, but the whole future. Symbolic destruction of the future is literally enacted at the end of the play, when Hedda kills herself, and destroys her own future.

Repetition, attention to endings of various divisions, the unexpectedly overemotional: these methodological approaches have led, in this case, to a host of analytical conclusions about technical aspects of the play, through the identification of a symbol—a symbolic act that defines Hedda's character, reveals her motivation, foreshadows the catastrophe of the plot (her suicide), thematically implies that living is looking to the future, and makes the play tragic—for Hedda is true to her inner nature when she kills herself. This example may fittingly conclude the discussion of drama. It shows that the suggested methods and the technical terms lead not to dissection, but to an understanding of the essential unity of dramatic art.

4. Poetry

A. Presentation

Poetry has been identified as involving the presence of the author and of the work, but not of the audience.* (Remember that "presence" does not mean literally there, but treated as though there.)

Lyric poetry is most typical of this genre. Lyric poems are songlike. It is the nature of the poetic genre to require performance, as a song requires performance, and to have form, as a song has form; in these ways the work is present. It should be thought of as sung by one person, as the expression of one person's attitudes and beliefs, like a love song; in these ways the author is present. And just as songs do not usually address the audience who is hearing them, in this sense, no matter how many people are in fact in the auditorium, the audience is not present.

Since this genre is probably the least familiar, both theoretically and practically, let's go over its definition again. As previously mentioned, poetry is meant to be said and heard.

* See pp. 87ff.

English teachers tell students to read poems out loud and to listen to the sound for two reasons.

First, whether in fact read silently from the printed page or in fact recited, poetry is meant to exist as audible sound. It is not to be experienced as something internal and subjective, but as something existing outside the reader. It has objectivity just as drama has objectivity, because it is to be performed. That is what "the work is present" means with regard to poetry: the poem is overheard, just as drama is witnessed.

Secondly, poetry is not only to be heard, but also to be spoken. Poetry implies a speaker—not actors, but a speaker. If the poem contains the words "I weep," the speaker cannot omit the words and cry artificial tears instead. Nothing in a poem corresponds to the stage directions that can be omitted from dramatic performance once the set has been created. If a scene is described in a poem, a speaker cannot omit the words describing it just because he has picked some posies or painted some rocks on a backdrop. The poem is not enacted to be seen, but spoken to be heard. The speaker of a poem stands for the author, the creator of the poem and its sound. This is what "the author is present" means for poetry.

When you read something out loud, you are no longer functioning as audience; you are functioning either as character within the work or as author-speaker. Of course, if you read a play aloud, you are speaking as a character in the play. Now, why isn't the speaker simply part of the poem in the same way the character is part of the play? When you read a poem aloud, you speak as whoever says the poem. The speaker of the poem says the whole poem, and therefore creates it, is responsible for all of it. In contrast, the character in a play does not say all of the lines, and is not responsible for what the other characters say. He reacts to what they say, but the work consists of the interaction between the characters of the play, and not of what any one character says; the character in a play does not speak as author.

Reading plays aloud does not work as well as reading poems aloud, because of the difference in genre. A play is supposed to be a work seen by an audience. As soon as you read the play aloud, you stop being audience, and become part of the work as one of the characters in the play; in a sense, you are one of the actors playing a part in the production of the play. It is very hard both to read the play as one of the characters in it (or as several in succession) and, simultaneously, to see it mentally the way the audience sees it, as witnessed event. But with poetry the situation is different. A poem is a work recited by an author. Therefore, you can read the poem aloud and become in effect the author, the speaker of the work, without becoming schizophrenic.

Then, why not say the poem is part of the speaker, since he says it all? Why not say "Only the author is 'present' in the genre of poetry"? The poem is more than part of the speaker-author, because the poem has a kind of independence from what the speaker wants to say. That is, the poem has a form which controls what may be said. Certain words must rhyme; certain patterns must be followed. When a speaker recites a sonnet, he is not simply pouring forth his emotions and thoughts. He is very explicitly creating an art work, reciting a sonnet. The formal independence of the poem means that poetry is to be experienced as a created work that is recited by an author.

Is the audience never "present" in poetry? The answer depends on whether the work in question addresses an audience (not another character in the work). If it does address an audience, then its genre is not poetry, but epic. An epic might begin "I sing to you of ancient warriors. . . ." Consider a poem that begins:

> Listen, my children, and you shall hear
> Of the midnight ride of Paul Revere.
> 'Twas the eighteenth of April, in seventy-five;
> Hardly a man is now alive
> Who remembers that famous day and year.

This poem is less typical of the genre of poetry than it is of epic, in that there is a speaker, a tale to be told—the work— and an audience that is not part of the work's contents but is addressed explicitly within the poem. To the audience the author-speaker can make comments about the work he is performing for them (e.g., how long ago all this happened) as Homer does. If the poem does not address the audience in this way, then it is truly poetry in the sense in which the genre is being defined.

Note that the poem may be addressed to someone, and still be in the poetic genre. A love poem that is addressed to the beloved is speaking to her not as the poem's audience, but as part of the work. The audience is therefore still "absent" from the experience of the work.

A simple way out of the difficulties of this definition is to give up the whole affair and say that "poetry" means simply versification. However, versification, although a very useful concept, is not a genre. It is part of a different system of classification, which distinguishes making verses from writing prose. The difference between verse and prose, of course, cuts across the present classification into genres. Therefore, either we don't think of poetry as a genre, and we handle it as a different kind of term (versification), or we think very closely about the way poetry is presented, along the lines suggested above.

B. Structure

Fiction is experienced; drama is witnessed; poetry is overheard. The oral-aural aspect of poetry—that poetry is to be spoken and heard—makes sound very important. Sound is physical, and different sounds have different physical qualities. For example, "keest" and "rulm" are different physically, just as red and blue are different physically. The interrelationships of sounds, considered purely as sound, can be interesting simply in themselves. In James Thurber's short story "The Secret Life of Walter Mitty," the protagonist daydreams constantly. In most of his dreams, there is a piece of equipment (an airplane, a surgical mechanism) which goes "ta-pocketa-pocketa-pocketa" until it begins to break down and starts going "ta-pocketa-pocketa-queep, pocketa-queep." These sounds are fun, even if meaningless.

But sounds are most interesting when they express something human, when they express some aspect of the psyche; particularly, when they express states of mind, or moods. The anguished cry of Linus deprived of his blanket or Charlie Brown when his kite tangles in the omnipresent tree—"ARRGH!"—expresses a mood or state of mind. Therefore it is more interesting than "keest" or "rulm," which as far as I know express nothing. At least, they express no mood of mine as I write them. In a given context they might turn out to be very expressive, just as red and blue can be very expressive in context. Think of someone red with anger or blue with cold; or, in a different context, someone red with shame or in a blue funk. If I stubbed my toe, you would probably expect me to say "keest" rather than "rulm," because "keest" is a more violent sound: the *k* and *t* are explosive, and because unvoiced (the vocal chords are not used in saying them) they are sharp; the *e* is a tight sound, the jaws close together and the tongue held high and forward. But if you said to me, "You look like you have a hangover," you would probably expect me to say "rulm" rather than "keest," because "rulm" is a dull, depressed sound, practically a moan: the consonants are all voiced, all are continuants (the sound can be held, unlike *k* or *t* or *d*); the *u* is as dull as the word "dull" itself, hollow and relaxed. Even meaningless sound has an expressive quality in the right context.

Poems, of course, do not go very far before introducing sounds that are not merely physical, but also have meaning. "Diddle-diddle-dumpling" goes immediately into "my son John"; "Hi-diddle-diddle" goes immediately into "the cat and the fiddle."

But most poems are *words* all the way through: sounds that are not just physical, and not just expressive in context, but meaningful; sounds that are verbal symbols. The choice of words is diction.

Words are units of sound, and also units of meaning. As units of sound, we have said they have two aspects: the sound itself, which is purely physical; and the mood the sound may express in context, which is psychic. As units of meaning words also have two aspects: the message they communicate, and the mood they express. For the individual word, that message is the denotation, its dictionary definition. The mood a word expresses is its connotation. "Negro woman" and "Negress" have the same denotation: a female member of the Negro race. But they have different connotations: the former is neutral, the latter is critical and condescending. As another example, consider two adjectives with identical denotations but quite different connotations, *canine* and *doggy*.

These aspects of words may be summarized in outline:

I. Sound.
   A. Physical quality (liquid, like *l* and *r*; voiced, like *r*, *d*, and *th* in *the*; explosive, like *d* and *t*; sibilant, like *s* and *z*; guttural, like *k* and *g*; open, like *aw*; closed, like *ee*; unvoiced, like *s*, *t*, *k*, and *th* in *thin*; continuants, like *l*, *m*, and *ng*).
   B. Expressive quality: mood.

II. Meaning.
   A. Denotation: message (unaffected by translation or substitution of synonyms).
   B. Connotation: associated mood.

Poetic diction is the selection of words in view of their expressive sounds and expressive connotations in order to produce a particular tone. Tone is the mood communicated; it is the basis of structure in poetry.

The expressive quality of words is tone. Poetic tone is closely related to "tone of voice." The way someone says "hello," his tone of voice, tells the visitor whether he is welcome or not. The throaty, sustained invitation of a "Hello" by a movie siren; the neutrally interrogative "Hello?" of someone answering the phone; the angrily interrogative "Hello?" of someone who has emerged from the shower and is holding the phone in one corner of the towel as he drips puddles on the hall rug; the discouragingly disappointed "Hello" of the girl who expected her fiancé and finds at the door the creep from the apartment upstairs; the friendly "Hello!" of a boyhood chum—all express mood through sound. The poet tries to control mood through his choice of words, that is, through the poetic tones of his diction. By choosing words which have come through usage to have certain connotations, he tries to specify and require certain tones of voice. The differences between "Well, hello-hello-hello, there," "How do you do?" "Yes, darn it!" "Oh. Hello, I guess," and "Hi, ole buddy" specify different tones of voice.

Poetic tone also controls mood through the qualities of the sounds themselves. Laughter that "cackles" is different from laughter that "gurgles"; to "murmur lullingly of love" is different from "whispering secrets of sex." "Murmuring" and "whispering" are almost synonyms; but "whispering lullingly of love" and "murmuring secrets of sex" use sound far less effectively than when the two verbs are switched.

So far, we have considered tone as a quality of individual words. How does tone determine structure in the poem as a whole? Tone affects structure in two ways: poems are structured in terms of both sound and connotation.

Consider first the structuring of poems in terms of sound. Sound as structure is versification. Since the most useful technical concepts (such as iamb, blank verse, assonance, and sonnet) are defined in Part I under the heading "Versification," those definitions will not be repeated here. It might be noted that poetic forms are so much more explicit than dramatic and fictional forms that some of the methodological questions suggested earlier are virtually incorporated into the technical concepts themselves. Thus, attention to beginning and end appears in technical versification as alliteration and rhyme (word beginnings, line and word endings); repetition is the basis of the definitions of most of the terms; and any scansion must identify the parts—rhyming, metrical, or stanzaic—which define the form.

Effective versification arranges sound in order to produce a desired tone. That is, the specific pattern and sounds used should not be chosen arbitrarily, but as effective means to defining one particular tone. For example, Shelley's "Ode to the West Wind" aims (in part) at a sense of the haste and urgency of the wind, and concludes talking about its relationship to the future. In choosing his verse pattern, Shelley did not select the heroic couplet, which because every rhyme comes in successive lines tends to stop the movement after each couplet. Instead, Shelley chose to use *terza rima*. His opening stanza is:

> O wild West Wind, thou breath of Autumn's being,
> Thou from whose unseen presence the leaves dead
> Are driven, like ghosts from an enchanter fleeing,
>
> Yellow, and black, and pale, and hectic red,
> Pestilence-stricken multitudes: O thou,
> Who chariotest to their dark wintry bed
>
> The wingèd seeds, where they lie cold and low,
> Each like a corpse within its grave, until
> Thine azure sister of the Spring shall blow

Her clarion o'er the dreaming earth, and fill
(Driving sweet buds like flocks to feed in air)
With living hues and odors plain and hill:

Wild Spirit, which art moving everywhere:
Destroyer and preserver: hear, oh hear!

The mood to be communicated is the sense of dynamic forward movement. At the end of the poem, this dynamic forward movement is expressed with an evaluation, in terms of hope:

The trumpet of a prophecy! O Wind,
If Winter comes, can Spring be far behind?

In content, the first stanza is more ambiguous than the conclusion, emphasizing about equally the wind as destroyer (it blows the leaves from the trees; as the breath of autumn, it is killing most vegetation) and the wind as preserver (it spreads seeds that will grow in the spring). But Shelley wishes to establish the tone of forward motion, appropriate here for the physical nature of the wind, and appropriate in foreshadowing the end of the poem, which looks forward to the spring. "Looking forward" is the basic quality of terza rima. Its rhyme scheme (*aba, bcb, cdc,* etc.) presents tercets in which the middle line anticipates, looks forward to, the rhyming pair of the next tercet. Thus, no tercet is complete in itself. The reader whose ear is attuned to rhyme should hear the end words, and recognize the repetition of the first line in the rhyme of the third. More than this, he should also be anticipating the rhymes to come, which will rhyme with the second line of the tercet he is now reading. No tercet is rounded off without anticipating the sound of the next. Shelley has chosen a pattern which is appropriate in its very sound quality to the mood he wishes to express, and thereby has defined the tone of his poem.

Looking at endings is a good methodological approach in poetry. We find the theme stated at the end of this poem, and by looking at the endings of the lines we establish the rhyme scheme. Then, by asking how this rhyme scheme is appropriate to the tone of the poem, we come to significant conclusions. Line endings also affect tone by their relationship to syntax.

End-stopped lines correspond with major syntactical divisions, such as sentence endings. Run-on or enjambed lines do not correspond with major syntactical divisions. The difference is one of degree, since syntactical divisions (into paragraphs, sentences, clauses, and phrases) vary a good deal. The first and third lines in the passage quoted are more or less end-stopped, the second is not. The only completely end-stopped line in the whole section is the final line, for the verb of the main clause (*hear*) comes in the last three words of the last line, the whole section being one long sentence. Thus, all of the lines require some continuity, some forward movement to the beginning of the next line. Some of the more radically enjambed lines are those that separate verb from direct object (such as "chariotest . . . seeds," lines 6-7) or subordinating conjunction from its clause (such as "until . . ." at the end of line 8, governing line 9). Not only does the separation of "blow" from its direct object ("her clarion," lines 9 and 10) span the gap between two tercets, but the verb "fill" at the end of line 10 runs on not to line 11, but all the way to line 12, the last three words of which, "plain and hill," are the direct objects. The whole of line 11 is parenthetical; and the verb-object relationship is thus jam-packed with words that fill the syntax as full as plains and hills are being filled with living hues and odors. In all of these ways, Shelley is driving the reader on, hurrying him forward, and generating the tone of eager motion which characterizes the poem.

Not only pattern, but also the actual sounds of the versification should contribute to the tone of the poem. Tennyson's poem "The Charge of the Light Brigade" uses dactyls to create a sense of speed:

> Half a league, half a league,
> Half a league onward,
> All in the valley of Death
> Rode the six hundred.

This should not be read "DUM-di-DUM, DUM-di-DUM, DUM-di-DUM-DUM-di," but "DUM-diddy, DUM-diddy, DUM-diddy-DUM-di." The basic foot is part of the tone of this poem.

The sound qualities of the words, of the vowels and the consonants, also should contribute to the tone. Compare, for example, the following equivalent groups of lines from a pair of poems Milton wrote in contrasting moods:

From "L'Allegro":

> Haste thee, nymph, and bring with thee
> Jest and youthful jollity,
> Quips and cranks and wanton wiles,
> Nods and becks and wreathèd smiles. . . .

From "Il Penseroso":

> Come, pensive nun, devout and pure,
> Sober, steadfast, and demure,
> All in a robe of darkest grain
> Flowing with majestic train. . . .

The first poem celebrates (and apostrophizes) mirth, the second, melancholy. Of sixteen accented syllables in the joyous one, half are long *e*, long *i*, or short *i*; not one of the accented vowels in the second is a long *e*, long *i*, or short *i*. All of these vowels are tight front vowels, often called "bright." Of sixteen accented syllables in the sad poem, the vowel sounds of seven, or almost half, are long *o*, *aw*, *ow*, and the indefinite vowel (*e* as in *the*: the sound "uh"). All of these vowels are open and most of them are back vowels, often called "dull." The appropriateness of these contrasting sounds to the contrasting tones of the joyous poem on the one hand and the melancholy poem on the other is clear. Sound defines tone; or the desired tone governs the selection of sound.

Notice as a general principle that you can work from either end: either start with a good idea of the tone and check the sound to see how appropriate it is, or start with a good idea of the sound and check the tone to see how appropriate it is. Which one you start from depends on which one you grasp first. If you know the tone is sad, look to see if the sounds are sad; if you know the sound is hurried, look to see if the mood, the tone, is hurried.

The choice of consonants, too, is affected by tonal considerations. Hamlet, enraged that his mother has married his uncle, cries shame upon her marriage: "most wicked speed, to post/ With such dexterity to incestuous sheets!" (Act I, Scene 2). As the mouth frames the sibilant *s*'s and explosive *t*'s of this line, practically spitting, and particularly as the tongue moves with great effort from the final *s* of "incestuous" to the initial *sh* of "sheets," we feel with Hamlet the great disgust that thickens his tongue. The harsh, difficult sounds of these consonants make the effect cacophonous. A pleasing series of sounds, on the other hand, is euphonious, as in "So shows a snowy dove trooping with crows/ As yonder lady o'er her fellows shows . . ." (*Romeo and Juliet,* Act I, Scene 5). Or:

> Her gentlewomen, like the Nereides,
> So many mermaids, tended her i' the eyes,
> And made their bends adornings; at the helm
> A seeming mermaid steers; the silken tackle
> Swell with the touches of those flower-soft hands,
> That yarely frame the office.*

The "snowy dove" is dominated by long *o*'s, a sustained echo of sound; half the accented vowels are long *o*'s, and two of the unaccented, and the *o*'s of "dove," "trooping," and "yonder" are closely related. The description of Cleopatra in her river-boat (the "eyes" are part of the bow of the vessel) is dominated by *n*'s, *m*'s, and *l*'s, all voiced continuants—the vocal cords are used, and the consonants are not *stops* that interrupt the flow of breath, but may be sustained. Try reading the quote from *Hamlet* ("Most wicked speed") and then the first two and a half lines of the quote from *Antony and Cleopatra* ("Her gentlewomen . . . adornings"), holding your ears shut. The *Hamlet* passage hisses and checks; the *Cleopatra* passage hums and murmurs. The ratio of voiced consonants to unvoiced in the latter, by lines, is 13-to-2, 13-to-3, 18-to-2, 10-to-7, 10-to-9, and 9-to-3. The gentle, voiced sounds clearly dominate. Note that in lines 4 and 5, where the subject is the softness of the hands, the unvoiced sounds increase in number; the sound thus lightening as the touch lightens.

Meaning, of course, dominates our response to sound. Thus, the consonants of "spit" and "soft" are all unvoiced, two of the three being the same sound at the same place in the word.

* *Antony and Cleopatra,* Act II, Scene 2, lines 211-216.

But the difference in meaning makes it almost impossible to spit out "soft" or to whisper gently "spit." Moreover, even in these two words, besides the difference between the tight front vowel *i* and the open back vowel *o*, the one different consonant (*p* for *f*) also affects the quality of *s* and *t*. The *p* is explosive, the *f* a continuant. This difference qualifies the other consonant sounds. The *p* makes the preceding *s* share its explosive quality; the *f* makes it very hard to explode the following *t* with any force. Not just meaning, but also a sound's relationship to its immediate context affects its tonal qualities.

You should have noticed that I called the *s*'s in Hamlet's line "practically spitting" and "cacophonous," but the *s*'s in the description of Cleopatra's maids "lightening" and "euphonious." Why? First, the meanings of the words emphasize different aspects of the sounds, sibilance and softness, respectively. Secondly, the context of the *s*'s differs in the two quotations (as a little phonetic spelling helps to reveal):

> HAMLET: m*o*st . . . e*d* *s*peed . . . p*o*st . . . de*k*sterity . . .
> in*s*e*sch*uous *s*heets

> CLEOPATRA: A *s*eeming mermai*d* *s*teers; the *s*ilken . . .
> tackl*e*/Swell . . . flow*e*r *s*oft . . .

Hamlet's *s*'s are surrounded by explosive consonant sounds: *t, d, p, t, k-t, ch, t.* In contrast, the *s*'s of the euphonious passage are surrounded not by explosives (there is one exception), but by vowels and liquid continuants (*l, r,* and the semivowel *w*); *a-e, d-t* (the exception), *e-i, l-w, r-o.*

Because meaning and context strongly affect our sense of the quality of a sound, one cannot set up a table of equivalent connotations for each sound. A murmur of love and a spiteful whisper are both soft, yet have different effects. But in spite of this uncertainty, soft sounds are appropriate to one broad area of meaning, loud, hard sounds to a different one.

The most often quoted example of the choice of expressive sounds is probably a passage from Alexander Pope's "An Essay on Criticism," which practices what it preaches:

> 'Tis not enough no harshness gives offense,
> The sound must seem an echo to the sense:
> Soft is the strain when Zephyr gently blows,

And the smooth stream in smoother numbers flows;
But when loud surges lash the sounding shore,
The hoarse, rough verse should like the torrent roar;
When Ajax strives some rock's vast weight to throw,
The line too labors, and the words move slow;
Not so, when swift Camilla scours the plain,
Flies o'er th' unbending corn, and skims along the main.

In looking at tone as the basis of structure in poetry, we have concentrated thus far on the various aspects of sound (versification). We have examined rhyme, rhythm, and pattern in their relationship to tone; and the appropriateness of individual sounds. In the next section of this chapter the discussion will turn to diction, which expresses the relationship of meaning to tone and structure, just as we have seen versification reflect the relationship of sound to tone and structure.

C. Diction

Diction has been defined as choice of words. Words are, of course, chosen partly for their sounds; they are also chosen for their associations. These associations, or connotations, contribute largely to tone; words are selected with the desired tone in mind. To make the most effective use of language, the poet therefore chooses words that do not literally communicate his message. By saying things figuratively, he makes a richer statement, including not only a literal message but also all the connotations of the figuratively used words. The process of analyzing poetry consists of identifying structural aspects of sound, or versification; of identifying structural aspects of diction, including all the figures of speech and patterns of imagery in the poem; and of relating these to the poem's tone. Then, other critical concepts may be applied, as appropriate. But before analysis can be attempted, the reader must first master the simple literal sense of what he is reading.

Understanding what you read at a literal level is frequently harder than it seems. Sometimes, overfamiliarity will obscure the sense. Consider the famous line from Hamlet's soliloquy, "To be or not to be: that is the question" (Act III, Scene 1). Sheer familiarity has led many readers to accept the line without wondering what it means. *What* is to be or not to be?

In context, of course, Hamlet. He contemplates suicide, as the soliloquy continues, with thoughts of stabbing himself with a dagger. "To continue to exist or not to continue to exist: being or nonbeing; life or death: that is the question." The late Albert Camus expressed much the same idea in *The Myth of Sisyphus*, which begins with the memorable assertion, "There is but one truly serious philosophical problem, and that is suicide. Judging whether life is or is not worth living amounts to answering the fundamental question of philosophy." * The power of Shakespeare's line, which has made it one of the most famous in English literature, comes from its quintessential condensation. It is hard to imagine a more profound, universal, and sweeping problem condensed into less space—thirteen letters, in fact.

If you are one of those who have encountered that line but did not know what it meant, beware. It is usually a mistake to accept words without expecting them to mean anything; very few writers put down words without caring what they mean. Understanding the literal sense precedes any interpretation, sophisticated or naïve, of higher (or lower) meanings and hidden beauties.

Judicious use of the dictionary may help you meet this necessity for understanding the literal sense. Your instructor will probably urge you to keep a dictionary handy, and to refer to it when uncertain of a word's meaning. Consider, for example, the lines by William Blake,

> The harlot's cry from street to street
> Shall weave old England's winding sheet.

Undoubtedly you know that a harlot is a prostitute, but do you know what a "winding sheet" is? If you don't know that it is a cloth in which the dead are wrapped for burial, you may completely misunderstand the couplet. You may think the harlot is going to spend a very merry night indeed with old England, bundling, perhaps. What Blake means is that the social conditions responsible for the wretchedness of prostitution are killing England.

* Albert Camus, *The Myth of Sisyphus and Other Essays*, tr. Justin O'Brien (New York: Alfred A. Knopf [Vintage Books], 1959), p. 3.

Sometimes, unfortunately, you don't know that you need a dictionary. Here, only your instructor or a well-annotated text can help you. Macbeth moans about "sleep, that knits up the ravelled sleave of care . . ." (Act II, Scene 2). Knowing that Shakespeare, like all the Elizabethans, was rather a sloppy speller (he spelled his own name half a dozen different ways), you may immediately identify "sleave" as "sleeve." Unfortunately, if you do you will be wrong. "Sleave" is a conjectured correction, for the early text reads "sleeue," which would be modernized "sleeve." "Sleave" means tangled thread or untwisted silk, or perhaps just coarse silk. Really, though, you would understand the general sense of this line even if you have the wrong visual image.

In other cases, you may miss the point entirely, as in Juliet's famous line, "O Romeo, Romeo! wherefore art thou Romeo?" (Act II, Scene 2). Most students read this, "Wherefore art thou [pause], Romeo?" considering the final "Romeo" as parallel to the first two. Actually, the last "Romeo" is a predicate nominative. The confusion centers on the meaning of the word "wherefore," which does not mean "where" but "why." Not "Romeo, where are you?" but "Why do you have to be Romeo, son of my father's enemy?"

And sometimes you may overlook a meaning which qualifies the basic sense. For example, Hamlet, rejecting his innocent girlfriend, Ophelia, tells her, "Get thee to a nunnery" (Act III, Scene 1). A contemporary audience's response to this line would be conditioned by the fact that "nunnery" was a slang term for "brothel." The line therefore has a certain ambiguity.

Having urged the use of the dictionary upon you, even when you don't know you need it, I must contrarily urge restraint in its use. The student who looks up so many words that he does not get his assignment read errs badly. Most words are learned in usage, from context. (However, note well the importance of learning precise formal definitions of technical vocabulary.) After all, you learned to talk pretty well before you could read at all, much less use a dictionary; and you learned some of the hardest words in the dictionary that way. (The word "in" gets a whole column in a full-size dictionary.) The strength of ordinary language is the flexibility of usage and meaning that makes precision in definition almost impossible. In this respect, common language differs from the language of mathematics, whose strength is its precision. Mathematical symbols have a perfectly precise meaning, and are learned dictionary fashion or not at all. But mathematical language is also completely inflexible, and can express no concepts that are not already implicit in the postulates and definitions that establish it. In contrast, the language we speak—the language you now read—is frequently very imprecise; but it is fertile and various. As poetry, that language continually creates new experiences, and records the unrealized dreams of mankind.

Since the strength of poetry comes from flexibility and multiplicity of meaning (the "nunnery" is not just a nunnery, nor just a brothel; somehow, it is both, which it could never be in an equation), too rigid adherence to a dictionary may create a strict literalism of reading that hampers rather than helps.

Therefore, regard the dictionary as a substitute for the broad reading you should already have done, in a perfect world, but probably have not. Literally, "sensuous" and "sensual" mean just about the same thing: "having to do with or providing gratification of the senses." But their usage differs: "*sensuous* implies delight in beauty of color, sound, texture, or artistic form; *sensual* stresses indulgence of appetite, especially for sexual pleasure." * The distinction might matter to the girl whom you had meant to describe as having the soul of a painter, but who thought you meant she was oversexed. As a supplementary substitute for your verbal experience, therefore, the dictionary will enrich your understanding and help you when you are completely baffled when faced with an exotic word. As a tool rather than a crutch, the dictionary will be of great assistance, but don't look up every word, or you will remember none. The only methodological approach to understanding the literal sense is a variation on looking closely at the unexplained. The "unexplained" in this context means what you don't understand. If you do not understand at first reading, do not pass on, but try to decipher the literal intent.

Frequently, mastering the literal sense will not depend simply upon vocabulary, but upon mastering the figurative use of language. The number of figures of speech is legion, but the ones commonly identified are fairly few: irony, symbol,

* Webster, *Seventh New Collegiate Dictionary* (Springfield, Mass.: G. & C. Merriam, 1963).

metaphor, and simile have all been defined elsewhere in this book (see Chapter 7).

For an example of careful choice of figurative uses of language (including imagery), consider Shelley's "Ode to the West Wind." The first section appears on p. 175. The rest of the poem is:

II

Thou on whose stream, mid the steep sky's commotion,
Loose clouds like earth's decaying leaves are shed,
Shook from the tangled boughs of Heaven and Ocean,

Angels of rain and lightning: there are spread
On the blue surface of thine aery surge,
Like the bright hair uplifted from the head

Of some fierce Maenad even from the dim verge
Of the horizon to the zenith's height,
The locks of the approaching storm. Thou dirge

Of the dying year, to which this closing night
Will be the dome of a vast sepulcher,
Vaulted with all thy congregated might

Of vapors, from whose solid atmosphere
Black rain, and fire, and hail will burst: oh, hear!

III

Thou who didst waken from his summer dreams
The blue Mediterranean, where he lay,
Lulled by the coil of his crystalline streams,

Beside a pumice isle in Baiae's bay,
And saw in sleep old palaces and towers
Quivering within the wave's intenser day,

All overgrown with azure moss and flowers
So sweet, the sense faints picturing them! Thou
For whose path the Atlantic's level powers

Cleave themselves into chasms, while far below
The sea-blooms and the oozy woods which wear
The sapless foliage of the ocean, know

Thy voice, and suddenly grow gray with fear,
And tremble and despoil themselves: oh, hear!

IV

If I were a dead leaf thou mightest bear;
If I were a swift cloud to fly with thee;
A wave to pant beneath thy power, and share

The impulse of thy strength, only less free
Than thou, O uncontrollable! If even
I were as in my boyhood, and could be

The comrade of thy wanderings over Heaven,
As then, when to outstrip thy skyey speed
Scarce seemed a vision; I would ne'er have striven

As thus with thee in prayer in my sore need.
Oh, lift me as a wave, a leaf, a cloud!
I fall upon the thorns of life! I bleed!

A heavy weight of hours has chained and bowed
One too like thee: tameless, and swift, and proud.

V

Make me thy lyre, even as the forest is:
What if my leaves are falling like its own!
The tumult of thy mighty harmonies

Will take from both a deep, autumnal tone,
Sweet though in sadness. Be thou, Spirit fierce,
My spirit! Be thou me, impetuous one!

Drive my dead thoughts over the universe
Like withered leaves to quicken a new birth!
And, by the incantation of this verse,

Scatter, as from an unextinguished hearth
Ashes and sparks, my words among mankind!
Be through my lips to unawakened earth

The trumpet of a prophecy! O Wind,
If Winter comes, can Spring be far behind?

Marked as it might be by a student concerned with structure, the poem would look like this:

I

O wild West Wind, thou breath of Autumn's being, *[looks at foreground]*
Thou, from whose unseen presence the leaves dead
Are driven, like ghosts from an enchanter fleeing,

[PLANTS (EARTH)]
Yellow, and black, and pale, and hectic red,
Pestilence-stricken multitudes: O thou,
Who chariotest to their dark wintry bed

The winged seeds, where they lie cold and low,
Each like a corpse within its grave, until
Thine azure sister of the Spring shall blow

Her clarion o'er the dreaming earth, and fill *[long look forward to Spring]*
(Driving sweet buds like flocks to feed in air)
With living hues and odors plain and hill:

Wild Spirit, which art moving everywhere: *more a destroyer*
Destroyer and preserver: hear, oh, hear! *in II & III*

II
pt. III; see l. 45?   *pt. I; see l. A3*

Thou on whose stream, mid the steep sky's commotion,
Loose clouds like earth's decaying leaves are shed,
Shook from the tangled boughs of Heaven and Ocean,

Angels of rain and lightning: there are spread *by wind or wild motion*
On the blue surface of thine aery surge,
[WEATHER SKY] Like the bright hair uplifted from the head

[Celebrant of or for futility & destruction] Of some fierce Maenad even from the dim verge
Of the horizon to the zenith's height, *looks at distance*
The locks of the approaching storm. Thou dirge
Of the dying year, to which this closing night *[?]* *Short look forward to winter*
Will be the dome of a vast sepulcher,
Vaulted with all thy congregated might

Of vapors, from whose solid atmosphere
Black rain, and fire, and hail will burst: oh, hear!

III
more remote: seen in imagination   *tense*

[(see l. 36)] Thou who didst waken from his summer dreams *looks back to summer*
The blue Mediterranean, where he lay
Lulled by the coil of his crystalline streams,

[handwritten: MOSTLY SEA]

Beside a pumice isle in Baiae's bay,
And saw in sleep old palaces and towers *[handwritten: see l. 45]*
Quivering within the wave's intenser day,

All overgrown with azure moss and flowers
So sweet, the sense faints picturing them! Thou
[handwritten: power] For whose path the Atlantic's level powers

Cleave themselves into chasms, while far below *[handwritten: remote view]*
The sea-blooms and the oozy woods which wear
The sapless foliage of the ocean, know
Thy voice, and suddenly grow gray with fear,
And tremble and despoil themselves: oh, hear!

IV

[handwritten: from geographical distance to distance in age]

If I were a dead leaf thou mightest bear; *[handwritten: picks up 1st 3 pts; anticipated in ll. 15-17?]*
If I were a swift cloud to fly with thee;
A wave to pant beneath thy power, and share

The impulse of thy strength, only less free *[handwritten: more geographical expansion of view in pts I-III]*
Than thou, O uncontrollable! If even
I were as in my boyhood, and could be

The comrade of thy wanderings over Heaven,
As then, when to outstrip thy skyey speed
Scarce seemed a vision; I would ne'er have striven

As thus with thee in prayer in my sore need. *[handwritten: = TIME: see progress from I-IV]*
Oh, lift me as a wave, a leaf, a cloud!
I fall upon the thorns of life! I bleed!

A heavy weight of hours has chained and bowed
One too like thee: tameless, and swift, and proud.

V

Make me thy lyre, even as the forest is:
What if my leaves are falling like its own!
The tumult of thy mighty harmonies

Will take from both a deep, autumnal tone,
Sweet though in sadness. Be thou, Spirit fierce, *[handwritten: like leaves & seeds of I]*
My spirit! Be thou me, impetuous one!

Drive my dead thoughts over the universe
Like withered leaves to quicken a new birth!
And, by the incantation of this verse,

Scatter, as from an unextinguished hearth
Ashes and sparks, my words among mankind!   = burned
                                              out & igniting;
Be through my lips to unawakened earth   dead & reborn

i.e.,
in this
poem

The trumpet of a prophecy! O Wind,   power linked
If Winter comes, can Spring be far behind?   with promise

The structure of the poem presents three parallel stanzas: I, images of plants and earth; II, images of air, atmosphere, weather; III, images of ocean and sea. The next, IV, contrasts the natural world of the first three to the speaker's own situation; and the last, V, resolves the contrast by seeing a parallel between the wind and the speaker's poetry. Clearly, the structure through line 45 is an imagistic structure, based on the diction of the poem.

But the structure is somewhat more complicated. The first stanza is a foreground shot, surrounded by blowing leaves and seeds; the second is a long shot, looking from horizon to the zenith of the sky; the third goes so far that it is imaginative rather than literally seen (the sense faints picturing them), all the way to the Mediterranean and on to the Atlantic. The fourth then makes explicit that such distance is not possible to the speaker, who cannot be a comrade in such wanderings. But in the fifth stanza he anticipates that his words can travel over the earth as the wind does, even though he cannot.

Time is important in the poem: the personification of spring breezes, in I, represents a long look forward; the approaching storms that will burst in rain, fire, and hail in II take a short look forward, to winter; III looks back to summer; and in IV the poet looks back to his own youth, before coming in V to look forward to the future himself, both in terms of the effect of his poetry and in the relationship of autumn to spring. In effect, he says at the end that in this poem the wind will become a symbol of hope for the future.

Note that although in terms of earth, sky, and sea imagery the first three sections are parallel, in time and distance they are progressive, moving steadily back in time (the present appears to some extent in all stanzas) from next spring, to coming winter, to last summer, and away in distance from the leaves around the speaker, to the horizon, to other parts of the earth. The climax of the progressions comes in the fourth section, which looks back to the remotest past and sees the greatest gulf or psychic distance between need and reality. Although the time progression is obvious, the distance progression is less clear: what happens is that stanza IV turns the great physical distance of lines 49-51 (the possibility of going with the wind) into the psychological distance between the poet's sense of helplessness and his desire to accomplish things. In the couplet ending IV, time (the loss of his former youth) is identified as what now discourages the poet. The fourth section thus is the climactic résumé, in personal application, of the earlier sections. In the fifth section, the poet again looks to the future, and now sees time not as failure in the past but as a promise for the future, and sees the greatest distance ("the universe") as conquerable by poetry.

In controlling the tone of his poem, Shelley has made the first section a combination of death and rebirth. For example, the wind is the *breath* of autumn (the breath of life), but drives *dead* leaves like plague victims; the word "chariotest" suggests a vitality that "who drives the hearse," for example, would not; and the "winged seeds" are clearly more vital— partly because winged, and they are winged because of the wind that blows them—than the dead leaves; the pestilential colors of line 4 are contrasted to the "living hues and odors" that spring will bring; and the contrast of corpses and buds is made explicit at the end of the section, in "Destroyer and preserver. . . ." (The end of the section is linked to the opening of the section by the opening tercet's "breath—enchanter" and the concluding couplet's "spirit"—from the Latin for "breath" and "blow.")

The second and third stanzas are much less ambiguous, emphasizing the destructive and frightening aspects of the wind's power (a huge tomb in II, bringing fear even to the ocean floor in III), building toward the agonized cry of part IV. The last section, V, echoes more of the first section than of the middle three, precisely because it is reaffirming the positive things suggested of the wind in I, now in personal terms that apply to the poet. The imagery therefore looks back twice (three and a half lines out of fourteen) to the dead, falling, blown leaves of part I.

All of these conclusions about the poem's structure can be reached simply by exploring the diction and questioning the reason for the figures of speech and imagery of the poem, that is, simply by applying technical concepts. Many of them, however, could be reached by less technical methods. First, one could look for differences between the parts; second, one could look closely at the beginning and end (I and V) and compare them; also, one could look at the beginning and end of each section, noting the difference between the "destroyer and preserver" in I, the "black rain, and fire, and hail" in II, the sea plants "gray with fear" in III, the "heavy weight" that has "chained and bowed," in IV, and the "trumpet of a prophecy" of spring, in V.

Moreover, a close look at the beginning of IV should show that instead of addressing the wind directly, as the first three sections did ("O wild West Wind, thou . . ." "Thou on whose stream," "Thou who didst waken"), IV begins differently: "If I were . . ." Section IV emphasizes this difference by beginning the next line with the same words: "If I were . . ." The first three lines of IV are a clear identification of the underlying image of each of the first three sections: leaf, cloud, and wave. On the same reasoning, the end of IV, which also differs from the injunction "oh, hear!" with which each of the first three ends, can be considered important: since it introduces the time metaphor ("the weight of hours"), one might well look back through the early sections to find other time references, and forward to the future prophecy of the fifth.

Looking for repetitions, besides bringing out some of the above points, might also turn up two recurrent metaphorical vehicles: the magic-religious, and the musical. The "unseen presence" of the "enchanter" in I, the violent Angels and gigantic Maenad (an ecstatic worshiper of a god of destruction and rebirth) in II, the shimmering unreality of the palaces and towers in III, the vision and prayer in IV, and the incantation and prophecy of V, both unite the poem and roughly parallel the structure thus far identified. Musically, spring's clarion in I, the reawakening sound, is replaced by the "dirge of the dying year" in II; in III the music has gone and only a terrifying voice is left; in IV there is neither; in V the wind plays a lyre, producing "mighty harmonies," "a deep autumnal tone" that is sweet though sad, and which by combining with the poet's thoughts in the poem itself will become the trumpet of the concluding optimistic prophecy. Again, a recurrent metaphor (wind as musician) unites the poem, but is varied in its details (clarion, dirge, voice, none, lyre-harmonies-trumpet) in order to contribute to the structure of the whole.

By using such imagery and figurative language, the poet introduces all sorts of connotations and associations that greatly enrich his statement. Indeed, his poem is poetic precisely because it is given this quality, and the quality of structured sound, to distinguish it from factual statement. This is what Robert Frost calls the "pleasure of ulteriority": the metaphorical statement, that says one thing but means another.

Not all structures are as ordered and progressive as Shelley's poem. For one thing, many poems do not have the clear progression that moves from a beginning through a series of steps toward a fitting conclusion. The structure of Alexander Pope's poetic "An Essay on Criticism," which is written in heroic couplets, is not progressive. Instead, it is structured in separate pieces, each couplet tending to form a unit, antithetically balancing one attitude or tone against another just as the two lines of the couplet balance against each other. For example:

> As on the land while here the ocean gains,
> In other parts it leaves wide sandy plains;
> Thus in the soul while memory prevails,
> The solid pow'r of understanding fails;
> Where beams of warm imagination play,
> The memory's soft figures melt away.

Although the middle couplet is basically literal, roughly stating the tenor or literal sense of the simile in the first couplet and of the metaphor in the third, each of the couplets is virtually complete in itself; and in each, just as the versification divides it into two equal halves, so the sense of each is a contrast or antithesis.

This balance is most clearly a matter of diction in Pope's satiric works, in which he balances the serious against the trivial:

> Here Britain's statesmen oft the fall foredoom
> Of Foreign Tyrants, and of Nymphs at home;

> Here thou, great Anna! whom three realms obey,
> Dost sometimes counsel take—and sometimes Tea.

The connotations of a queen's taking counsel on the one hand and tea on the other contrast radically. Within the couplet, Pope's poems are tightly structured; but as a whole, they may not be. This looser overall form does not, of course, make them inferior, simply different. As a matter of fact, romantic poets like Shelley are sometimes characterized as breaking formal rules in favor of irregularity, and neoclassical poets like Pope are characterized as sticking to rigid forms. The difference between the poems of these two lies in how each poem has been structured: in Shelley's "Ode" the structure is a structure of the whole; in Pope's poems, it frequently tends to be a structure of the parts.

In analyzing poetic structure, the basic method is as follows:

1. Ask what the literal meaning of each sentence or phrase is, pharaphrasing or restating it as clearly as you can.

2. Ask why the poet chose to express his literal meaning in the way he did. What did he expect to gain from those words as sounds? What did he expect to gain from the connotations of those words?

D. Other Technical Concepts

Irony in poetry derives most characteristically from a conflict of tone, either between two vehicles or between vehicle and tenor. The poetry of John Donne and of other poets who wrote what is called metaphysical poetry abounds in such tension and conflict. A conflict of tone between two figures of speech is found in the progression from the first to the last stanza of Donne's "The Sun Rising," which moves from a playfully colloquial personification to an expansively serious metaphor. The poem opens with the speaker in bed with his love, chiding the sun for awakening him:

> Busy old fool, unruly sun,
> Why dost thou thus
> Through windows and through curtains call on us?

But the opening and concluding lines of the last stanza are quite different from that first stanza in their connotations and in their mood:

> She is all states, and all princes I;
> Nothing else is.
>
> .   .   .   .
>
> Shine here to us, and thou art everywhere;
> This bed thy center is, these walls thy sphere.

The bedroom has become, metaphorically, an entire universe, building from the whole world (the lovers are all states and princes) to the whole solar system (the bed is the center of the sun's movement, the walls the sphere or space within which it moves). The ironic tension between the playful tone of the first stanza and the serious tone of the last stanza can be traced throughout the poem, which is structured in terms of the progress from the tone of the beginning to the tone at the end.

The tonal contrast in "The Sun Rising" involves two figures of speech: the initial apostrophe and the final metaphor. The basic conflict is between the connotations of the two vehicles, the "old fool" in contrast to the statelike solar system. A poetic irony may also set up a tension between vehicle and tenor. Such irony may have a partly humorous, partly satirical intent, as in this list (from another poem by Donne—"Song: Go and Catch a Falling Star") of impossible and fantastic deeds necessary in order to find honesty:

> Go and catch a falling star,
>   Get with child a mandrake root,
> Tell me where all past years are,
>   Or who cleft the devil's foot,
> Teach me to hear mermaids singing,
>   Or to keep off envy's stinging,
>   And find
>   What wind
> Serves to advance an honest mind.

The tenor of the poem is: Wherever you may go and whatever you may do, you will not find honesty prospering. The idea itself is bitter. But the opening hyperboles are extrava-

gant and witty; the tone of the vehicle is therefore lighter
than the tone of the tenor.*

But the contrast of the tone of the vehicle with the tone of
the tenor need not be either satirical or humorous, and may
indeed be quite earnest. At the end of "A Valediction For-
bidding Mourning," in which the poet, going on a trip, assures
his love that there is no reason to be upset—the poem apparently was written for Donne's wife before he took a trip
to the Continent—there appears a famous extended simile
working out several similarities between them as lovers and
the two halves of a draftsman's compass or dividers:

> If they [our two souls] be two, they are two so
>   As stiff twin compasses are two;
> Thy soul, the fixed foot, makes no show
>   To move, but doth if the other do.
>
> And though it in the center sit,
>   Yet, when the other far doth roam,
> It leans, and hearkens after it,
>   And grows erect as that comes home.
>
> Such wilt thou be to me, who must
>   Like the other foot obliquely run:
> Thy firmness draws my circle just,
>   And makes me end where I begun.

Donne is being neither satirical nor pedantic; the peculiar
quality of this poem comes from the tension between all your
associations with a mechanical compass and mechanical drawing, the vehicle of the simile, and the spiritual bond between
the lovers, the tenor of the simile. The tension is so acute in
this case as to constitute a nonsatirical semi-irony.

Clearly, what seem jarring notes—words or ideas that do
not fit—should be examined closely, in order to determine

---

* You might note that there is also some contrast in the connotations of the vehicles of alternating lines: lines 1, 3, and 5 are
romantic, suggesting aspiration; lines 2, 4, and 6 deal with threat-
ening evil (mandrake roots, being fork-shaped, suggested human
forms, and were associated with magic; e.g., they were alleged to
scream when uprooted, and to promote fertility in women).

whether the poet may have been trying to establish precisely such a conflict.

Character in poetry usually involves the speaker (except, of course, in narrative poems, which may be analyzed in this respect like fiction). The speaker's imagery, the figures of speech he employs, will tend to reveal his habits of thought. Thus, Polonius, in *Hamlet*, perpetually uses metaphors from commerce; he thinks in dollars and cents. Diction as level of usage often identifies a character as educated, fastidious perhaps, or uneducated, manly or effeminate, boorish, or blunt, or what-have-you. Metaphor and level of usage are both very relevant to poetic drama, and to some extent to dramatic monologues such as Browning's, in which the speaker is imagined to be in a particular historical and personal situation, addressing people. The dramatic monologue differs here from the typical poetic genre, since the speaker in the former is not consciously creating a work of art.

The best method of identifying character as it is expressed poetically consists of looking for repetitions. To draw again from *Hamlet*, the flowers that surround Ophelia characterize her beauty, innocence, and fragility.

Character also is reflected in poetic diction in many verse satires and some comic verse. (See the comments on mock-heroic in Part I, "Satire.")

Narrative forms of poetry tend toward another genre, epic, in which a narrator recounts a tale to an audience. Indeed, most epic works are poetical: that is, they are poetic in structure (in versification and use of figurative language) although not in presentation (since the narrator speaks to the audience, instead of being overheard by an audience that is ignored). Because epic and drama are both objective—that is, they are presented, performed in one sense or another—they accept poetic structure easily. For poetic structure is also objective. Versification and nonliteral statement, figurative language, draw attention to the surface of the communication; they make language significant in its own right, independently of literal content. Since drama and epic both are objectively presented, they adapt to the objective emphasis that poetic structure gives to the surface pattern of the work.

In drama, the poetic structure of the imagery may come to be clearly noticeable, beyond the plot structure. See, for example, the remarks in the discussion of drama about the movement from eye-metaphor to blindness-symbol in *King Lear*.

Plot has no special relevance for poetry, and need not be discussed in detail. Poetic devices may have some relevance for plot. The prose work *The Stranger*, for example, comes to a climax at the end of Part I when the protagonist, Meursault, kills a stranger, an Arab, on the beach. This climactic moment is marked by a sudden outburst of vivid metaphors expressing the oppressive heat and blinding brilliance of the sun, giving emphasis to the turning point in Meursault's life. The unexpectedly emotional quality of this change in language should help the reader notice it in analysis, just as it emphasizes the impact of the climax whether he is analyzing or simply reading the story through. The technical concepts are diction and metaphor; the methodological clue is the unexpected (in this case, unexpected emotionalism), and its appearance at the end of a part.

Sometimes a shift in vehicle may have an effect so strong that the illusion is that something has happened, that plot has developed. Arnold's "The Scholar Gypsy" divides into two major parts, the first describing the scholar gypsy's wandering through the world of nature, seldom spotted by those who stay with civilization, and then only fleetingly; the second describing the fatigue, sickness, and death brought on by involvement in the affairs of the modern world. Then, in the last two stanzas, with a sudden swoosh, a long and vivid simile compares the scholar gypsy to an ancient Tyrian trader, urging the scholar gypsy to act like the Tyrian trader, who left when the Greeks came and disappeared into the wilderness of the Atlantic coastline, leaving Mediterranean civilization behind him:

> Then fly our greetings, fly our speech and smiles!
>   —As some grave Tyrian trader, from the sea,
>   Descried at sunrise an emerging prow
> Lifting the cool-hair'd creepers stealthily,
>   The fringes of a southward-facing brow
>   Among the Aegean isles;
> And saw the merry Grecian coaster come,
>   Freighted with amber grapes, and Chian wine,
>   Green bursting figs, and tunnies steep'd in brine;
>   And knew the intruders on his ancient home,

The young light-hearted Masters of the waves;
  And snatch'd his rudder, and shook out more sail,
  And day and night held on indignantly
O'er the blue Midland waters with the gale,
  Betwixt the Syrtes and soft Sicily,
   To where the Atlantic raves
Outside the Western Straits, and unbent sails
  There, where down cloudy cliffs through sheets
    of foam,
  Shy traffickers, the dark Iberians come;
   And on the beach undid his corded bales.

The poem, in this simile, does what it advises the scholar gypsy to do: it leaves the world (in this case, the rest of the poem) behind, and takes flight. This radical change gives the illusion of sudden development very much like an escape in plot. Figuratively, it is a change in scene; literally, of course, it doesn't happen.

Poetry structures by mood; plot is structure by cause and effect. Poetry echoes both sounds and associations, producing a kind of simultaneity of perception—we hear and remember multiple sounds and meanings. Plot plods, stepping from one event to another, producing not simultaneity but succession, one event coming after another, as its very essence. For this reason, narrative forms are not, per se, poetic, and plot does not function distinctively in poetry, however useful poetry may be as an overlay to plot.

Just as poetic irony is most characteristically a conflict between moods or tone, so poetic satire sets two moods or attitudes against each other. The most typical poetic satire is the mock-heroic,* which treats a mediocre or trivial subject as though it were terribly important, thereby ridiculing the attitude of excessive concern for a trivial matter.

"Burlesque," which means treating a subject incongruously, is a broader term, and includes both mock-heroic and parody. Parody is the imitation of another work by applying its language or style to things with different connotations from those of the original subject; the result is a usually humorous discrepancy.

* See pp. 56–58.

Parody may be sheer play. Edmund Waller wrote a poem entitled "On a Girdle," which begins:

> That which her slender waist confined
> Shall now my joyful temples bind.

My father wrote a parody of this poem which begins:

> That which once her waist confined
> Doth now a bale of cotton bind.

This is not an attack on Waller's charming poem; it's a joke.

Parody may, however, be a satiric attack, aimed either at the spirit of what the original said or perhaps at the way it was written, at its style. Lewis Carroll wrote some very effective parodies, one of them on Isaac Watts's poem "How Doth the Little Busy Bee." Watts's poem goes:

> How doth the little busy bee
> Improve each shining hour,
> And gather honey all the day
> From every opening flower!
> How skillfully she builds her cell!
> How neat she spreads the wax!
> And labors hard to store it well
> With the sweet food she makes.
>
> In works of labor or of skill
> I would be busy too;
> For Satan finds some mischief still
> For idle hands to do.
> In books, or work, or healthful play,
> Let my first years be passed,
> That I may give for every day
> Some good account at last.

Carroll's devastating parody of this treacly poem with its "healthful play" is called "The Crocodile."

> How doth the little crocodile
> Improve his shining tail,
> And pour the waters of the Nile
> On every shining scale!

> How cheerfully he seems to grin,
> How neatly spreads his claws,
> And welcomes little fishes in
> With gently smiling jaws!

By talking of gobbling up fish as though it were a sweet thing to do, Carroll establishes the parodic, and in this case satiric, discrepancy. Echoing the language of Watts's poem, he implies that Watts's sentimental view of nature is erroneous.

Mock-heroic and parody are not quite the same. Both mock-heroic and parody apply a certain style to an inappropriate subject; both are, that is, burlesque. But mock-heroic sets a high traditional style against a trivial subject at the expense of the subject, whereas parody sets an individual's style against an inappropriate subject (whether trivial or not) at the expense of the style or the attitude it implies.

Spotting parody is easiest when you know the original. If you don't know the original, then the major clue to the burlesque, as in the case of mock-heroic, is the unexpected, the disparity between diction and subject matter.

The method of Byron's poetic satire is to treat potentially serious subjects very casually, creating a satiric and ironic tension between the alleged importance of the topics—such as social prominence—and the lightness, even the frivolity, of his diction. For example,

> I say—the future is a serious matter—
> And so—for God's sake—hock and soda-water!

Or, as the titular hero of *Don Juan* is carried away by ship from his first love,

> "Belovèd Julia, hear me still beseeching!"
> (Here he grew inarticulate with retching.)

Or,

> Christians have burnt each other, quite persuaded
> That all the Apostles would have done as they did.

Byron rhymes "lost your" with "imposture," "evil is" with "syphillis," "merry tin" with "heroine," and in a comment on his hero's parents that he applied to his own marriage,

But—Oh! ye lords of ladies intellectual,
Inform us truly, have they not hen-pecked you all?

Most often, the humorous rhyme of the *ottava rima* stanzas of *Don Juan* comes in the concluding couplet, which is particularly emphasized in the rhyme scheme (*abababcc*) because it is the new and unexpected sound, because it comes at the end of the stanza, and because the immediate rhyme is more strikingly repetitive than the earlier alternations. Here, too, Byron usually puts the specifically satiric comment.

Distinctively poetic comedy usually plays with unexpected sounds, versifying in unanticipated ways. Byron's ingenious rhyme for "intellectual," virtually a quadruple rhyme (four syllables), is surprising and amusing. Ogden Nash's humorous verse plays with the relationship of rhythm to rhyme, crowding as many as fifteen or twenty extra syllables into a line in order to get the desired rhyming sound at the end. His insistence on achieving the rhyme does not seem like a mechanical fixation, but like a triumph of flexible ingenuity over the restrictions imposed by the form. By giving up the rhythm, he achieves the rhyme. The poet as singer here is analogous to Miss Langer's comic hero, the form he overcomes corresponding to the blows of fate. The sense of human accomplishment in managing to find a triple rhyme for "bespectacled" gives the reader of comic poetry exactly that sense of comic expansiveness, of the potentials of human adaptability, that Miss Langer describes. If you can't think of the rhyme Nash found, check the bottom of this page.* Comic poetic forms of versification tend to be quite rigid, as are the limerick and the recently repopularized clerihew.

Tragic poetry tends toward drama, as in Tennyson's "Ulysses." The poem presents two incompatible goods: the domestic life at home, which Ulysses' son Telemachus wants, and the life of adventurous exploration, which Ulysses himself chooses. Since the goods are incompatible, a choice must be made between them. Ulysses genuinely faces a tragic dilemma: pining away in boredom, or giving up wife, family, friends, security, and possibly life itself. In the last line of the poem, his determination expressed in slurp and heavily accented iambs, Ulysses virtually affirms the spirit of the

* Neck tickled.

tragic hero as Arthur Miller describes him: "To strive, to seek, to find, and not to yield."

Of course, these qualities—the dilemma and the self-affirmation—are not peculiarly poetic. The devices of versification and imagery are used to enrich the tragic statement, but do not themselves carry the tragic structure. They may, however, define a tone appropriate to the tragic situation. The elegy, essentially a poem of mourning (frequently with a final consolation) for someone's death, has a tone appropriate to tragedy: sad at the reality of the loss, but consoled with the knowledge that value still exists. The poet suffers his individual loss, but learns by the end of the elegy that consolation is possible. In their combination of real loss (which is evil) and recognition of value (in consolation), elegies fit Richard Sewall's definition of tragedy quite well.

For example, Milton's "Lycidas" mourns the accidental death of a young man, finding in the death cause for bitter reflection on the number of evil people left alive and the promising future that was cut off. But at the end of the poem, Christian confidence in the dead man's resurrection consoles the speaker. Comparing the diction of beginning and ending, you may note that the grammatical person changes from first person to third person. Why? The effect is a concluding objectivity, as the speaker who has been composing the elegy is seen preparing to move on. There is a parallel in tone here to the effect of catharsis—the grief and the bitter reflections have been transcended with the thoughts of immortality; and they have been objectified in the written poem. Since they are now expressed, the poet has learned to live with them, they are outside him now. He has learned acceptance. If the poem ended with hymns of joy at salvation, the effect would be not that of tragedy, but of a happy ending. Therefore, the consoling thoughts move the poet-speaker beyond a personal identification (much as Oedipus' transfiguration in *Oedipus at Colonnus,* in which he leaves the world mysteriously, somehow ennobled by suffering), move him into a state of blessedness that cannot be fully understood. He can only be seen from the outside, from the third person. This tendency toward objectivity is dramatic.

Actually, "Lycidas" does not involve the depth of feeling that a great dramatic tragedy like *Oedipus* does. The tone of the poem is formal and muted, not loud and dramatic. Milton was fully conscious of the tone he sought. Invoking the muses, he urges them to "Begin, and somewhat loudly sweep the string" of their instruments. ("Lyric" comes from "lyre.") Not the "howl, howl, howl, howl," with which Lear challenges the universe to match him in grief, but a more restrained and a specifically artificial tone: Lear is not composing a song, but the shepherd-singer in "Lycidas" is. Much poetry is extremely personal; but in its self-consciously formal creation of a work of art to express grief, "Lycidas" represents the elegy as the form in which tragic tone is transmuted into the genre of poetry. The poet and the work are both present; and the poet creates a container, the poem, to embody his grief, thereby lessening it. The elegy is thus subdued; and emphasizing the objectifying process of creating the song of grief, Milton shifts from the opening *I*-will-sing-of-grief to the closing *he*-went-on-his-way.

Scene often structures poems, because of the specific connotations associated with particular settings. There are happy places and unhappy places, busy places and quiet places, and so forth. We have already noted the shift of scene at the end of "The Scholar Gypsy," The widening view of the scene in "Ode to the West Wind" structures its parts. Consider the following Shakespearean sonnet:

> That time of year thou mayst in me behold
> When yellow leaves, or none, or few, do hang
> Upon those boughs which shake against the cold,
> Bare ruin'd choirs, where late the sweet birds sang.
> In me thou see'st the twilight of such day
> As after sunset fadest in the west,
> Which by and by black night doth take away,
> Death's second self, that seals up all in rest.
> In me thou see'st the glowing of such fire,
> That on the ashes of his youth doth lie,
> As the death-bed whereon it must expire,
> Consum'd with that which it was nourish'd by.
> > This thou perceiv'st, which makes thy love more strong,
> > To love that well which thou must leave ere long.

If the technical concepts of versification are applied to this poem, you will quickly identify the rhyme scheme (*ababcdcd-*

efefgg) and the foot (iambic) and the meter (pentameter). As a fourteen-line poem, with that rhyme scheme and meter, it is of course a sonnet. Since it is by Shakespeare, you should not be surprised to discover that the rhyme scheme in question typifies the so-called Shakespearean sonnet. A Shakespearean sonnet consists of three quatrains and a couplet; a check of the rhyme scheme shows that the rhymes do divide the sonnet into these four parts. Checking the ends of the parts, the quatrains, you note that each one ends a sentence. Checking the beginnings of each part, you note a verbal repetition at the beginning of the second and third quatrain: "In me thou see'st the twilight . . ." "In me thou see'st the glowing . . ." Then, looking back at the beginning of the first part, you see that the first line expresses the same idea, although without the striking verbal repetition: ". . . thou mayst in me behold . . ." Clearly, a kind of parallelism is being established among the three quatrains.

Checking the beginning of each one again, you look for what is seen: "time of year," "twilight of . . . day," "glowing of . . . fire." Isn't this a progression? The scope narrows in each quatrain: first the season of the year, a broad unit of time; then the twilight of the day, a much narrower unit of time; then the last moments of a dying fire, a still smaller unit. Now check the quatrain endings: the sweet birds are gone; death's second self (night, perhaps sleep) has come; a simile comparing the ashes of the fire to a deathbed on which it must die. This is harder, perhaps, to see, but there is a progression here too. The progression moves toward death. First, the departure of youth (and we note that the leaves, too, are going or gone); then, a deathlike state; then the statement that death itself is coming.

What are the scenes described by each part? First, the empty branches; then the sunset; then the dying fire. There is an order here. The first scene looks up, at the boughs; the second looks at the horizon, where the sun sets (in the west); the third looks down at the embers of the fire on its deathbed.

The thematic repetition is obvious in each of these parts, which literally state the same idea: I am not young, but old, and nearing death. But there is a repetition of imagery that unifies the pictorial scene: light and heat are contrasted to darkness and cold. Yellow leaves, the twilight after sunset, and the glow of the fire, are all fading yellow-oranges. The shivering of the branches, the taking of the last light by black night, and the expiration of the fire on and into ashes, all are heat losses, and also color losses (even the yellow leaves are virtually gone).

By this examination, you have identified the structure of the poem, as defined by diction; for most of the language is figurative, and all of these progressions and many of the parallels depend on the relationships among the vehicles of the metaphors and similes.

The preceding discussion, by the method of looking at parts, at beginning and endings, and at repetitions, and by keeping in mind the various technical concepts of versification and the general concept of theme, described the sonnet's poetic structure. In the process, it was incidentally noted that the literal statements of each quatrain are repeated, emphasizing the *theme* of approaching death. Thus, attention to parts of poems and to what is repeated is relevant to theme as well as scene. But what about the concluding couplet? First, since it comes at the end of the poem, it ought to be important; its distinctive rhyme (that is, that it is a couplet and not a quatrain) also makes it stand out. It's unusual in another respect, too: it contains no figures of speech. Does it deserve such emphasis?

Some critics think the basic structure of the versification of the Shakespearean sonnet is weak, precisely because (they say) the last couplet cannot deserve such emphasis. But it can. If the couplet is simply a tacked-on idea, then it is weak, and not part of the figurative structure of the poem. But if it ties together the preceding quatrains, if it is the unifying factor, then it should be emphasized. Now, this particular idea —seeing that I am getting old and approaching death, you love well that which you will have to leave—does not sum up the preceding quatrains, for they all said "I am getting old and approaching death"; and the conclusion here is a consequence, but not an otherwise missing unity—they are already unified.

There is another possibility which can make the couplet deserve its emphasis. Even if it does not unify, if it re-unifies in different terms, then it is indeed important. What is it the person addressed loves better? It could be the speaker-poet, for he is dying. But just as well, it could be youth, for that is what the person addressed sees the poet leaving—youth and life, the vigor of vitality. "You see me getting old, and that makes you love youth and life better." Reread the poem with this idea in mind. Now the tone changes somewhat, moving farther from pathos and closer to an ironic paradox. Age is inevitable; but seeing the inevitability makes one cling to youth harder. And note what happens when you reach the final quatrain—youth is what has brought age. Age lies on the ashes of its youth, dying on the remains of its youth, destroyed by what gave it life ("Consum'd with that which it was nourish'd by"). So youth eats itself up just as a fire burns itself out: and if loving youth better means trying to be more youthful, then it also means trying to become old faster. If you don't like the dark, burning your candle at both ends to make things brighter will make it get dark faster.

Thematically, then, the last couplet introduces a new idea that gives a different total significance and a different tone to the figurative statements of the quatrains.

Note that the last quatrain comes somewhat closer to the theme of the couplet than do the first eight lines. In general, the literal parts (in the case of the Shakespearean, the quatrains and couplet defined by the versification) do not *necessarily* correspond to the thematic units of the poem. In fact, some Shakespearean sonnets use the Shakespearean rhyme scheme, but are structured in units of eight lines and six lines, like a Petrarchan sonnet. Therefore, use the parts of the poem as clues to thematic statements, not as proof.

Symbolism is akin to poetry. A symbol's ratio of meaning, as stated in the glossary, is one-to-many; one symbol, but many meanings. Poetic diction works in the same way: by figurative statement, it introduces a host of connotations, all of which work to define the tone of the whole poem.

Recognizing poetic symbolism is as hard as recognizing any other kind, and the same cautions are in order. Don't over-interpret. Be specifically careful not to call metaphors symbols; it won't kill anyone, but it is sloppy thinking.

The basic clue to symbolic status is overemphasis, usually an overemotional statement. Thus, Blake's "Tiger, tiger, burning bright" seems an overemotional approach to the literal animal. Or consider his poem "The Sick Rose":

Rose, thou art sick!
The invisible worm
That flies in the night
In the howling storm

Has found out thy bed
Of crimson joy,
And his dark secret love
Does thy life destroy.

The emotional intensity of this poem should lead you to conclude that the worm "that flies in the night in the howling storm" is not the common ordinary garden variety but something special, perhaps evil itself.

Poetry does so much in such small compass that analysis is easy to make—not perhaps good analysis, but at least lengthy analysis; pages of prose can and have been turned out about very few lines of poetry. This chapter has itself turned out a substantial number of pages about not too many poems. In conclusion, therefore, a reminder may be needed. If the methods illustrated in this chapter—looking at endings, looking for repetitions, and so forth—are means to the end of seeing how the technical terms apply to a given poem, so too are the technical terms themselves means to a different goal: the experience of the poem itself. Dr. Johnson said that poetry's business is not to number the streaks of the tulip. He meant poetry was not concerned with particulars, and he was wrong about an awful lot of great poetry. I quote his words with a different thought. If analysis numbers the streaks of the poetical tulip, the reader may then see changes in color he had not noticed before; and, putting the statistical count, once made, out of his mind, the reader may then see the whole flower and all its complex colors in their fullest radiance.

5. The Essay

The *essay* as an art form doesn't receive as much attention in English courses as do novels, short stories, poems, and plays. There are two reasons. First, the essay as art form (typically, the familiar essay) merges with the essay as pure information or as practical persuasion (e.g., how you should vote). The essay thus does not have as clearly defined a position in a course in literary art as do poems, plays, and fiction.

Secondly, essays are often used in conjunction with writing instruction. They may serve as examples of the kind of writing the students should imitate, or provide topics for the student to write about. In neither case is the artful essay the best one to use. Most student writing is supposed not to be artistic, but to be clear communication. So a beautiful essay that really communicates the author's personality, his religious faith, say—Sir Thomas Browne's *Religio Medici*, for example, or one of John Donne's sermons—does not show the freshman how to write an essay exam in history. Suppose a student wrote, like Browne,

But, because the name of a Christian is become too general to express our faith,—there being a geography of religions as well as lands, and every clime distinguished not only by their laws and limits, but circumscribed by its doctrines and rules of faith,—to be particular, I am of that reformed new-cast religion, wherein I dislike nothing but the name; of the same belief our Saviour taught, the apostles disseminated, the fathers authorized, and the martyrs confirmed; but, by the sinister ends of princes, the ambition and avarice of prelates, and the fatal corruption of times so decayed, impaired, and fallen from its native beauty, that it required the careful and charitable hands of these times to restore it to its primitive integrity.*

Or, like Donne:

When God who is all blessing hath learned to curse us and, being of himself spread as an universal honeycomb over all, takes an impression, a tincture, an infusion, of gall from us, what confection of gnawing worms, of gnashing teeth, of howling cries, of scalding brimstone, of palpable darkness can be so, so insupportable, so inexpressible, so unimaginable as the curse and malediction of God? †

On tests and papers the student may actually be marked down for communicating his personality. As for writing topics, essays that deal either with controversial social and moral problems or with academic problems are much more stimulating in the first case and much closer in the second case to what the student must wrestle with for the next four years, than are beautifully done personal essays.

Since the essays you will actually encounter in your courses are not as clearly within the scope of the genre classification as the plays and other literature you read, this chapter, in

* Sir Thomas Browne's *Religio Medici, Urn Burial, Christian Morals, and Other Essays*, ed. John Addington Symonds (London: Walter Scott, 1886), p. 12.

† John Donne, Sermon XXVI, folio of 1649, quoted in *Seventeenth-Century Prose and Poetry*, ed. Robert P. Tristram Coffin and Alexander M. Witherspoon (New York: Harcourt, Brace, 1946), p. 111.

addition to analyzing the genre, will make some specific suggestions for reading other kinds of prose.

A. Presentation

The essay as an art form, like all literature, exists for the sake of the experience it offers. It is to be read for what the reading provides in itself. Essays written primarily for other purposes are nonliterary. Essays written for the purpose of providing information are usually classified as *expository* writing; essays written for purposes of persuasion are usually classified as rhetorical writing, or propaganda, or perhaps hortatory prose (prose which ex*horts* you to do or believe something).

Artistic and nonartistic essays differ with respect to the presence or absence of author, work, and audience. The artistic essay involves the presence of author and audience, and minimizes the work. That is, the artistic essay is apparently a communication directly from the author to the reader. The reader does not see the essay as an objective art work, but instead looks through the words to see the experiences and attitudes the author is trying to communicate.

The nonartistic essay, the nonliterary essay, on the other hand, involves the absence of all three: no author; no work; no audience. Since its function is purely communicative, its content is what counts—not content as an artistic creation, but content as purely independent truth. The author's personality, his evaluations and opinions, are supposed to be completely irrelevant. The ideal style of expository prose has long been completely impersonal, on the assumption that the truth is the truth no matter what the author, or for that matter the audience, thinks about it. Therefore, in theory, the best expository prose simply presents that truth, without involving either author or audience, in a neutral and transparent style that minimizes the reader's sense of the work. Second- and first-person forms (you and I) are supposed to be excluded from formal expository prose.*

* The most effective propaganda, like expository prose, is neutral and impersonal; the reader does not even realize that he is being persuaded of something. Subtle editorializing may effectively channel the reader's evaluations into agreement with the evaluations and

You may have noticed that I do not conform to this standard. I have written this book in a personal style partly because I suspect that most of its readers, perhaps you, are more interested in people and personal communication than you are in the techniques and methods of literary analysis. Frankly, I am trying to entertain. Partly, however, my practice reflects a growing consensus that the implied objectivity of completely neutral third-person exposition is misleading; that the pure truth is never presented purely, but always as understood by the speaker, and perhaps further modified in the understanding of the hearer. The writer who presents his views rather than objective truth is denying reality. The writer who presents as objective truth views which are necessarily tinged by his individual perception is not only unrealistic but dishonest.

To avoid these pitfalls of expository writing just using first or second person is not enough. If every other sentence begins with "I" you probably are too wrapped up in yourself and too little concerned with what you are saying. (Imagine my chagrin, when reviewing the manuscript for this book, at finding one passage of less than 150 words that included all of the following: "I propose . . . I began . . . I base . . . I recognize . . . I distinguish . . . I base . . . I mean. . . .") Your instructor may insist that you write exclusively in the third person to give you practice in attending to content rather than to your subjective intuitions and reveries. In an art work, in a personal essay, you may very properly attempt to express your own attitudes just because they are yours; but in expository prose, you should be expressing your attitudes not because you think them, but because you think them true. This basic difference, between writing that is a meeting of two minds (author and reader), and writing that states

standards of the presumably straightforward account. Propaganda of a more obvious sort moves closer to the literary essay as a genre, since the more aware the reader is that he is being persuaded, the more he experiences a difference, at least a relationship, between himself as audience and the persuader as author. The more explicit the author's standards, the more the propaganda tends toward communicating "this is how I feel," and the less it is a manipulation *masquerading* as expository objectivity.

truths (with no emphasis on author or reader or even the work as a form), is the difference between the essay as a literary genre and the essay as expository prose.

A quotation from *An Anatomical Disquisition on the Motion of the Heart and Blood in Animals,* by the seventeenth-century physician and anatomist William Harvey, startles modern readers because of the author's personal intrusion into a work of expository prose, violating our sense of the appropriate style for medical treatises:

> And, above all, how can they say that the spirituous blood is sent from the arteria venalis by the left ventricle into the lungs without any obstacle to its passage from the mitral valves, when they have previously asserted that the air entered by the same vessel from the lungs into the left ventricle, and have brought forward these same mitral valves as obstacles to its retrogression? Good God! how should the mitral valves prevent regurgitation of air and not of blood? *

B. Structure

In its orientation toward communication, the essay differs from fiction, which emphasizes experience; from drama, which emphasizes enactment, deeds; and from poetry, which emphasizes the expression of mood and feeling. Shared experience, witnessed deed, and overheard feelings all differ from statement, the address of one man to another, that characterizes the essay as genre. In this emphasis on explicit communication, the essay appropriately enough bases its structure on theme.

E. B. White's essay, *Once More to the Lake,* † informal in style, shows a thematic structure in the pattern of the whole, working toward a vivid symbolic image that defines the

---

* Reprinted in *Great Books of the Western World,* ed. Robert M. Hutchins (Chicago, Ill.: Encyclopaedia Britannica, 1952), vol. 28, p. 272.

† In *One Man's Meat* (New York: Harper & Bros., 1941), reprinted in Sachs, Milstead, and Brown, *Readings for College Writers* (New York: Ronald Press, 1962).

essay's theme. Paragraph by paragraph, it may be summarized as follows:

I decided to return to the lake where I used to vacation as a child. Taking my son, on the way there I remembered what it had been like. (Not really wild, the lake had seemed so to me then.) My son acted as I had, so that I began to feel he was me, and I was my father. We fished, and I had the same illusion of swapped identities, so much was the same. The lake seemed unchanged. Dinner seemed the same. Summertime *is* unchangeable. I realized that the past summers deserved to be preserved. The noisy outboard motors were the only big difference from the way it used to be. I remembered everything; it was the same now; I felt my son to be me. A thunderstorm came, just as it used to.

That summarizes all but the last paragraph. (The barren quality is my summary, not White's richly detailed account.) In the last paragraph, White, watching his son don swimming trunks soaked by the rain, "saw him wince slightly as he pulled up around his vitals the small, soggy, icy garment. As he buckled the swollen belt suddenly my groin felt the chill of death."

The last paragraph states the essay's theme symbolically: Change in the life of a man is his replacing of his parents, and his children's replacing him; although things may seem the same, the sameness is not the identity of the individual, for he grows up, grows old, and dies, leaving his children behind him to do the same. White, looking at his son pulling on the cold bathing suit, identifies with his son, sees his son as himself; in doing so, he empathically shares his son's feeling of cold. That cold is a suggestion of death. Thus, by seeing his son as himself, he is seeing that he has been replaced, and his ultimate replacement will occur when he has died. Appropriately, the feeling of death is in the "vitals," the life organs, including the reproductive ones. Since reproduction would not be necessary if individuals lived forever, the very fact of reproduction itself implies the death of the individual parent. The symbol is vivid, compact, and so rich with meaning that spelling it out literally is tedious. Obviously, this vivid symbolic imagery of cold is the climactic expression of the essay's theme, and the essay is structured by theme in the sense that the main punch is the thematic symbol at the end.

Moreover, the relationship of the rest of the paragraphs to each other also shows the dominance of theme in the structure of this essay. The structure of the paragraphs may be outlined as follows:

Introduction: basic situation (return to lake, par. 1).

I. The sameness.
 A. I remembered the past, in anticipation of returning (pars. 2 and 3).
 B. My son was like me, I was like my father, all was the same (pars. 4, 5, 6, 7).

II. My evaluation of this sameness.
 A. A universal truth: such summer vacations never change (par. 8, introduced by an emotional apostrophe of summer).
 B. This changelessness is good (with an ironic hint that the situation is not quite the same now) (pars. 9, 10, 11).

III. The difference.
 A. The thunderstorm (itself an ironic symbol, since storms are associated with dire change, but are interpreted by White as expressing sameness; the dire change does occur in the next paragraph) (par. 12).
 B. The intuition of personal death (par. 13).

The essay is clearly structured, and the structure is thematic. The theme is, "Things seem unchanging, as I would like them to be; but they are not, for I will die." The style of most of the essay is easy, informal, fairly simple, with many concrete illustrative details, sometimes in short sentences, sometimes linked in longer ones, usually by "and." Part II (as outlined above), the expression of the desire for the preservation of the past, for the permanence of the idyllic summers, is introduced by a highly poetic apostrophe of "Summertime, oh summertime, . . ." which is much more emotional and quite different in style from what has gone before. The unexpectedness of this stylized apostrophe marks a progression toward a new idea about the apparent sameness: its emotional importance to the author. Part III (in the above outline), the difference, is not marked by a change in style, but it is marked in content, by a summary (in paragraph 11) of what has been said thus far: the remembering, the identity of father and son, the sameness. Then the thunderstorm, which "was the big scene, still the big scene," and the climactic revelation of the idea of personal death.

Summarizing, outlining, noting repeated words and ideas, checking particularly the ending (the last word is "death"), looking for the unexpected—these methods of approaching the essay can bring out its thematic structure.

C. Syntax

A sense of essay style requires an ear for the quality of words, for their connotations and sound qualities, just as a sense of poetic style does. More strongly, however, it requires a sense of syntactical relationships, for *syntax* is the basis of the organization of ideas, and ideas are the essence of theme, and theme is the basis of structure in the essay. Sir Thomas Browne's *Religio Medici* is an example of careful syntactical structure that communicates theme. Consider the following paragraph:

> For my religion, though there be several circumstances that might persuade the world I have none at all,—as the general scandal of my profession,—the natural course of my studies,—the indifference of my behavior and discourse in matters of religion (neither violently defending one, nor with that common ardor and contention opposing another),—yet, in despite hereof, I dare without usurpation assume the honorable style of a Christian. Not that I merely owe this title to the font, my education, or the clime wherein I was born, as being bred up either to confirm those principles my parents instilled into my unwary understanding, or by a general consent proceed in the religion of my country; but having, in my riper years and confirmed judgment, seen and examined all, I find myself obliged by the principles of grace, and the law of mine own reason, to embrace no other name but this: neither doth herein my zeal so far make me forget the general charity I owe unto humanity,

as rather to hate than pity Turks, Infidels, and (what is worse) Jews; rather contenting myself to enjoy that happy style, than maligning those who refuse so glorious a title.*

Careful subordination and parallelism communicate the reflective balancing of rational introspection. What is my religion? Browne asks himself, and tries as accurately as possible to express it. The basic ideas are expressed in the three sentences:

I. My religion is Christian.

II. My Christianity is derived from conviction.

III. But my conviction does not make me intolerant.

Each sentence is qualified by possible objections or conflicting ideas:

I. My religion,
   A. although you might not think so,
   B. is Christian.

II. My Christianity is
   A. not due to externals,
   B. but derived from conviction.

III. But my conviction
   A. does not make me intolerant;
   B. instead, I rejoice in my own conviction.

And within each sentence, complex parallelisms develop the completeness of the statement:

I. My religion,
   A. in spite of
      1. the bad reputation of doctors,
      2. what my studies [because materialistic, e.g., anatomy?] might imply, and
      3. my habits and remarks about religions,
         a. in which I have neither supported one
         b. nor denied any,
   B. is Christian. (The independent clause and the main idea occur at the sentence's end.)

* In Symonds, *op. cit.*, p. 11.

II. My Christianity is
   A. not due simply to such externals, as
      1. baptism ("the font")
      2. education, or
      3. surroundings, whether
        a. parental or
        b. social-national,
   B. but derived
      1. after mature reflection,
      2. on the basis of
        a. grace and
        b. reason,
      3. from conviction.

III. But my conviction
   A. does not make me
      1. forget my duty to be tolerant,
      2. nor make me hate
      3. rather than pity
        a. Turks
        b. Infidels
        c. (parenthetically emphasized) *Jews:*
   B. instead, I
      1. enjoy the name ("style") of Christian,
      2. rather than criticizing non-Christians.

Notice the balancing of conflicting ideas in the last sentence: not zeal overcoming charity, making hate overcome pity, but enjoyment instead of maligning.

Now, the point of this long-drawn-out triple outlining of a mere three sentences is that the sentences are carefully structured, in a complex syntactical pattern. If you read the work perceptively, you should feel the give and take, the thrust and counterthrust of opposed ideas and tendencies, ordered and restrained by the various syntactical subordinations and parallelisms.

The style itself embodies Browne's gentle reflectiveness, his tolerant consideration of both people and ideas. (A little later he says, "I could never divide myself from any man upon the difference of an opinion, or be angry with his judgment for not agreeing with me in that from which, perhaps, within a few days, I should dissent myself.") *

Both White's informality and Browne's formality are excellent writing; and both men structure their essays thematically, although the structure of the one shows most clearly in the pattern of the whole, the structure of the other most clearly in the pattern of the sentence.

D. The Essay as Persuasion

When reading any essay or expository prose, the first question to ask, and perhaps the last as well, is: "What is the purpose of the essay? Is it to entertain? to inform? to persuade?" The literary essay, the essay as art form, primarily entertains; its purpose is intrinsic. The other two purposes, to inform and to persuade, are extrinsic. The purpose of informing preeminently characterizes textbooks. The purpose of persuading preeminently characterizes a campaign speech. The difference matters.

The Appendix contains suggestions for reading textbooks. Here we are concerned with essays that persuade. Some essays attempt to persuade, but do so disinterestedly. The author of a disinterested essay wants, of course, to persuade the reader that his view is the right one, but that is the extent of his interest. The goal is knowledge of the truth, not some further practical action. Disinterested literary scholarship and criticism, for example, argue the validity of a given interpretation purely for the sake of a better understanding.

In contrast to scholarly works, writings in the areas of politics, social action, and advertising can be assumed to have ulterior motives, hopes for practical consequences resulting from the author's success in convincing the reader. The author wants you to vote for someone, to join a group, to buy a product. Like literature, such writing may affect the reader's response without his realizing how the response is controlled. Unlike literature, however, such writing aims at controlling subsequent actions. If a man is to be free, he must realize how persuasive prose directs his responses. Only then can he react rationally out of the strength of his own convictions.

* *Ibid.*, p. 16.

One of the first questions to ask when analyzing persuasive prose is, "Who is the author?" The answer contains a clue to the real implications of what is said. Consider two widely disparate examples. During the Republican National Convention that nominated Barry Goldwater for President, Senator Peter Dominick read to the delegates a statement purportedly from an old copy of *The New York Times*. The statement criticized the extremism of a hero of the American Revolution, and was taken by the delegates as parallel to criticism by contemporary news media of the Republican nominee's "extremism," considered by the delegates to be as patriotic as that of the Revolutionary hero. Demonstrations followed Senator Dominick's reading, including much shaking of fists at reporters, cameramen, and the booths occupied by television commentators.

Now, a large part of the force of the statement the senator read depended on its having been published by one of the supposedly hostile news media. The senator said he was quoting from an issue of *The New York Times* published during the Revolutionary War. But *The New York Times* published its first paper more than half a century after the American Revolution was over. Obviously, the senator was not telling the truth (he ultimately said he had been joking). The enthusiastic response of the delegates, however, depended largely on their belief that not one of the senator's staff writers but an editor of *The New York Times* was the author of the statement.

As a second example of the importance of knowing who the author is, consider the first creation story in Genesis 1. The account of the creation of the heavens and the earth and all living creatures during six days of activity was actually written during the Babylonian Exile. Prior to the Exile, Jewish worship had been centered around the Temple in Jerusalem, but that was now destroyed. What does the story say in this context? Some things it says in any context: Man is the most important creature; the whole of the universe is God's. But in the historical context of the Exile, it says that a new center of worship and observance can replace the Temple— the holy day. For on the seventh day, God rested. The exiled Jew could not go to the Temple, but he could observe the Sabbath. Knowing who the author is here means in particular knowing the historical context in which he writes, the practical situation he faces. Note that identifying the author is not necessarily a debunking or exposure but that, as in this latter case, it may reveal additional significance.

In some cases, however, knowing the identity of the author may lead to a discrediting of evidence. To support its own political slant, the book *None Dare Call It Treason* cites the *Congressional Record*. Probably many readers of the book do not realize that any printed matter whatsoever can be reprinted in the *Congressional Record* without ever having been heard on the floor of Congress. The fact that material is in the *Congressional Record* guarantees only that one congressman requested that it be included. In no way need it express consensus or even deliberation by Congress or any of its committees.

Knowing who the author is means knowing whether he has an ulterior motive (perhaps the nomination of Barry Goldwater); knowing the context in which he writes (perhaps the exile of his people); and knowing his relative claim to authority (perhaps one politician's opinion in contrast to the deliberate conclusions of the entire Congress of the United States). Knowing these facts enables you to judge sincerity, to understand the problem the writing tries to solve, and to evaluate testimony. None of these is a substitute for knowing simply what is said. The most important question is: "What is the author's thesis? What is he trying to persuade me of?"

Identifying the thesis of an essay or speech is primarily a matter of close reading. Particular attention should be paid to beginnings and endings, both of paragraphs and of the whole work. The thesis statement (or the topic sentence) will most often be found in one of those two places. If the thesis is not stated at the beginning, it will almost always be stated at the end.

At least, the thesis probably will be stated in one of those two places if the author states his thesis explicitly. Much writing implies a thesis, rather than stating it explicitly as a scholarly article or a textbook should. The techniques of persuasion are a little different in the two cases. When the thesis is explicitly stated, the arguments for it are usually explicitly stated, too. When the thesis is merely implied, the unwary reader may not even realize he is being persuaded:

News reports sometimes convey an editorial attitude without explicitly stating it. The implied thesis is suggested by the selection of information and by slanted language. Such is Dale Wittner's article (accompanied by photographs) "The killing of Billy Furr, caught in the act of looting beer." * In a race riot in Newark, Billy Furr was shot by a policeman as he fled with beer he had taken from a liquor store. Mr. Wittner, a *Life* photographer as well as a reporter, happened to witness the shooting. The implied thesis of the report is that Mr. Furr did not deserve to be shot. How is that thesis communicated?

First, there is some selection of event.

> When he noticed me, Billy thrust a can in my hand.
> "Have a beer on me," he said. "But if the cops show up get rid of it and run like hell."
> I opened the beer and went off. . . . [The arrival of a squad car] was the first sign of police authority on the block in more than an hour, except for a young Newark police trainee who had sipped beer and watched the looting with me. †

No reference is made to smoking, although one of the pictures shows Billy Furr with a cigarette in his mouth. The reporter obviously thought that fact irrelevant, but the fact that he and a rookie policeman drank beer quite relevant. Although Mr. Wittner draws no conclusions from these details, they strongly imply an evaluation. The taking of the beer was not condemned by a decent, respected member of society like the author, nor by a representative of the very enforcement agency that shot the looter.

The inclusion of these details is not a trick, for they *are* relevant to the situation. But their selection does involve an editorial attitude, a conviction, an implied thesis. Presumably, someone who felt that Billy Furr deserved to die for stealing beer could have included details about the incidence of looting, the breakdown of civil order, the threats to property and life itself that unrestrained lawlessness creates. After all, the fact that a reporter and a rookie policeman condone theft

* *Life*, July 28, 1967, pp. 20–23.
† *Ibid.*, p. 21.

does not mean that theft is right or permissible. These considerations are not explored by Mr. Wittner. He sees the shooting as unjustified; and he includes in his reports facts that imply that evaluation.

Language too can be slanted, just as the selection of information can. Before firing, the policeman who shot told the reporter to duck. " 'Get down,' he screamed." The implications of "screamed" are quite different from the implications of other verbs that might have been used: *warned, called, shouted,* even *cried.* Hysterical and vicious men scream; strong, stalwart defenders of law and order call loudly or warn. Even punctuation can imply an editorial attitude. My own parenthetical contrast between "one politician's opinion" (*politicians* are sneaky and *opinions* are usually ill-founded) and "the deliberate conclusions of the entire Congress of the United States" (*deliberate conclusions* sound so judicial they must be right; *the Congress of the United States* is very official and impressive, and anything *entire* is overwhelming) was unfair, since the hypothetical politician was himself a member of Congress.

One reason I have used the report of Billy Furr's death as an example of how a thesis, an evaluation, can be implied is that I agree with the implied thesis. No human being deserves death for running away with stolen beer. And the fact that Mr. Wittner does not explicitly discuss the rights and wrongs of the situation does not make either his presentation or his evaluation improper. But both those who read the article and were moved by it and those who read the article and were annoyed by it could respond more thoughtfully if they understood how the selection of information and the choice of words affected their response.

Faulty arguments offered in support of a thesis are of many types. For example, "If an accused man is guilty, he will protest his innocence. This accused man protests his innocence. Therefore he is guilty." Or: "Fascists jeer at Joan Baez and her protest songs. Al Capp makes fun of Joan Baez with Phoney Joanie in *Li'l Abner.* Therefore Al Capp is a Fascist." In both cases, the erroneous assumption is that one shared attribute proves another attribute is shared. The conclusions are non sequiturs—that is, they do not follow from the premises and evidence.

A slightly different form of fallacious argument is called

post hoc, ergo propter hoc—after this, therefore because of this—or more briefly, a *post hoc* argument. Its assumption is that because one event follows another, the later event is caused by the earlier. In its most persuasive form, such an argument is partly implicit. "Franklin Roosevelt took office for an unprecedented third term in January 1941; and before the year was out, the whole nation was involved in total war." Spelling out the argument makes it much less alluring. "Because we entered World War II after the start of Roosevelt's third term, it must have been his third term that involved us in the war."

The red herring, dragged across the argumentative trail to deceive the noses of truth-hounds, is an irrelevant distraction. The classical scholar F. M. Cornford, in a satire on academic politics, suggests that any action proposed in writing at a university senate meeting can be stalled off indefinitely by "comma-hunting." *

The "straw man" is a position or argument invented just for the sake of demolishing it. An author who uses a straw man to disprove someone else's views may introduce it by saying, "Does he think that . . ." and offer a position his opponent never dreamed of asserting, a position that can now be torn convincingly to shreds. The unwary reader is led to equate the straw man with the opponent's position.

Perhaps the most common fallacy is the hasty generalization. This fallacy in thinking underlies much prejudice. "They're all alike. . . . Well, you know how *they* are. . . ." Governor Reagan of California is said to have answered a conservationist's objection to selling state parks and timberlands, saying, "When you've seen one tree you've seen them all."

Argument by example, however, is very persuasive. It is effective because of its concreteness and vividness. Sir Philip Sidney, in his work *An Apology for Poetry*, argues that poetry is a better teacher of virtue than history:

> For, that a feigned example hath as much force to teach as a true example . . . let us take one example wherein a poet and a historian do concur.

* F. M. Cornford, *Microcosmographia Academica, Being a Guide for the Young Academic Politician* (Chicago, Ill.: University of Chicago Press, 1945), p. 28.

Herodotus and Justin [historians] do both testify that Zopyrus, King Darius's faithful servant, seeing his master long resisted by the rebellious Babylonians, feigned himself in extreme disgrace of his king; for verifying of which he caused his own nose and ears to be cut off, and so flying to the Babylonians, was received, and for his known valour so far credited, that he did find means to deliver them over to Darius. . . . Xenophon excellently feigneth such another stratagem, performed by Abradates in Cyrus's behalf. Now would I fain know, if occasion be presented unto you to serve your prince by such an honest dissimulation, why you do not as well learn it of Xenophon's fiction as of the other's verity and, truly, so much the better, as you shall save your nose by the bargain; for Abradates did not counterfeit so far.*

How much more memorable is this than would be the barren abstract statement: "Poetry teaches virtue as well as history, because the poet can tell fictionally all of the instructive events and models of morality that history can; morever, the fictional account can alter details to make a more effective or more palatable lesson."

And yet, however vivid, argument by example does not prove the universality of what it illustrates. Even Sidney's example, for all its effectiveness, is not proof; for although Cyrus' enemies believed Abradates in the fiction, the Babylonians might not have believed Zopyrus had he not cut off his nose; and even if they would have, your captors might not believe you if you didn't cut off your nose.

Therefore, although examples and illustrations are evidence, their basic function should not be proof. As explanation, the example is perfectly legitimate and extremely effective.

The distinction between proving and explaining or clarifying applies to many essays. The essay that states its thesis explicitly need not be trying to prove its point; it may be simply explaining the author's position, his convictions. In evaluating effectiveness and legitimacy, this distinction must be made: Is the example offered as proof? If so, is it

* Sir Philip Sidney, *The Defense of Poesy otherwise known as An Apology for Poetry,* ed. Albert S. Cook (Boston: Ginn, 1898), p. 20.

really typical? Or is the example offered simply as explanation? In the latter case, the essay probably falls into the category of "disinterested" attempts to persuade, presenting new ideas for consideration.

A simile or analogy may serve as a comparative example, and, like the good example, can communicate vividly.

> Esau, it has been observed, was a gentleman. He was, in fact, an amiable, manly fellow, who addled his wits with outdoor sports and attached small importance to his spiritual heritage—very like an English gentleman indeed. And he sold his birthright for a sodden mess.*

Thus Dorothy L. Sayers wittily compares the man who traded his inheritance for some food to the typical Englishman. The paragraph ends by dumping a bowlful of mush into the reader's attention. If you did not know the title, "The English Language," you might not immediately realize that Miss Sayers is equating the sodden mess with the way the contemporary Englishman uses his native tongue. She continues:

> The birthright of the English is the richest, noblest, most flexible and sensitive language ever written or spoken since the age of Pericles. Every day sees it sold, not only to Brother Jock and Brother Paddy, and young Brother Jonathan, but to the sob-sisters of Fleet Street, to the aged and doddering Mother of Parliaments, to the wicked Uncles of the B.B.C., to the governors, teachers, spiritual pastors and masters of the Board of Education, and to all the myopic old women of both sexes who cannot tell a purposeful hawk from an ill-regulated handsaw. †

Esau, of course, proves nothing about the language of the twentieth-century Englishman. But as Esau's bowl is upturned and the reader's nose rubbed in the mush, the comparison aptly expresses Miss Sayers' attitude.

* Dorothy L. Sayers, *Unpopular Opinions* (New York: Harcourt, Brace, 1947), p. 107. Miss Sayers puns on the meaning of *mess* as dirty slop, the biblical usage meaning simply a serving.

† *Ibid. Cf. Hamlet*, Act II, Scene 2: "I am but mad north-northwest: when the wind is southerly I know a hawk from a handsaw."

Parenthetically, we may note the control of rhythm in the length of sentence and phrase. The opening paragraph is a sandwich: two short sentences, the first announcing the topic of the comparison (Esau), the second at length comparing him to an Englishman, and the last tersely and emphatically dumping the sodden mess. And in the last sentence quoted, the parallel phrases gradually lengthen, building toward the climactic generalization—"to all"—with its sarcastic contempt for those who cannot tell purposeful language from ill-regulated language:

> not only to Brother Jock and Brother Paddy,
>   and young Brother Jonathan,
> but to the sob-sisters of Fleet Street,
> to the aged and doddering Mother of Parliaments,
> to the wicked Uncles of the B.B.C.,
> to the governors, teachers, spiritual pastors and
>   masters of the Board of Education
> and to all the myopic old women of both sexes
>   who cannot tell a purposeful hawk from an
>   ill-regulated handsaw.

The concrete illustration is one of the most effective means of communicating. The illustration must of course be anchored in place by a statement of the general principle or idea it illustrates. But without particularity there is no life, and the writing dies.

As in Miss Sayers' essay, the concrete illustration or analogy frequently provides an effective introduction to the topic. This introduction may be gradual and even roundabout, or it may be terse and emphatic, as the occasion or the personality of the writer requires. Compare these two beginnings:

> When the right virtuous Edward Wotton and I were at the Emperor's Court together, we gave ourselves to learn horsemanship of John Pietro Pugliano, one that with great commendation had the place of an esquire in his stable. And he, according to the fertileness of the Italian wit, did not only afford us the demonstration of his practice, but sought to enrich our minds with the

contemplations therein which he thought most precious. But with none I remember mine ears were at any time more loaden, than when (either angered with slow payment, or moved with our learner-like admiration) he exercised his speech in the praise of his faculty. He said, soldiers were the noblest estate of mankind, and horsemen the noblest of soldiers. He said they were the masters of war and ornaments of peace; speedy goers and strong abiders; triumphers both in camps and courts. Nay, to so unbelieved a point he proceeded, as that no earthly thing bred such wonder to a prince as to be a good horseman. Skill of government was but a pedanteria in comparison. Then would he add certain praises, by telling what a peerless beast a horse was, the only serviceable courtier without flattery, the best of most beauty, faithfulness, courage, and such more, that if I had not been a piece of a logician before I came to him, I think he would have persuaded me to have wished myself a horse. But thus much at least with his no few words he drove into me, that self-love is better than any gilding to make that seem gorgeous wherein ourselves are parties. Wherein if Pugliano's strong affection and weak arguments will not satisfy you, I will give you a nearer example of myself, who, I know not by what mischance, in these my not old years and idlest times, having slipped into the title of a poet, am provoked to say something unto you in the defence of that my unelected vocation, which if I handle with more good will than good reasons, bear with me, since the scholar is to be pardoned that followeth the steps of his master.*

My words today were written to the music of that moving American folk-song, "I'm Bringing You a Big Bouquet of Roses, One for Each Time You Broke My Heart." Since some of you said that you could not grasp the piece we wrote about the press because my style was dark and dense, I shall try to tell you what I think of you in words both few and short.

I shall begin by paying you the greatest compliment

* Sidney, *op. cit.*, pp. 1–2.

in my power. I think you are teachers. I did not say you were good teachers.*

In Latin rhetoric, the introduction, which is to gain the listeners' or readers' attention, is called the "exordium." Both beginnings call for attention. But one does it gracefully, gently, casually; the other tersely, wittily, abruptly. Partly, the difference between the two openings may depend on the different sizes of the respective essays, for Sidney's is close to 20,000 words, Mr. Hutchins' is 3,500. Partly this very difference in length may reflect a difference in the relative leisure of the two audiences. But partly the difference comes from the personalities and purposes of the authors. Sir Philip Sidney was a cultured aristocrat, a man of letters in his leisure time; Robert M. Hutchins is an aggressive intellectual, a brilliant executive who believes that now is the time for decision. As President of the University of Chicago, he might stick his head into a vice-president's office to say, "Give me three reasons why we shouldn't send all our juniors to Stuttgart for the year" and the startled second would realize that if he didn't come up with three reasons, next September all of the juniors would be in Stuttgart. This same intellectual ruthlessness is reflected in the opening of the speech, "The Lack of Public Confidence in Newspaper Editorials."

The endings show the same contrasting features. Sidney's summary leads into a graceful exhortation, adorned with allusions and quotations:

> So that since the ever-praiseworthy Poesy is full of virtue-breeding delightfulness, and void of no gift that ought to be in the name of learning; since the blames laid against it are either false or feeble; since the cause why it is not esteemed in England is the fault of poet-apes, not poets; since, lastly, our tongue is most fit to honour Poesy, and to be honoured by Poesy; I conjure you all

* Robert M. Hutchins, "Freedom Requires Responsibility: The Lack of Public Confidence in Newspaper Editorials," a speech delivered before the National Conference of Editorial Writers, Louisville, Kentucky, November 19, 1948; in *Vital Speeches of the Day*, vol. XV (January 1, 1949), p. 175.

that have had the evil luck to read this ink-wasting toy of mine, even in the name of the Nine Muses, no more to scorn the sacred mysteries of Poesy, no more to laugh at the name of "poets," as though they were next inheritors to fools, no more to jest at the reverent title of a "rhymer"; but to believe with Aristotle, that they were the ancient treasures of the Grecians' Divinity; to believe, with Bembus, that they were first bringers-in of all civility; to believe, with Scaliger, that no philosopher's precepts can sooner make you an honest man than the reading of Virgil; to believe with Clauserus, the translator of Cornutus, that it pleased the heavenly Deity, by Hesiod and Homer, under the veil of fables, to give us all knowledge, Logic, Rhetoric, Philosophy, natural and moral, and *Quid non?*; to believe, with me, that there are many mysteries contained in Poetry, which of purpose were written darkly, lest by profane wits it should be abused; to believe, with Landino, that they are so beloved of the gods that whatsoever they write proceeds of a divine fury; lastly, to believe themselves, when they tell you they will make you immortal by their verses.

Thus doing, your name shall flourish in the printers' shop; thus doing, you shall be of kin to many a poetical preface; thus doing, you shall be most fair, most rich, most wise, most all; you shall dwell upon superlatives. Thus doing, though you be *libertino patre natus,* you shall suddenly grow *Herculea proles,*

Si quid mea carmina possunt.

Thus doing, your soul shall be placed with Dante's Beatrice, or Virgil's Anchises. But if (fie of such a but) you be born so near the dull-making cataract of Niles that you cannot hear the planet-like music of Poetry, or rather, by a certain rustical disdain, will become such a Mome as to be a Momus of Poetry; then, though I will not wish unto you the ass's ears of Midas, nor to be driven by a poet's verses (as Bubonax was) to hang himself, nor to be rhymed to death as is said to be done in Ireland; yet thus much curse I must send you, in the behalf of all poets, that while you live, you live in love, and never get favour for lacking skill of a Sonnet, and, when you die, your memory die from the earth for want of an Epitaph.*

Mr. Hutchins, in contrast, drives forcefully and tersely to his conclusion:

What causes this? The reason the people who buy your newspapers do not take your advice is that they do not believe what you say. They do not believe what you say because they do not believe you are disinterested. They do not believe you are responsible. They will not accept you as teachers because they know that editorial writers do not operate within the tradition that is necessary for good teaching. They may buy the papers for countless reasons: to find out what has happened to Dagwood, or who won the fifth race at Santa Anita, or what is on sale at Gimbel's. They do not buy them for the editorials. They read the editorials, if at all, for amusement; they do not read them for instruction. Yet I think you are teachers. If you are to have pupils, public confidence in you must be established. The major recommendations of the Commission on the Freedom of the Press aimed at this result. If you do not like these recommendations, think of something else that will give this result. The Commission on the Freedom of the Press showed that freedom requires responsibility. You do not need a commission to tell you that influence requires responsibility, too. †

And, indeed, the whole of any essay must live up to the tone set by its opening. Either gentle persuasiveness or aggressive insistence may be convincing; but the good writer, having taken his stance, does not carelessly shift his ground. And the good reader is neither cajoled nor bullied into his beliefs, but responds to the tone of what is said while recognizing what that tone is.

This discussion of the essay as persuasion has stressed the importance of knowing who the author is, distinguishing

* Sidney, *op. cit.*
† Hutchins, *op. cit.*, p. 178.

between implicit and explicit theses, recognizing the editorial slant governing selection of detail and language, seeing through several types of faulty argument, appreciating the limitations and legitimacy of example, and recognizing and responding to overall tone, particularly as reflected in the opening and closing. Most important is remembering that the effort to persuade is itself a legitimate and often praiseworthy undertaking. One candidate is better than the other, most of the time; and the campaigner who urged you to vote for that better candidate is trying to get you to do what is in fact better. That he urges as persuasively as he honestly can is not to his discredit. But it is to your discredit if you are persuaded without knowing why.

Finally, the ultimate concern of us all should be the truth. The good reader reads critically, not for the sake of one-upmanship but to replace opinion with knowledge. The good writer states the truth as he sees it. The Greek historian Herodotus reports an account of a voyage circumnavigating Africa, a report he does not believe. Apart from the improbability of the feat itself, he disbelieves because the account said that at the bottom of Africa the sun rose and set to the north, instead of to the south as in Mediterranean waters (north of the equator). This geographical fact is, of course, exactly what someone moving from the northern hemisphere to the deep southern hemisphere would notice. Only because Herodotus honestly and impartially reported both the account he rejected and the evidence on which he based his evaluation has the record of this human adventure been preserved for the history of man.

In the last analysis, truth resembles beauty. Perhaps they are not identical, as Keats's Grecian urn proclaimed they were. But just as beauty that is not true contains in its falsehood the germ of its own destruction, so truth that is simply ugly is partial and incomplete. Therefore, this book concludes with the mention of truth in persuasive writing. For at a profound level all literature seeks to be true.

Truth and beauty are two of the Platonic triad of values. The third is goodness. The man who seeks truth and beauty participates in that goodness by the seriousness of his dedication. To read critically, to write honestly, to entertain perceptively the whole work of literature in all its complexity, these are the pursuits of the man who knows that literature concerns the world in which it originates and toward which it points. For the very stuff of literature's beauty is the very truth of life itself. You are the better for seeing both.

Appendix

A. Classroom Instruction

Although college emphasizes reading and assigns more reading per class hour than is possible in high school, much college learning is still aural. Listening well is therefore important. It requires more than the passive receptivity of a bottomless hole, where everything goes in but nothing comes out. Nor is the unassimilated regurgitation of the sea cucumber much better, the sea cucumber being an omnivorous creature which takes in everything it is physically capable of ingesting, and, when it eats something which disagrees with it, vomits its entire stomach, contents and all. The good listener listens thoughtfully, assimilating and digesting what he hears. (Even the sea cucumber, incidentally, will starve to death if it has not digested a wholesome meal just before abandoning its stomach.) The good listener listens critically, always trying to decide what is important and what is not.

What he thinks important, of course, he writes down, whether in formal lecture, informal discussion, or some combination of the two. The principle of writing things down is essential to effective study, not only in listening but also in reading. The process of writing helps to formulate thoughts, to translate them slightly perhaps into one's own words, which are always so much more memorable, and helps one to re-member—whether one goes back to review the notes or not.

Last-minute remarks deserve particular attention; the in-structor may be summarizing the whole period, thus giving you a chance to fill in gaps in the notes you have taken. Even if not summarizing, the reason he is perhaps talking a bit faster or perhaps holding the class a minute or two after the bell has rung is that he thinks he has something worth saying to you. If he is not summarizing, he may be thinking to him-self: "I've just got to tell them this point, for they have to know it; and I can't examine them on it if I haven't at least mentioned it in class." Or he may be giving an important assignment.

For all of these reasons, the conscientious student pays not less and less attention as the end of the period approaches but more and more. This requires special effort, especially if there is much shuffling of feet or collecting of books and assembling of papers as the bell rings. But as long as the instructor talks, it's best to keep your notebook open and your pen poised.

When a teacher enters a discussion class, he usually has clearly in mind several major points which he wishes to get across. By suitable questioning, he will try to make the students think of these points for themselves. This question-and-answer technique progresses quite slowly. The students don't think as fast as they could be told; the instructor may have difficulty relating what they say to what he expected them to say, and irrelevant questions may be raised.

A prepared lecture, on the other hand, moves rather quickly. Without the danger of irrelevant student questions, without the obligation to adjust his approach to student attitudes, and without the necessity for going any slower than he himself can think, the lecturer will usually cover a much larger quantity of material than the discussion leader. In fact, he may cover so much that the student has great difficulty keeping up with him. The problem the lecturer faces is not "What shall I say?" Rather, it is "What shall I leave out?"

Note-taking is therefore more critical. How much should the student try to convert into black and white? Although the answer depends largely upon the particular lecture, a very few general principles may be cited:

First, do not take it all down. You can't, unless you take

shorthand; and even if you can take shorthand, trying to get everything will divert your attention from the content of what is said, where your attention should be, to transcription of the exact sounds, which don't matter.

Second, concentrate on getting down anything that is repeated. If the lecturer takes the trouble to say something twice, he must think it especially important.

Third, distinguish between examples and the principles they illustrate (the lecturer is usually obliging enough to tell you which is which). English, fortunately, is a discipline that lends itself to exemplification, particularly in introductory courses. All the details of an example need not be reproduced. Jotting down a catch-phrase, a title, that may recall the whole to you later will usually suffice. If it doesn't, the loss is probably trivial.

Fourth, take your notes in outline form if possible, listening very carefully for transitional phrases (such as "Next we will consider . . . The third part . . . Others have taken a different attitude . . ."); announcements of what is to be taken up (such as "First I will, . . . and then . . . Before taking up such and such . . ."); and summaries of what has been said thus far. Organized knowledge is retained; disorganized knowledge is lost. Returning from Europe, I put my traveler's checks in the case with my typewriter, so that I would not lose them. Then I had to borrow the fare from New York to Chicago, because I could not remember where I had put the checks. I carefully explained that they weren't *lost*—I just didn't know where they were. The same thing happens to ideas when they are not appropriately organized.

Taking notes in class is easier than taking notes in lecture because there is less to be noted. Unfortunately, it is also harder: like the professor preparing a lecture, the student in class must decide what to leave out. Since students will be volunteering information or trying to answer specific questions, the note-taker must evaluate their responses. Remember that some of what they say will be wrong; but remember too that some of what they say not only will be right, but also may be important.

The instructor should tip off his evaluation of student response. Frequently an instructor will repeat whatever good points have been made by a student, in order to insure that other students have heard it. Just as often, however, he will content himself by saying, "That's right." Obviously, it's important to know which your instructor does. If he does not repeat, you must listen closely to what your peers say (personally, I think this a good reason for the instructor's not repeating a student's valid point). Even if he does not explicitly confirm what the boy on your right said, he may show acceptance of it by dropping that topic and going on to another point. Unless he returns later on to correct it, this procedure usually means that he agrees.

The one exception to this rule comes when the instructor discovers he is running out of class time and still hasn't accomplished what he intended. He may then move on to a new point without settling the previous one. Usually, though, he will say that is what he is doing. If a point is left unsettled, approach him after class and try to get it settled. In any event, looking over class notes while they are still fresh in your mind (this can profitably be done with lecture notes, too), and trying to discern some organization, some ratio of greater to lesser importance in what is written, will help organize the ideas more clearly and memorably. For example, in a freshman course, the clarification of a critical term—say, dramatic irony, would be more important than the examples that might be examined in detail—say, Oedipus cursing the criminal that he himself unknowingly is. In this case, so many examples of dramatic irony dependent upon Oedipus' ignorance might be cited in class that they should be subsumed in your notes under such a heading:

"dramatic irony—when a character says things that are true or appropriate in ways he doesn't know. Ex: all Oedipus' remarks about the killer, which the audience knows him to be, although he doesn't (says to punish him if he doesn't punish the killer, curses killer no matter who, etc.)"

And, finally, if anything in your notes confuses you, you can ask the instructor for clarification.

The principle of thinking critically applies not only to notetaking but also to preparation. Since most courses in literature aim at least partly toward improving the student's ability to read critically, simply memorizing the instructor's insights is, more often than not, inadequate. You have not learned enough if you simply write down the specific interpretations of poem or play that he offers. As he interprets, explains, analyzes, consider constantly how you might have thought of those points for yourself. Being well prepared for class means having tried in advance to think of everything the instructor might say. As he tells you the things you didn't think of (not historical or biographical facts, but details of analysis and interpretation), ask yourself what clue you might have pursued to come to his conclusions. Sometimes the point will be one no student could think of for himself. More often, particularly in beginning classes, a student who started looking in the right place could have come up with the idea himself. This book has suggested, as your instructor will, the places to look and what you may find.

A final word about learning in discussion class. I have said that taking notes helps the mind both to store and to digest. The same benefits come from taking part in discussion. Grasping a new idea is a process that requires involvement. The student who does not participate orally in a discussion is not really involved. And if his involvement is really total, if he cares for the advancement of learning, he will acknowledge a responsibility to his fellow students to share his own understandings and formulations with them.

B. Textbook Assignments

Textbooks tell no tales. Presumably neither fanciful nor false, they tend to be much easier—if much less challenging—reading than literature and propaganda, both of which almost always work somewhat indirectly and may very well lie. A textbook may therefore be approached with a naïve acceptance, and probably should be, in introductory courses. Because it is explicit, the textbook first announces its topic, then says what it means, and then tells you what it has said. Look, therefore, for topic sentences, thesis statements, and summaries.

As in all writing, the place of greatest emphasis is the end. This applies to expository prose (such as a textbook) as well as to literature, and to the parts as well as to the whole. When reading a textbook assignment, therefore, look very closely at the end of the assignment. The place of next greatest emphasis is the beginning: look well there, too. I don't recommend omitting the middle (this is intended as an understatement), but ordinarily it will contain details. The universality of this ratio of emphasis comes not from a conspiracy on the part of authors but from the psychology of human attention. What comes first hits us fresh, with all the impact of novelty on unwavering attention; what comes last lingers, which is why adults eat their dessert after the rest of the meal. Children, who just don't know any better and can't imagine that far into the future, eat their dessert first, if Mama will let them. But nobody eats his dessert in the middle of the meal.

Still, the middle of the meal is often the most healthful; so it should be eaten, too. What does this distribution of emphasis mean for the student confronted by his text? Since the author of the text knows what portions of his work will receive the greatest emphasis in the reader's mind, he puts in those places the most important points. Before reading in detail, scan the section assigned. Read the introductory and concluding paragraphs, then go through the sections and do the same for each paragraph. Skip (while scanning) obviously illustrative material, such as quotations from poems. You should find announcements of what the topic is; thesis statements where a single major point is to be made; and topic sentences within the individual paragraphs. Don't confuse transitions with beginnings or endings. For example, the first sentence of this paragraph is transitional, and not the topic of the paragraph. The second sentence announces that topic. And this final sentence states the paragraph's thesis: After scanning the beginnings and endings of all parts of the assignment, you should have an organized grasp of the major points, and then not only read the assignment through with better understanding but remember longer what you have read.

Making written notes helps fix ideas in your memory, even if you never review what you have written. This point applies to reading textbooks and, indeed, anything. You will remember your assignments better if you take outline notes on them. If you do not have time to be so thorough, a good halfway step is to mark significant passages as you read them, either by underlining or by side-lining. Side-lining, which for probably unmentionable neurotic reasons I prefer, is much neater; but underlining facilitates more precise selection of words for emphasis. Mark with a question mark anything you don't understand, and if objections or qualifications occur to you, write them down, too. Buying someone else's thoroughly marked-up book has this great drawback: it discourages you from making your own selection of important statements. The fact that you make that selection and mark it yourself will do more than anything else to fix it in your mind. Always study with a pencil in your hand.

Some textbooks, of course, practically demand that you study with pencil at hand, for they continually ask questions on what you have just read, or perhaps ask that you apply to exemplary material the principles just explained. Always try to answer these questions, even if your instructor has not specifically directed that you do so. Write down the answers to those you can answer, and ask about any you cannot. In working on a question, look for the author's motive in asking that question. If you don't know why a good study question (of course you might hit a few bad ones) has been asked, then you have not understood either the answer or the general context. Consider specifically whether the question is based on the context of that chapter or whether it reminds you of something studied earlier. If a poetry text, for example, defines overstatement and understatement, and then asks for a comment on the figurative use of language in the lines, "And I will luve thee still, my dear,/ Til a' the seas gang dry," don't begin by inventing hidden symbolic significance, or wrestling with whether the lines are metaphor or simile. Consider the question first in terms of the immediate context, and decide whether the lines may be overstatement or understatement. If neither (they are, of course, overstatement), consider the possibilities discussed in earlier chapters.

This principle, of understanding relevance to context, applies to other aspects of the text. For example, if examples are offered be sure you understand what they are intended to illustrate.

Sometimes a text will have done your underlining for you, by printing significant words or statements in italics or boldface type. Clearly, it would be foolish to ignore such clues.

Since a text is a study-aid itself, few study-aids are appropriate for use with a text. This chapter is one; a good dictionary is another. The dictionary should always be used in conjunction with technical and semitechnical vocabulary. While reading your text, ask yourself what words are being used in apparently special senses, or what analytical concepts —perhaps, in the case of a sophomore survey text, historical characteristics—are expressed in catchwords. Work toward as precise an understanding of those words as possible, and start with a dictionary. Frequently, your text will provide a glossary of terms at the end. When it does, use this in preference to the dictionary for all words you can find in it. Some words are used in different ways by different writers; some cannot be defined with very great precision. For these, rely primarily upon your text itself, using the dictionary for the rest. But in any case, identify what seems to be technical vocabulary, and learn those words. Indeed, some texts are very largely dictionaries of critical concepts, with examples.

As this discussion of studying textbooks indicates, many of the methods suggested for the study of literary art also apply to expository prose. Attention to beginnings and endings, trying to understand what at first seems unexplained, noting carefully the unusual (at the simplest possible level, unusual print, such as italics), looking for repetitions, checking part divisions for what unifies them—all of these methods may help you to understand both literary and nonliterary writing.

The major difference in method involves the initial contact. A textbook assignment may well be skimmed in advance, and you will understand and remember it better if you do preview it. But literature should not be previewed. Art should be given the chance to make its fullest impact through a direct confrontation. Then the student reader or the professional critic tries to increase his understanding by the process of analysis. Ideally, the analysis completed, he returns to the work, ready to meet it again with greater understanding. Even more ideally, the process of analysis becomes an almost un-noticed part of the initial understanding.

C. Examinations

1. Preparation

In Goethe's *Faust*, Mephistopheles advises a student to prepare, for his professor. The devil's advice is ironically intended (he is mocking all formal education); but as long as it is not taken exclusively, and as long as the student remembers that it is ultimately for himself that he prepares, it is good advice. Nowhere is preparation more immediately practical than in the examination room.

A good examination allows each student to show what he has learned and how well. Such an exam does not necessarily test everything the student may have learned during the course. The instructor's preference in neckties may have been outstanding, but it will not appear on the exam. Nor will all that the student has learned about the course material, about the reading assignments, appear on the exam. Not everything is important. The less important, the less likely to appear on an exam, and the less reason for appearing on an exam.

For a number of years I have taught Dante's *Inferno*, the first part of his *Divine Comedy*. Every class has wanted to know how much to remember. In one sense the question is legitimate. Indices of proper names in this tightly packed work, rich with allusions, contain about 700 entries. Clearly, memorizing the entire list would be an exhausting grind, of little significance. In another sense, the question is improper. Every course tries to communicate more than can be compressed into a final examination. To ask "What should we remember?" implies that there are only two types of information: important things, which will be on the exam, and unimportant ones, which won't. Actually, there are many, many degrees of importance, and a good examination will sample some of all, with greatest emphasis on the most important.

My answer to the student who wants to know how many of the names in the *Inferno* he must remember goes as follows. First, the student is theoretically responsible for knowing everything that goes on. In theory, that is, the instructor will not present something in class unless he has some interest in the student's hearing it. Since the examination is a *sampling* of the student's learning in the course, some trivia may be included. Second, although the student is responsible for everything, he is most responsible for the most important things. The instruction should indicate what those most important things are. Part of the purpose of the examination is to determine whether the student has learned to tell what is important and what is not. The real question, then, is how to tell what is of greater importance.

One course may emphasize one aspect of a work, and another course a different aspect. For example, in presenting the *Inferno* one course might stress its historical position, as a bridge from Middle Ages to Renaissance; another might stress the poem's allegorical aspect. In the first course, allusions to classical characters would be important because rediscovery of the classical world is one of the ways in which the Renaissance differed from the Middle Ages. In the second course, characters related to recurrent themes would be important because allegory depends on the relationships among a number of symbols. Therefore, a student learns to tell what is important partly by listening to what his instructor emphasizes. Facts relevant to that emphasis, even if not used as examples by the instructor, are more important to the purposes of that course than other facts are. It follows that in studying for an examination a student should review the reading in the light of the general ideas (such as historical characteristics or allegory) presented by the instructor.

In addition, a few simple principles indicate what is important. In the *Inferno*, some characters are mentioned once only; many characters are simply named; some do not speak; some receive only half a line of text. These are surely less important than characters whom Dante mentions several times, who are graphically described, who engage in lengthy dialogue, who occupy a whole canto or section of the poem. Importance, that is, is defined not only by the instructor and the course, but by the work itself.

Finally, the more ways in which something is important, the greater its total importance. Virgil matters in the *Inferno* because he reflects Dante's interest in classical figures; and because he functions at several levels of allegorical meaning; and also because he receives great emphasis in the text, present as he is throughout virtually the entire poem. A student who forgets Virgil has simply forgotten the *Inferno*.

Preparing for the instructor and his examinations requires judgment. I suppose any student could memorize all of the characters mentioned in the *Inferno*. But he wouldn't have time for much else, including other courses. Both studying and reviewing, therefore, must involve critical reading, asking: "Is this important? why?"

2. Types of Examinations

Probably the most useful way to categorize examinations is according to the length of the answers: long, short, and selected—commonly called "essay," "short-answer," and "objective." In spite of the preference of some students (and instructors) for one type over the others, all are valid, if in slightly different ways. The longer the answer, the more the student's ability to develop ideas is tested; the shorter, the more the material that may be covered. Essay tests reveal scope, objective tests require precision and specificity. They are equally fair, although again in different ways. Although the essay test allows the student to show what he has learned in personal terms, not forcing him into the straitjacket of limited alternatives, nevertheless the grading standard has to be subjective. The objective test reverses the situation: although it forces the student to choose among few alternatives, no one of which may be the total truth, not allowing for the student's unique insight, nevertheless the grading standard is fixed and impartial, unaffected by the teacher's reactions to the papers he graded first. The objective test has been defined (in contrast to an essay test) as one in which the instructor's subjectivity comes into play before giving the test rather than after. No type of test is perfect, but all are legitimate and effective.

Most students have at least some acquaintance with all three types of exams, but many make unnecessary mistakes in taking a given type. Here are some suggestions.

A. ESSAY TESTS

In most English courses, the person who can write a decent essay will get a decent grade. Therefore, grammatical correctness and clear organization are very important.

Your instructor will comment on what he expects, and will probably suggest outlining. In addition to making a preliminary outline before starting to write out the answer, you can achieve greater clarity by incorporating the outline into the answer itself: topic sentences, transitional sentences and phrases, and anticipations and summaries structure an answer just as they do any essay, making it clearer and therefore more impressive.

Just as clear organization requires preliminary outlining and attention during the writing process, so grammatical correctness and stylistic smoothness require attention during the writing process and proofreading afterward. You should allot time for proofreading at the end of the test period. One danger of essay exams comes from making editorial changes without the appropriate adjustments. Thus a student might first write "Fortinbras is a foil for Hamlet," then go back and insert after "Fortinbras" the words "and Laertes," without changing the verb to agree with the now plural subject. Sometimes a student makes such an error by changing his mind in the middle of the sentence as he writes it, even though he knows better. Only careful proofreading can prevent such unnecessary mistakes.

Legibility insures a fairer grade (and illegibility is annoying). However, if your instructor will accept legible corrections, time need not be wasted on making a perfect copy.

The two most common errors in writing answers to essay

examinations both involve time. The student who finds he has finished long in advance of the allotted time may be tempted to keep going, to expand by padding, to repeat, to say again, in verbose convolvulaceous sesquipedalianism. Any teacher worth his salt can spot such stuffing at once. The only good expansion adds additional content or clarifies structure.

In contrast to the student who finishes early, the student who never finishes at all runs out of time somewhere in the middle of Point Two, Example A. He either has not had the sense to bring a watch to the exam or has tried to put down everything he knows about the course. Either is a mistake. A well-prepared student should select what he will include in his essay answer. This need is part of the reason for outlining in advance.

Finally, the best essay answers operate at two levels: general principle and specific example. An essay without generalizations is a hodgepodge of unassimilated and disorganized fragments; an essay without examples is empty wind, meaningless and imprecise. The generality expresses significance; the example proves and clarifies.

B. SHORT-ANSWER TESTS

The length of the "short" answer required may vary from a single word to a paragraph. The single word or fill-in-the-blanks test is more restricted in its scope than the others, resembling a simple objective test. The paragraph answer, of course, is virtually several little essay tests. The single-sentence answer is in many ways the hardest, both to write and to grade. If you do not understand the point of the question, your answer will simply be wrong. Whereas an essay will provide a context that may make your own interpretation of the question comprehensible and perhaps legitimate, the single sentence does not allow you to justify your unconscious misreading by what you do with it. A moment's second thought— is my answer what the question was aimed at?—is the only safeguard (besides, of course, thorough preparation in advance of the test).

Since most short-answer tests are graded by assigning a certain number of points to each question, answering all of the questions is very important. Conceivably, you might be able to spend the entire exam period writing a beautiful essay in answer to the first question. But if there are ten questions, and the instructor has assigned ten points to each, your score is a maximum of ten out of a hundred. The examiner may include a question that tempts you to spend so much time precisely because answering such a question requires selection.

C. OBJECTIVE TESTS

Contrary to some students' opinion, good objective questions can be written on literature. At the University of Chicago when I was an undergraduate, even the philosophy course had objective questions; they averaged two a page, and each alternative was a short paragraph. Most objective tests on literature, however, offer less daunting alternatives. Some rules of testmanship for objective tests are:

1. *Read all the alternatives before answering.*

2. *Look for patterns in the alternatives that make understanding the question easier.* A simple and readily understandable pattern links one thing with two others in various combinations. For example:

Shakespeare is
    A. both a playwright and a poet
    B. a playwright, but not a poet
    C. a poet, but not a playwright
    D. neither a playwright nor a poet

Sometimes this pattern appears as follows, linking two things with one:

Shakespeare and Dickens may be compared in that
    A. both are playwrights
    B. Shakespeare is a playwright, but Dickens is not
    C. Dickens is a playwright, but Shakespeare is not
    D. neither Shakespeare nor Dickens is a playwright

Basically similar is the pattern linking two with two:

Shakespeare and Dickens may be compared in that
    A. both are playwrights
    B. Shakespeare is a playwright, but Dickens is a novelist

    C. Dickens is a playwright, but Shakespeare is a
       novelist
    D. both Shakespeare and Dickens are novelists

These are examples of extremely simple factual questions. However, when the alternatives get more complicated or sophisticated, noticing some pattern such as those suggested above may help substantially.

Some questions, of course, have no such pattern, but simply list five disparate alternatives. For example:

Shakespeare
    A. wrote only three tragedies
    B. died in the year Queen Elizabeth was born
    C. rejected the Renaissance concept of the Great Chain
       of Being
    D. came close to following the neoclassical unities in
       The Tempest
    E. tried unsuccessfully to obtain a divorce

In answering such a question, each alternative must be considered separately. Again, though, it's best to check all alternatives before selecting one. The first may be right, but the second may be righter, and the best alternative is the one that scores. For example:

Shakespeare wrote
    A. tragedy
    B. tragedy and comedy
    C. tragedy and romance
    D. comedy and romance
    E. tragedy, comedy, romance, and satire

When the alternatives are groups of answers in different combinations, eliminating wrong answers is often the fastest approach. For example:

Shakespeare wrote
    A. plays, sonnets, and novels
    B. sonnets, novels, and narrative poems
    C. novels, narrative poems, and plays
    D. narrative poems, plays, and sonnets

After reading the first alternative, and spotting the incorrect item "novels" you may eliminate alternatives #2 and #3 at a glance, simply by noting that they include the wrong answer.

3. *Skip a question that gives trouble and come back to it after answering the easy ones.* As with all tests, watching the time is important.

4. *Be aware of certain psychological tendencies.* Students tend to pick the longest answer, as the one most carefully phrased; they tend to regard a large number of the same answer in a row as unlikely (on one test I took, the correct answer was D for twenty questions in a row!); the examiner may actually have a preference for or against making a certain alternative the right answer. But your instructor knows all of these things. Therefore, trying to outguess him without a computer and a ten-year supply of keyed tests is a grievous error. Indeed, most single tests are much too short to warrant statistical inferences, such as "Professor Jones likes answer *B;* I'll guess that whenever I don't know the answer." This may be the day Professor Jones sets out to eliminate B from his key.

5. *Guess, if all else fails.* Guessing has a legitimate place. Most objective tests are scored by subtracting a fraction of the wrong answers from the right answers. The purpose of this subtraction is compensation for random guessing. If a student marks at random, he will average 20 questions out of 100 if there are 5 alternatives for each question. Subtracting ¼ of the wrong (¼ of 80 is 20) from the right corrects his score to 0. But the student who answers only when he is willing to stake his life on the correctness of the answer will do poorly. In general, if any of the alternatives can be eliminated as clearly wrong, it is better to make an informed guess from among the remaining alternatives than to leave the item blank.

Examinations have many functions. Motivating the student to study, rewarding the outstanding student, helping graduate schools make their selection, reminding the instructor to keep his course focused and not wander off down the byways of learning, all are legitimate reasons for testing. An exam can also be a stimulating educational experience. A good test both reviews a course and puts it in perspective; it also suggests new insights. You don't have to be an honors student to anticipate a little mind-stretching. Yes, folks (delivered in a rich fruity tone of voice whose irony allows you to disagree without concealing my basic conviction), you too can have fun at finals!

D. The Term Paper and the Oral Report

Both the term paper and the oral report require the student to present formally the results of his own independent study and thinking. Since the term paper is far and away the more massive undertaking of the two, usually requiring a wider variety of skills, let's consider it first.

1. Term Papers

Writing a term paper involves five rather different processes, which are performed more or less consecutively. Although they may overlap, the steps in chronological order are:

1. Selecting a topic

2. Taking notes

3. Stating the thesis and outlining the paper

4. Writing the draft

5. Making the properly annotated final copy in correct format

1. Selecting a workable topic is much harder than most students assume. A good topic is one which has not already been thoroughly covered by a scholar. It has aroused enough interest to produce material for the student to work with—but not so much interest that it cannot be covered adequately within the length restrictions of the assignment. How on earth is the student to know whether his topic is a good one until he has tried to write the paper?

First, there is virtually no way of knowing whether a topic includes a possible thesis of your own until you are just about ready to work on the final draft. Most instructors therefore do not require complete originality of insight in a freshman or sophomore term paper.

Second, if your instructor recommends some topics, it is a good idea to work with one of his suggestions. Presumably he suggests them because he knows they are workable.

Third, you may pick an area that interests you, with the expectation of narrowing it. Almost all original topics are too broad in their scope. Scanning as much relevant material as possible will then help you to state the topic precisely. The advantage of knowing as much as possible before settling on a specific task is clearer perhaps in the area of science. Who, without knowing anything about biochemistry, would try to state a topic he planned to write on? In less radical form, the same problem arises in literary study. Therefore, scanning, browsing, and miscellaneous poking around should precede precise formulation of the topic.

Fourth, the process of browsing is itself a preliminary survey of how much material is available. The best topic does not appear as the title of someone else's book, chapter, or essay, but is discussed, perhaps even indexed.

Finally, the nearest thing to a ready-made topic is an explication of a particular short story, poem, or play. Some instructors make use of casebooks, collections of critical material dealing with a particular work or problem, for a term-paper exercise.

Locating material is of course a matter of familiarity with the library and its catalogues and with such bibliographical sources as those listed in Appendix E.

2. Even if the topic is ready-made, it is very hard to know what notes should be taken until most of the material has been

read. Even when working with an assigned topic, therefore, scanning a good bit of the material before even beginning to take notes is advisable. "A good bit" means "at least most" and "preferably all."

Many students, when annotating, run into trouble that careful note-taking would have prevented. They fail to distinguish clearly between directly quoted phrases or sentences and their own recasting or paraphrasing. The author's exact words, of course, must always be in quotation marks, whereas rephrased material is introduced as indirect quotation. Changing one or two words and the position of one phrase does not constitute rephrasing. Since the paper will be written from notes and not from the texts of the sources themselves, notes must discriminate between direct and indirect quotation.

Most texts suggest a mechanical procedure that I personally have rarely used, but which most writers apparently find helpful, to wit, the use of note cards. The reasons for using note cards are good: enforced brevity, portability, easy separation of distinct ideas which can therefore be reshuffled in the writing process without the need for cutting up huge pieces of paper into irregular little snippets. Moreover, most instructors and texts specify the way cards should be labeled. Obviously, one could use different sizes of paper or card, and one could number note cards in lower left rather than upper right. But even though in subsequent semesters you may modify such mechanical procedures for your own convenience and taste, the format suggested by your instructor deserves a conscientious try.

3. The problem of organizing a term paper is not radically different from the problems involved in organizing other written assignments. As in all writing, intelligent structuring depends on what the point is. The thesis must be stated clearly before the outline can be prepared. Both thesis and outline may subsequently be revised, but the first step cannot be plotted until the goal—the conclusion to be reached—is known.

One trap for the unwary lies in the possibly conflicting opinions of the sources. Since much of the material presented in the final paper will be the words and thoughts of others, and not of the student, he may inadvertently include contrary ideas. If the contradiction or conflict is not explicitly recognized in the way the ideas are introduced, the result is chaotic. This trap can be avoided by remembering that not everything in print is gospel, and that interpretations of literature, in particular, may conflict. Perhaps the hardest thing for the novice student of literature is keeping a balance between arbitrary authoritarianism and irresponsible subjectivity. That critics disagree means neither that one is absolutely wrong, or the other absolutely right, nor that the question of who is right doesn't apply. One of them may be simply wrong, but it is more likely that the views of both have some degree of validity. When critical interpretations differ, it is the commentator's task—in this case, the term-paper author's task— to show what amount of validity belongs to each view.

4. Writing the draft of a term paper is just like writing the draft for any other paper. Since much of the material will be cited from various sources, there will be many phrases identifying the person whose idea is stated: "Jones thinks . . ."; "According to Jones . . ."; "Jones goes on to say . . ."; "In Jones's view . . ."; "Jones would have it that . . ."; "Jones regards literature as . . ."; "Jones interprets this as . . ."; "Jones claims . . ."; "Jones argues . . ."; "Jones maintains . . ."; "Jones persuasively urges the view that . . ."; "Jones tries to show that . . ."; "One critic, Brown . . ."; "One writer [identified in a footnote as Brown] . . ."; "In contrast, Smith thinks . . ."; "Smith agrees, adding the point that . . ."; "On the other hand, according to Smith . . ."

As with any composition, writing the term paper as much in advance as possible, so as to let it gel before proofreading, gives you a fresher perspective and a more critical eye. Proofreading something you have just written is much less effective, for you will persistently see not what you have written, but what you meant. The period after completion of the final draft is virtually the only time in the term-paper process when incubation may help, and even then too much delay may enforce hasty typing with all of the errors haste implies.

5. Preparing the final copy in correct format is a simple matter of following instructions. The most common error I have encountered, apart from leaving the final copying until the night before the paper is due, is the assumption that the format this instructor uses is the same as the format used by

the last instructor. One of the virtues of a particular format is its internal consistency. While there are a number of accepted formats and guides to annotation, mixing them or following one when your instructor uses another can only lead to confusion. Therefore, prepare the final copy with the instructions and model footnotes required by your instructor right by the typewriter. Memorizing format is unprofitable unless your instructor requires it. In the field of literature, the *MLA Style Sheet* is increasingly the authority for recommended form. Every idea that is learned from another source must be annotated. Everything that the student does not think of for himself, or observe himself, or that is not common knowledge, he must annotate. The reasons are two: honesty, in acknowledging that the idea is someone else's; verification, in making it possible for the reader to check the original source for its authority, the accuracy of the term-paper's report, and the significance of the original context. Failure to provide the necessary footnote is dishonest, because it falsely claims originality, and conceited, because it demands belief without authority.

In theory, a term paper is a public utterance. It should be written as though for publication. When well executed, with thoughtful arguments and documented evidence, it marks the student's participation in the search for understanding that animates the world of scholarship.

2. *Oral Reports*

Like all compositions, the oral report should be interesting, clear, and accurate. Although the three characteristics overlap and in some respects are inseparable, examples and forceful language keep interest; generalizing and stating organization clarify; and careful notes on preparatory research insure accuracy.

Some graduate courses call for oral reports that are virtually term papers read aloud in class. The only distinctive guide for the content of such a report is the rule that significant points should be repeated. The listener who scratches his ear may not have heard the point then being stated, and since no page is before his eyes, he cannot check back to pick it up on his own. The speaker must state it again.

Undergraduate classes call for reports varying from exercises in speaking before a group, with little emphasis on the content, to participation in the actual instruction in, say, a senior seminar. But even in the most informal report, what is said matters. The contents should therefore be planned in advance, with all of the careful organization, selection of detail, choice of phrasing, and timed rehearsal that adequate preparation requires. In this case, the medium is *not* the message.

One can, of course, distinguish between the delivery and the content of what is delivered. Most students could improve their performance by attending to the following:

1. *Eye contact.* To maintain contact with the audience. To keep it and the speaker aware of each other, the latter must constantly look up from notes or text—not at the ceiling or back wall, but at the individual listeners.

2. *Vocal melody.* Speech has musical pitch. The typical melody differs from language to language. French rises at phrase endings, settling only at the end of the sentence:

English intonation, in contrast, drops at phrase endings, rather more at sentence end:

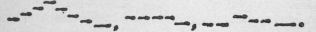

Even English English and American English differ, most markedly perhaps in the melodic pattern of a question:

Have you been to the cinema lately, Aunt Susan?

Have you been to the movies lately, Aunt Sue?

The American interrogative intonation rises steadily, in contrast to the graceful reverse curve of English pitch. The student delivering an oral report should listen to the melody

SPEECH EVALUATION FORM

SPEAKER ―――――――――――― DATE ―――――

SUBJECT ――――――――――――――――――

CONTENT	Minimum				Maximum
Effective opening	1	2	3	4	5
Organization	1	2	3	4	5
Soundness of ideas	1	2	3	4	5
Clarity of language	1	2	3	4	5
Interest	1	2	3	4	5
Adequate length	1	2	3	4	5
Effective conclusion	1	2	3	4	5

DELIVERY					
Appropriate volume	1	2	3	4	5
Appropriate rate of speaking	1	2	3	4	5
Enunciation	1	2	3	4	5
Expression and variety	1	2	3	4	5
Contact with audience	1	2	3	4	5
Posture, gesture, facial expression	1	2	3	4	5

Time began――――― Ended――――― Total time―――――
Total score―――――

COMMENTS

EVALUATOR――――――

of his own voice, and consciously vary it, for interest and emphasis. Monotones are monotonous.

3. *Personal expression.* A report that is read seems impersonal and distant, and is in danger of losing attention. Speaking from abbreviated notes may ruffle the smoothness of the delivery, but it insures that you personally are talking to the people before you.

The following evaluation sheet was developed by one professor for use in freshman classes. Copies of the form are distributed to the reporting student's classmates, who mark it as he speaks.

All of the criteria we have mentioned concern communication. The goal of both the term paper and the oral report is communication. First you have something to say, and then you say it. Content before expression; clarity before elegance.

E. A Brief Annotated Bibliography

A *bibliography* is a research tool. For the serious scholar, inclusiveness is the criterion by which bibliographies are measured, with convenience and informative comments serving as secondary standards. Unfortunately, informative comments and inclusiveness virtually rule each other out. The *Publications of the Modern Language Association of America (PMLA)* for May 1966 lists 3,381 separate entries, books and articles, concerning English literature published in the previous year. And to round things off, it adds 1,544 entries on American literature. It is just not possible to provide summaries, with or without criticisms, of that many works every year. Critical (or annotated) bibliographies are therefore very incomplete, and bibliographical appendices, like this, are bare samplings.

The function of a bibliography is to tell you where to go and, if annotated, to suggest what you may find there. Standard sources for advanced students of English literature are the *Cambridge Bibliography of English Literature*, edited by F. W. Bateson, which with the supplementary fifth volume covers literature (primary material) up to 1900 and criticism and scholarship (secondary material) up to roughly 1955;

and the annual bibliography published in the May *PMLA,* mentioned above, which since 1956 has included non-American scholarship. Other general bibliographies for students of English (there are special bibliographies for particular topics) include inexpensive one-volume listings by Arthur G. Kennedy and Donald B. Sands, *A Concise Bibliography for Students of English,* and Tom Peete Cross and Donald F. Bond, *A Reference Guide to English Studies.* For American literature, consult Volume II (Third Edition) of Spiller, Thorp, Johnson, Canby and Ludwig's *Literary History of the United States.*

The least depressing general bibliography of English I know is *A Guide to English Literature,* published in 1965, by the same F. W. Bateson who edited CBEL. (The government, as you can see, has no monopoly on alphabetese.) This excellent book is a critical bibliography with chapters of text characterizing each historical period. The title listings, emphasizing the best annotated text for each author, are invaluable to the beginner. In addition to the period bibliographies, there is a chapter on criticism, listing books concerned with each of the major genres. As always, one should hesitate to take the evaluative comments as gospel, but this lively, clear, and useful book is probably the least terrifying and the best bibliography for the beginning student.

For periodical listings, the beginner will probably be happiest working with the *Social Sciences and Humanities Index* (formerly the *International Index*). This bibliography of articles in professional journals falls somewhere between the nonscholarly *Reader's Guide to Periodical Literature,* which lists general interest magazines and the *PMLA Index,* which is compiled only in one-year units and is therefore more tedious to use for the average freshman or sophomore who cannot afford to look up all articles dealing with *Hamlet.* As a matter of fact, since over forty articles or books on *Hamlet* were published in 1964 alone, even the junior or senior English major might have some difficulty doing that.

The subject-index of the library card catalogue is of course a basic source of books (although not of periodical articles), and each book of secondary material or annotated primary material is apt to provide its own bibliography. Summaries of selected work can be found in *The Year's Work in English Studies* and *Abstracts of English Studies.*

One word of warning. When consulting bibliographies, expect to spend some time learning how to use them. The student who grabs six unfamiliar ones off the shelves at 10:40 and expects to have a working bibliography for a term paper by the time the 11:00 bell rings may cry a lot.

Standard reference works include the various encyclopedias (such as *Britannica*) and dictionaries. The *Oxford English Dictionary* is a massive compilation of the first printed use of words in each of their meanings (that is, it is a historical dictionary). The two-column *Shorter Oxford English Dictionary* is handier, although of course much less thorough. The historical dictionary is particularly useful for poetry with archaic or obsolete vocabulary. In spite of the furor over its permissiveness, Webster's *Third New International Dictionary* is probably the best one-volume, all-purpose dictionary of English. College students consult it if their own "collegiate"-size dictionary doesn't have the word they need to know. A collegiate dictionary, incidentally, is one that is too big to fit into the pocket and has over 1,000 pages of rather small print. Smaller dictionaries are inadequate for college purposes.

The Thrall, Hibbard, and Holman *Handbook to Literature* (revised 1960) lists critical vocabulary, including the names of periods and movements. One page, for example, has the entries Originality, Ossianic Controversy, Otiose, Ottava rima, and Oxford Movement. *The Oxford Companion to English Literature,* together with its companion, *The Oxford Companion to American Literature,* is the place to look up literary authors, titles, and characters.

Literary histories are numerous, the massive, graceful, and somewhat dated *Cambridge History of English Literature* being the grandfather. *The Oxford History of English Literature* is sufficiently more recent that it is still in process. A. C. Baugh's *A Literary History of England* compresses its coverage into one volume, as does the latest edition of *The Literary History of the United States* by Spiller et al., mentioned above for its bibliography.

David Daiches' *A Critical History of English Literature* is very readable, with liberal quotations, "critical" because it evalutes the works discussed. The author states in the preface that he intended the book "less as a work of reference than as a work of description, explanation, and critical inter-

pretation. It is not meant to be looked up, but to be read." *
In this respect it differs from most of the books cited so far.

When working on a term paper, you may find various
paperback collections helpful. A number of publishers are
issuing series of either criticism with a common topic or literary texts plus relevant criticism. Prentice-Hall's "Twentieth
Century Views" series reprints articles and chapters dealing
with the writer named in the title. W. W. Norton's "Norton
Critical Editions" series combines a text (say, of Shakespeare's *Henry IV, Part 1*) with critical discussions of the
play and relevant source material. Others, such as D. C.
Heath's *Discussions of . . .* , Thomas Y. Crowell's *A Casebook
on . . .* , the Scribner Research Anthologies, the *Harbrace
Sourcebooks,* and various Wadsworth publications, are similar
or may focus on broader (e.g., comedy) or more problematic
(e.g., literary symbolism) topics.

For the form of footnotes and bibliographical entries, the
MLA Style Sheet, published by the Modern Language Association, is the standard on many campuses and for many
scholarly periodicals. (Graduate schools specify the more exhaustive manuals they require for theses and dissertations.)
The college student who expects to write term papers for
science courses, too, may find *A Short Guide to Manuscript
Form and Documentation* by Eliot D. Allen and Ethel B.
Colbrunn convenient, for besides incorporating the MLA
recommendations for papers in the humanities and social
sciences, it illustrates the more common forms of annotation
in the natural sciences.

Shakespeare appears in most general courses. The best
single-volume editions of the plays are those in the New Arden
Edition, formerly under the general editorship of Una Ellis-
Fermor, now of Harold F. Brooks and Harold Jenkins. These
heavily annotated, critical editions should not be confused
with the slim, pocket-sized D. C. Heath Arden Edition, a
much older series that is not at all comparable. The New
Arden is published by Methuen in London and by Harvard
University Press in Cambridge, Mass. Something over half
of the plays are now available. Each volume, in addition to
reproducing all of the significant textual variations in footnotes, contains a long introduction covering not only the

---

* Daiches, *op. cit.*, p. 2.

scholarly problems such as date, source, and text, but also the critical questions of meaning and form, with summary of the major critical interpretations. (Since the original English Arden edition, which the New Arden is replacing, was completed in 1916, it is much less helpful to the nonspecialist, concentrating as it does on scholarly rather than critical problems.) *The New Cambridge Shakespeare,* edited by J. Dover Wilson, is also worth consulting.

Among the best-known criticisms of Shakespeare's work are those of A. C. Bradley, E. E. Stoll, Harley Granville-Barker, and G. Wilson Knight. A visiting lecture given by Knight when I was a student inspired me to stay up most of the night studying (the only time I recall this happening), and his books have some of the same inspirational quality. D. A. Traversi and H. C. Goddard have written stimulating books on Shakespeare: Traversi's treating the plays as poems, Goddard's discussing Christian themes.

What follows should be considered a reading list rather than a reference list. If you desire to explore the various genres, the following may interest you:

1. *Drama:* Cleanth Brooks and R. B. Heilman's critical anthology, *Understanding Drama,* intended as an introductory text but worthy of anyone's attention. Books by Francis Fergusson and by Eric Bentley assume a little more literary sophistication.

2. *Fiction:* E. M. Forster's *Aspects of the Novel* makes an excellent introduction; Brooks and Warren's *Understanding Fiction,* a companion to *Understanding Drama,* analyzes a number of short stories very closely and perceptively. *Writers at Work: The Paris Review Interviews,* ed. Malcolm Cowley, provides the insights of the authors themselves.

3. *Poetry:* For illustrations of basic critical terms, Perrine's *Sound and Sense* is excellent, if elementary. A slightly more sophisticated text along similar lines (definition of concept, illustrative poem, study questions) is X. J. Kennedy's *An Introduction to Poetry.* Josephine Miles's *The Poem* is an anthology with less apparatus and less emphasis on detailed analysis. This makes her comments more readable, as she classifies poems by their point of view in very illuminating introductions. Elizabeth Drew's *Poetry* is very readable, if

elementary; Cleanth Brooks's *The Well-Wrought Urn* is an excellent introduction to close reading, and shows why the "new criticism," a movement rejecting history and biography in favor of analysis of the individual text, has been so influential.

4. *Critical theory:* If your interests run toward theory, David Daiches' *Critical Approaches to Literature* and George Watson's *The Literary Critics* make a clear contrast: Daiches stressing criteria of evaluation, Watson maintaining criticism is possible only when evaluation is set aside. Both are histories of criticism. A purely theoretical approach that is both short and clear appears in Wayne Shumaker's *Elements of Critical Theory.* For an extremely sophisticated presentation of a complete theory of literature, go to Northrop Frye's *Anatomy of Criticism.* Although definitely not for beginners, the book's index makes a large number of individual insights available to the student who is doing a paper on one of Shakespeare's plays, say, but does not have the theoretical interest that is the book's focus.

When you know what you are looking for—be it critical insight into a particular work, the meaning of a term, a research list, or an evening's reading—you can find it. Bibliographies, dictionaries, histories, criticism—all have their uses to students of literature. All, of course, are secondary to the work itself.

Index of Terms

Index of Authors

An invaluable reference library of illuminating study guides to enrich your understanding and appreciation of the great works of fiction

---

Each volume includes reviews of fifty novels containing: —*plot outlines*
—*character analyses*
—*critical evaluations*
—*author's biographies*
—*notes on selected works by the same author*

PLUS: an Introduction on "How To Read a Novel" and an index of titles, authors, and main characters.

A STUDENT'S GUIDE TO 50 AMERICAN NOVELS   W • 0901/75¢
Edited by Abraham Lass

Guides to such classics as *Billy Budd, The Scarlet Letter, Arrowsmith, The Bridge of San Luis Rey, Light in August, The Human Comedy, The Naked and the Dead, Invisible Man,* and *The Catcher in the Rye.*

A STUDENT'S GUIDE TO 50 BRITISH NOVELS   W • 0902/75¢
Edited by Abraham Lass

A collection of summaries ranging from *Pilgrim's Progress* to *The Lord of the Flies* and including such works as *Gulliver's Travels, The Pickwick Papers, Vanity Fair, The Return of the Native, Lord Jim, Of Human Bondage, Brave New World,* and *1984.*

A STUDENT'S GUIDE TO 50 EUROPEAN NOVELS   W • 0900/75¢
Edited by Abraham Lass and Brooks Wright

A remarkably comprehensive collation including classics such as *Don Quixote* and *Candide,* contemporary masterpieces such as *The Stranger* and *Doctor Zhivago,* and encompassing the most famous works of Russian, French, Italian, German, and Spanish fiction.

WSP
ⁿ **WASHINGTON SQUARE PRESS**

If your bookseller does not have these titles you may order them by sending retail price, plus 15¢ per book for mailing and handling to MAIL SERVICE DEPARTMENT, Washington Square Press, a division of Simon & Schuster, Inc., 1 West 39th St., New York, N.Y. 10018. Please send check or money order—do not send cash.   W 10/9